"Based on extensive data from 17,000 assessments and field-tested experiences, Botelho and Powell provide a compelling and concise road map to help you identify and develop your executive talent."

—Randall Stephenson, chairman and CEO of AT&T

"Botelho and Powell have brought big data and analytics to one of the critical bastions of business: the individuals who make it to the corner office. Their insights into business leadership have the promise to be a game-changer for companies, leaders, and everyone who aspires to get ahead."

—Thales Teixeira, associate professor, Harvard Business School

"A first-rate guide for aspiring CEOs as well as those who have already moved into the top spot. Botelho and Powell's compelling research and real-life stories provide a practical road map to leadership and career success that readers can apply in any setting."

—Art Collins, retired chairman and CEO of Medtronic, Inc.

"Botelho and Powell challenge conventional wisdom to deliver the most useful and credible book on career success I've seen in years! *The CEO Next Door* offers a rare view behind the scenes on how leaders get picked for coveted roles and how they really succeed and fail. . . . Refreshingly candid and deeply researched. Whether you aspire to a CEO role or are just starting out your career, *The CEO Next Door* will raise your odds of success and protect you from painful stumbles."

—Jacqueline Reses, Capital Lead and People Lead of Square, Inc.

"CEOs come from different backgrounds in terms of economic status, education, family, gender, race, color, country of origin, and sexual orientation. The majority of them do an adequate job, some of them perform exceptionally well, and a few are utter failures. Everyone has a unique story of their journey to get to this destination. So what differentiates the top performers from mediocre performers and the laggards? This seminal work by Elena Botelho and Kim Powell does an outstanding job of identifying habits and traits of superstars versus those of average performers. The frequent references to real situations and real people make the book even more credible. The book ends on the optimistic note that everyone in any leadership position with determination and drive can master the skills. A must-read for those who aspire to make a difference."

—Raj L. Gupta, chairman of Delphi Automotive PLC and Avantor, Inc., and board member of Arconic, Inc., Vanguard Group, and IRI

"*The CEO Next Door* contributes much-needed research and data to a subject long dominated by anecdote and conjecture. Your probability of success will rise substantially when you put these insights into action—whether you aspire to be a CEO or simply want to reach your full potential professionally, or you are charged with developing and selecting the next generation leaders as a board member or a CHRO."

— L. Kevin Cox, CHRO of the American Express Company

"With a 'Moneyball' approach to leadership, *The CEO Next Door* uncovers four well-researched CEO behaviors and shows the path to get to the top and stay there. A must-read for aspiring leaders, CEOs, board members, and anyone responsible for grooming future leaders."

—Jim Donald, former CEO of Starbucks and Extended Stay Hotels

"A clear, practical guide on how to run any company, large or small. It's not about credentials, breeding, looks, experience, or resources but about how one makes decisions, adapts to change, shows empathy, and collects information. *The CEO Next Door* explodes the myths behind what it takes to get to the top and provides what works, regardless of gender or background. Eye-opening and operational."

—Stuart Diamond, serial entrepreneur, author of the *New York Times* bestseller *Getting More: How to Be a More Persuasive Person in Work and Life*, and professor, Wharton Business School

"What an invaluable book. With colorful stories and interviews, and solid, in-depth data to back up its points, *The CEO Next Door* is the next must-read for business leaders of all types!"

—Susan Packard, cofounder of HGTV, author, and media executive

THE
CEO NEXT DOOR

The 4 Behaviors That Transform Ordinary People into World-Class Leaders

Elena L. Botelho and Kim R. Powell

with Tahl Raz

CURRENCY
NEW YORK

Copyright © 2018 by G. H. Smart & Company, Inc.

Published in the United States by Currency,
an imprint of the Crown Publishing Group,
a division of Penguin Random House LLC, New York.
crownpublishing.com

CURRENCY and its colophon are trademarks of
Penguin Random House LLC.

Currency books are available at special discounts for bulk purchases
for sales promotions or corporate use. Special editions, including
personalized covers, excerpts of existing books, or books with
corporate logos, can be created in large quantities for special needs.
For more information, contact Premium Sales at (212) 572-2232 or
e-mail specialmarkets@penguinrandomhouse.com.

Library of Congress Cataloging-in-Publication Data
Names: Botelho, Elena L., author. | Powell, Kimberly R., author. | Raz, Tahl, author.
Title: The CEO next door : the 4 behaviors that transform ordinary people into world-
    class leaders / by Elena L. Botelho and Kim R. Powell with Tahl Raz.
Description: New York : Currency, [2017] | Includes bibliographical references and index.
Identifiers: LCCN 2017035471 | ISBN 9781101906491
Subjects: LCSH: Chief executive officers—Case studies. | Executive ability. | Career
    development. | Success in business.
Classification: LCC HD38.2 .B6735 2017 | DDC 658.4/09—dc23
LC record available at https://lccn.loc.gov/2017035471

ISBN 978-1-101-90649-1
Ebook ISBN 978-1-101-90650-7

PRINTED IN THE UNITED STATES OF AMERICA

Book design by Andrea Lau
Jacket design by Mark Melnick

10 9 8 7 6 5 4 3 2 1

First Edition

To Mamulech, Baba Valya, Liolia, and Murochka—
for testament that impossible is nothing.

To my number one fan. And to AJN for everything.

contents

Contents

SECTION III

Get Results: Navigate the Challenges of the Role

THE CEO NEXT DOOR

GET STRONG

MASTER THE
CEO GENOME BEHAVIORS

DECIDE

ENGAGE FOR IMPACT

RELENTLESS RELIABILITY

ADAPT BOLDLY

No wonder we assume that we are not CEO material! We know at this stereotypical character is nothing like us.

But then there's Don Slager. When we first met Don in 2005, he dn't see himself as CEO material either. Walking into the meeting ith our team, Don stretched out the large hand of a laborer. Towing over six feet tall with the frame of an offensive lineman, Don oked formidable. Yet his handshake was surprisingly tentative. Don nfided to us that he was uncertain he was cut out for the CEO job. enjoyed his COO role and didn't see himself as a CEO. He quesned whether he was a worthy candidate and didn't think he would ously be considered for the opportunity to be CEO.

Don is *not* what one thinks of when one thinks of a CEO. He grew in a blue-collar community a short distance from Chicago and the y Works steel mills in Lansing, Illinois. He was surrounded by ders, truck drivers, and steel-mill workers—not college graduates. Don at the time, there was no CEO next door. He went to voca- al high school with aspirations to become a builder, but gradu- into a bum market for construction. Instead, he started his career ng a garbage truck. For the better part of six years, he punched in 45 A.M., started driving at 3:00 A.M., and endured the thankless otony of his route for ten to twelve hours a shift. At the end of week, he collected his paycheck and prepared himself to start the e again.

it here's the strange thing: Don *is*, in fact, a CEO. Don is a great Under his leadership, stock of Republic Services—a Fortune owerhouse in the waste services industry generating over $9 bil- annual revenue—outperformed S&P average returns between nd 2016. In 2015, Republic Services outperformed the S&P by imes. Since Don took the top job, Republic Services' market s nearly doubled from $11.5 billion to $22 billion as of mid- 017. Based on anonymous and voluntary reviews by Republic s' employees, Don was recognized with the Glassdoor Employ- oice Award and named to Glassdoor's 2017 highest-rated-CEO

Unlocking the Secrets of the CE

"You had the power all along, my dear.
—L. Frank Baum, *The Wonderful Wizard*

YOU WILL NEVER BE A **CEO**. THAT'S THE MESS
ternalize from an early age. You may be extrer
harder than anyone else, do everything right, I
you don't look the part, don't have the right
your résumé, don't possess the right pedigree,
ing the top are slim. And so we assume that b
the cards for "regular people" like us.

The world is changing faster than ever, b
ership remains dominated by talk of such
prophets as Steve Jobs and such executive
This iconic CEO is powerful and patrician,
vert with a flawless résumé. An oracle of b
around the globe from Davos to Detroit wit
A brilliant strategist who shapes the reality
the public, have been absorbing for decade

t
d
w
er
lo
co
He
tio
ser

up
Ga
wel
For
tion
ated
drivi
at 2:
mon
each
routi
B
CEO
500 p
lion i
2012
eight
cap ha
year 2
Service
ees' Ch

list.[1] Don didn't learn about leadership at Harvard Business School. He didn't even graduate from college. The foundation for his leadership success was built on the sturdy platform of his blue-collar beginnings and his six years of driving garbage trucks around Des Moines, Iowa, and Chicago, Illinois. Don's leadership behaviors and choices—not his pedigree—propelled him to the top of the waste services industry. Don's father, whose motto was "Show up every day," had always given his son a long leash as long as his grades were good and his chores completed, planting the seeds for unwavering reliability, a key attribute of successful CEOs. Don's reputation for always giving 110 percent attracted the notice of powerful mentors who pushed him to aim higher. Long hours that ended only when the trash bins were empty gave him the stamina not only to survive but to emerge as a leader during the dark days of restructuring at his company, when many others quit or were let go. More important, his roots gave him the authority to evolve the business in ways that the front line would have rejected coming from a more "typical" white-collar executive.

When Don became CEO of Republic Services, he had held almost every position in the company and had worked as the COO alongside four very different CEOs. In 2005, Don wasn't sure he deserved or wanted to be a CEO. There were some things about the CEO role that he found off-putting, such as the need to cater to Wall Street. So when he finally said yes, it was for one simple reason. His vision for how to make Republic Services "America's preferred choice" required him to be able to do what only a CEO can: set the strategy and build the team and culture that would take the company there.

And so it is that a garbageman without a degree becomes a CEO who is recognized by employees and competitors as one of the most passionate, respected, and effective leaders. Don's journey from the garbage truck to the corner suite may sound unusual, but it is not an anomaly. There are countless like him who came from unlikely backgrounds. CEOs such as Aetna's Mark Bertolini or Lear's Matt Simoncini. Seemingly ordinary people achieving extraordinary success. The

CEOs next door. How do we know? We know because, between the two of us, we have coached, advised, and vetted over three hundred CEOs. We are leadership advisors at a firm called ghSMART. Leading boards, outgoing CEOs, and investors count on our objective counsel to help them select the *right* CEO candidates, prepare them for the role, and coach them to perform at full potential. We deploy a rigorous analytical approach to first help our clients define what future business success looks like and the leadership profile it requires, and after that we assess candidates to help predict how they would perform if hired. We conduct extensive five-hour interviews to identify candidates' skills, accomplishments, mistakes, motivations, and mind-sets. We ask questions in a precisely defined sequence that cuts through a clever executive's artful spin. We hear the unvarnished truth of their greatest victories, their painful blowups, their challenges, and their regrets.

Our robust technique for data collection and analysis provides a "moneyball for leadership" solution that helps clients avoid the pervasive errors of gut feel that plague so many failed hiring decisions. Our clients' independent analysis shows that our approach is accurate at least 90 percent of the time—compared to a 50 percent error rate in a conventional interview process.[2] Since 1995, our team has advised and assessed over 17,000 C-suite executives, including over 2,000 CEOs and CEO candidates. Unlike a board member or a search firm, we analyze CEOs with a fully objective perspective, not invested in any particular outcome. When our analysis of a leader's capabilities indicates a fit with a CEO or leadership position in a company, we recommend her or him, whatever her or his pedigree, much as we did with Don.

When you encounter as many exceptional but seemingly unconventional CEOs like Don Slager as we have, you begin to question convention. If many of these CEOs had bought in to the existing stereotypes of leadership, they might never have attempted to win even the first promotion. Looking at Don's success today, nobody would guess that twelve years ago he questioned whether he belonged at the top. "You guys did my assessment and told me that I was a walking, talking symbol of the American Dream and that I had CEO potential. You are experts on CEOs. Thanks to your feedback, I changed my outlook, gained confidence and began to work on my gaps. I decided to go for it and see what I can do. The rest, as they say, is history."

We found ourselves inspired by these CEOs' stories of seemingly unlikely success. And that inspiration led to *the* foundational question behind this book: *Are the "unlikely" CEOs we know simply lucky exceptions? Or did conventional wisdom get it all wrong about what a successful CEO looks like and what it takes to get there?*

In our client work, we aim to solve a $112 billion problem. Hiring or holding on to the wrong CEOs costs shareholders an estimated $112 billion in lost market value annually, according to a study by PwC.[3] In May and June of 2017 alone, CEOs of General Electric, U.S. Steel, Ford, and J. Crew all stepped down under pressure from shareholders, prompting the *New York Times* to call the end of the American era of the baronial chief executive.[4] With this book, we aim to solve a much bigger problem. These prevailing stereotypes of CEOs—arguably the most prominent people in business—offer false role models and success guideposts for leaders at any level. Even worse, they deter millions of talented people like Don Slager from ever aspiring to senior leadership roles. *Stereotypical CEOs look nothing like me, so why even try?* they ask. That is the real tragedy.

One of the reasons for this is that we tend to limit our thinking to the companies and leaders that regularly appear in mass media. This view—typically focused on Fortune 500 companies—is very narrow. It is also very shallow: we know little about these leaders beyond their seemingly perfect public bios. We tend to ignore the vast universe of companies of all sizes. If you broaden the lens beyond the Fortune 500, there are, for example, over two million companies with more than five employees in the United States alone.[5] This means over two million CEOs: a broad, rich set of leadership experiences that don't often get talked about in the press. These smaller companies are an important engine of our economy, generating almost half of the U.S.

non-farm GDP.[6] When we expand our horizons to include companies of all sizes and apply a deeply analytical approach to understanding CEOs and their paths to the top, our profile of the "average" CEO changes radically, as do the odds of attaining the corner office. Instead of a 1 in 240,000 chance of becoming a Fortune 500 CEO, it means 1 in 50 odds of becoming a CEO if you broaden the company set.[7]

On our mission to separate facts from fiction on what successful CEOs *really* look like, we started asking a few pointed questions: How does one become that 1 in 50 who gets the CEO seat—or, for that matter, the 1 in 240,000? What allowed Don Slager and others like him to beat the odds and get to the top? How did they excel? How did they get noticed? What can each of us learn from them? What distinguished those who succeeded at the top from those who flamed out?

If we could answer these questions, we thought, we could tell a far more accurate story of leadership, one that would blow open the doors of the CEO suite to any talented person who wants to reach his or her full potential and is prepared to do the necessary work. Even better, we could provide the map to get there.

What Makes a Great CEO?

To uncover the answers to these questions, we turned to the ghSMART data set of 17,000 leadership assessments. The assessment interviews we conduct typically last roughly five hours and reveal vastly more than one could gather from traditional interviews or psychometric assessments. The *Wall Street Journal* called this information "coveted" for its unique breadth and depth of leadership data.[8] To mine this data, we engaged leading academics and researchers and deployed cutting-edge analytical techniques. For the first time ever, *The CEO Next Door* unveils insights on CEOs based on the world's most comprehensive leadership data set, powered by twenty-first-century state-of-the-art data-mining techniques.

Ten years ago we partnered with professors Steve Kaplan and Morten Sørensen and their research teams at the University of Chicago and Columbia University to study our data set of 17,000 leaders. To do that, they extracted a subset of 2,600 leaders to analyze in greater depth. Kaplan's research is based primarily on the thirty competencies measured in the ghSMART analysis.[9] As we read through transcript after transcript, we found ourselves wondering whether behavior patterns of CEOs compared to those of non-CEOs, and of low-performing to high-performing CEOs, held deeper insights than the competencies data alone could offer. To uncover these patterns would require analyzing almost one hundred thousand pages of text transcripts—a daunting challenge.

Much like mapping the human genome, uncovering secrets of the "CEO Genome" required cutting-edge science and technology. The solution came from an unexpected place. In 2013, ghSMART founder Geoff Smart and Elena interviewed Dr. Jim Goodnight, cofounder and CEO of SAS, for Geoff's book *Power Score: Your Formula for Leadership Success*. SAS Analytics power the predictive tools that major banks and tax agencies use to detect fraud, to name just one high-stakes application. In the conversation, it dawned on us that if the software could handle millions of tax records each year, it could handle thousands of CEO interview transcripts.[10] And so we unleashed the world's most powerful predictive-analytics software on a subset of what we believe to be the world's richest data set of leadership behaviors.

What we came to call the CEO Genome Project broke new ground in understanding what drives leadership success, uncovering insights that typical regression analysis never could have picked up. What we discovered surprised and inspired us. *Harvard Business Review* found our research compelling and relevant for today's leaders, featuring "CEO Genome Behaviors" in a cover article ("What Sets Successful CEOs Apart," *HBR* May/June 2017). This article and related press coverage got downloaded over 250,000 times by readers globally. The portrait of the successful CEO staring back at us from the data looked nothing like the glossy, unattainable image we'd all come to expect. In fact, the data burst a number of the myths surrounding CEOs:[11]

CEO Myths

- **Only Ivy Leaguers need apply.** In fact, only 7 percent of the CEOs we have analyzed graduated from an Ivy League college. Eight percent of CEOs in our sample did not even complete college or took unusually long to graduate. Ivy League graduates are more prevalent among the ranks of Fortune 500 CEOs, but outside of that small set of the largest companies, we see a much broader range of educational backgrounds and pedigrees.

- **CEOs were destined for greatness from an early age.** Over 70 percent of the CEOs we interviewed didn't set out to become CEOs early in life. Only when they came within reach of the C-suite—typically after fifteen-plus years of experience—did they start to feel that maybe they could achieve and thrive in the role.

- **CEOs are egotistical superheroes.** We were intrigued to uncover that the CEOs who saw "independence" as their defining character trait were twice as likely to underperform compared to other CEOs. The weakest CEO candidates used "I" at a much higher rate than "we" compared to the rest of the CEO candidates. For many successful CEOs, this team orientation has its roots in early organized athletics and in mentoring others.

- **Successful CEOs have a larger-than-life personality with exceptional charisma and confidence.** Wildly charismatic "masters of the universe" may prowl unchallenged in the boardrooms shown in Hollywood films, but, in real boardrooms, results speak louder than charisma. Over a third of CEOs in our study actually describe themselves as "introverted." And self-described introverts in our sample were even slightly more likely to *exceed* boards' expectations. When looking at CEOs who *met* expectations, we found no statistically significant difference between introverts and extroverts. High confidence more than doubles a candidate's chances of being chosen as CEO but provides no advantage in performance on the job.

- **To become a CEO you need a flawless résumé.** The reality: 45 percent of CEO candidates had at least one major career blowup that ended a job or was extremely costly to the business. Yet more than 78 percent of them ultimately won the top job.[12] What set successful CEOs apart was not their lack of mistakes but how they handled mistakes and setbacks when they did occur. CEO candidates who talk about a blowup as a failure are half as likely to deliver strong performance as a CEO.

- **Female CEOs succeed differently from men.** Women may deploy leadership styles and exhibit attributes different from men's, but statistically, gender has no impact on the probability of delivering strong results as a CEO. Successful CEOs exhibit the same four CEO Genome Behaviors, whether female or male. Where it matters, female and male CEOs appear more similar than different. Unfortunately, the one big difference remains. Depending on the year, only about 4 to 6 percent of the largest companies are led by female CEOs.[13]

- **Great CEOs excel in any situation.** A common misperception is that a great CEO is capable of handling any situation. Actually, we find that great CEOs are very thoughtful about identifying the roles and context where they can be successful. They have the self-discipline to turn down the wrong job even when it comes with a CEO title. Many CEOs who are great at turning around a struggling company may struggle in a high-growth context and vice versa.

- **To become a CEO, you need to check every box.** Everyone has areas for improvement, and CEOs are no exception. Even the best-performing CEOs have three to six key development areas to improve when they get the job. Those who succeed quickly surround themselves with the right teams to complement their skills and experience.

- **CEOs work harder than the rest of us.** CEOs, of course, work very hard, but so do others in a wide range of jobs. Analysis showed no predictive relationship between how hard a leader worked and how likely she or he was to become a CEO. Furthermore, 97 percent of *low*-performing CEOs in our sample scored high on work ethic.

- **For CEOs, the smarter, the better.** Above-average intelligence is an important indicator of C-suite potential.[14] However, once at the C-suite level, higher intelligence as measured by standardized tests does not increase the odds of being hired as CEO or performing well in the role. In fact, CEO candidates who "cut to the chase" and speak in clear, simple language are more likely to be hired than those with complex and cerebral vocabulary.

- **Experience trumps all.** Among the more shocking findings in our research: First-time CEOs were statistically no less likely to meet or exceed expectations than those with prior CEO experience.

We decoded the CEO Genome with the help of Professor Kaplan, SAS, and more than fourteen other researchers from the University of Chicago, Columbia, Cambridge, NYU, the University of California at Berkeley, and ghSMART. But we still weren't finished. To achieve the full purpose of our work, we needed to go beyond describing what a CEO looks like. Our goal was to create a playbook of tried-and-true and repeatable practices that anyone can benefit from. And so we spent an additional two years going through our findings and digging deeper with clients, cross-referencing their perspectives and ours against the insights yielded by thousands of pages of articles, transcripts, studies, books, and consolidated research. We reinterviewed several of the CEOs in our data sample and added one hundred new interviews. We documented techniques and practices we have used with the CEOs we coach. Over nine thousand people of all levels of seniority have taken a self-assessment on CEO Genome Behaviors on our website www.ceogenome.com and have found the advice immediately applicable.

Between the data and the field-tested experience, we believe we have produced a book that has the power to unveil what it really takes to get to the top—and who succeeds once there. More important, we hope this book has the power to accelerate your journey to the top of your aspirations—whatever they may be—and to protect you from some painful mistakes along the way.

If you aspire to become a CEO: You will learn how to prepare yourself and increase your odds of achieving your goal.

If you don't know yet where your professional path will take you: You will learn secrets of professional success and how to achieve your full potential from those who have reached the loftiest heights. Just as each of us can benefit from working out with experienced trainers, you will be able to raise your game by learning from today's successful CEOs.

If you recently landed in a CEO role: Congratulations! And fasten your seat belt! Here you'll uncover the costly and painful pitfalls that can await a new CEO. We will offer advice to protect you from predictable crises of the CEO role and help you accelerate your success.

If you are an experienced CEO or board member: Grooming the next generation of leaders is probably one of your goals. This book offers proven steps to help you do that, as well as insights to protect you from making painful wrong choices.

Our goal is to give you industrial-strength, evidence-based advice powered by two decades of combined experience advising CEOs, investors, and boards of directors, buttressed by thousands of hours of studies and research by an interdisciplinary team. We will unveil how you *get strong*, how you *get to the top*, and how you *get results* once in the role.

Section I:

Get Strong: Master the Four CEO Genome Behaviors

What are the behaviors that enable one to lead like a CEO? What separates the best from the rest? What are the skills or behaviors that really matter? Our research uncovers the **Four CEO Genome Behaviors** statistically associated with success: **Decisiveness**, **Engaging for Impact**, **Relentless Reliability**, and **Adapting Boldly**. Importantly, these are *not inborn traits.* They are behaviors and habits shaped by practice and experience, and they can be developed at any time in your career. We will explain and explore each behavior in the next four chapters and arm you with practical tools to improve your game. And you will learn which one of these behaviors works double-time to increase both your odds of success and your chances of getting to the corner office in the first place.

Section II:

Get to the Top: Win Your Dream Job

We have mined the data across thousands of leadership careers to unveil underlying patterns of success. Knowing these patterns can help anyone advance in her or his career. We also examine the career choices and experiences that got some CEOs to the top *faster.* Finally, we take you behind the scenes to unveil how boards really decide who gets the CEO job and how you can increase your chances of being chosen. What on the surface looks like a highly rational process is full of emotion and biases. To give you just one example, a candidate who speaks with a strong accent is twelve times less likely to be hired as a CEO.[15] We will help you anticipate and safely navigate these land mines, no matter what your background is.

Section III:

Get Results: Navigate the Challenges of the Role

A quarter of annual CEO departures are forced.[16] There is little margin for error at the top. The first two years are make-or-break for a new CEO. It's not enough to get to the top—we will show you how to succeed once you are there and how to avoid the hazards in your way.

In those inevitable "lonely at the top" moments, you'll have a trusted guide. Most of the first-time CEOs we work with see the board as their biggest challenge. And yet 75 percent of experienced CEOs tell us that their number one mistake in their first CEO job had nothing to do with the board! It was about picking the wrong people or moving too slowly to get their team in place.[17] We'll lay out how to avoid these and other pitfalls, nail the first two years in the job, and stay on course amid the distracting perks and challenges of the position. Many of the insights in this section will help you navigate any new leadership role.

Could It Be *You*?

We've helped some of the most unlikely CEOs succeed. People such as a nurse who became the first female CEO in the 160-year history of a preeminent children's hospital. The founder of one of the most respected investment firms who started his career by losing all of his parents' 401K savings. The son of an Italian immigrant shoemaker who ran a global helicopter company and a major technology company. A child actor and singer who ran one of the nation's most consistently profitable banks. Don Slager. The list is long. Each of them at times felt like an outsider or an underdog. Each of them at some point—much to his or her own surprise—realized, "*I* could be a CEO." Countless employees, pensioners, patients, and families are better off because these individuals stepped up to the plate despite all odds.

We believe that there are tens of thousands of leaders who could make effective—maybe even world-changing—CEOs if armed with the insights from this book. And there are millions more who can benefit from the lessons and advice and practices of those who do rise to the top to improve their own career trajectory and fulfill their career potential, wherever they ultimately land. *Our personal mission is to arm you with the full advantage of an insider's view on what separates the best from the rest.*

The fact is, CEO leadership requires outstanding capabilities—but capability isn't enough. To become a CEO, an individual must be able to see and believe in that possibility in order to believe it might be an achievable destination. That's why people who have parents who are professional athletes are statistically more likely than the rest of us to be professional athletes themselves.

Here's the key: Becoming a CEO isn't necessarily about background or good fortune. It's about performance, about behaviors that most of us can master with hard work, close attention, and the techniques we share in this book. We offer real-life stories of success and failure on the way to the top as a way of helping you shape your own career journey.

Even the most impressive CEOs often didn't start out knowing they were destined for greatness. Nor did most feel driven to pursue the corner office until later in their career. At some point along the way, though, they had their "I *can* do it" moment. Often it was when they got to see real CEOs "up close and personal."

Above all, by bringing you "up close and personal" with The CEO Next Door, *we hope this book will be the "I* can *do it" moment for you in pursuing your professional dreams.*

Research Approach

We've known for some time that the staples of talent selection—the résumé and the job interview—are essentially worthless. Since 1995, our firm ghSMART has been helping investors and boards pick the right *who* for the C-suite.

Throughout most of the twentieth century, businesses took a decidedly unscientific approach to hiring, relying mostly on intuition, or gut, as their primary criteria for making a selection.[18] Over the past several decades, as neuroscience has revealed the biases and irrationality of our choices,[19] leaders, from concert halls to baseball fields to boardrooms, have sought out ways to improve the rigor and specificity of the hiring process.

When clients call us for help on a hiring decision or to coach a CEO, our first step is to create a "scorecard." The scorecard defines success in the role. It includes the mission, business outcomes that the CEO must deliver, and the key leadership competencies required in the role. (A mission might be to position the company as the industry leader. An outcome might be to increase revenue growth from new products from 5 percent to 15 percent annually.) Each CEO scorecard is unique to every company, based on the specific needs of the organization and the company's performance at a given point in time. It crystallizes, often in quantitative terms, the expectations for financial, strategic, operational, product/service, people, and cultural results over an agreed-upon time frame.

The scorecard becomes the lens through which we assess the executives we interview. Our job is to determine whether a candidate has the track record, the skills, the competence, the trajectory, and the temperament to lead a particular company to success with the prioritized outcomes and to identify the ways to support and develop the executive team.

Armed with the scorecard, our senior consultants (each with at least ten-plus years of postgraduate professional experience) spend roughly five hours with each candidate conducting what we call a *Who Interview*™.[20] We ask candidates what they were hired to do, what they were most proud of, what their key mistakes were and lessons learned, whom they worked with, and why they left, for every job they held over the course of their career. We start with simple questions and eventually go deeply into their history, moving well beyond the résumé to capture an intimate personal history. A candidate who is presumed to be a star, we'll come to find out, was fired from three of his or her past five jobs. A $5 billion construction project almost came undone because of a bad call. A CFO saved a business by convincing the CEO and board to sell a marginally profitable division. Most find the process refreshing and thought-provoking—at last, they are encouraged to tell their full story. A few leave sweaty-palmed.

After completing the interview, we cull and analyze hundreds of data points to assign a probability of success against the scorecard we created. In addition, leaders are graded against more than thirty competencies, such as *holding people accountable* and *attracting strong talent.* Finally, we calibrate our findings with several colleagues and with relevant data from past assessments to ensure we are as accurate as possible. In addition, we often supplement our findings with 360-degree feedback data and factor in board-reported data about how the winning candidate went on to perform as the CEO.

After 17,000 of these executive assessments, we know who gets hired and why or why not. And we know how the candidates did once they landed the job. This allows us to connect the success we see today to the qualities we saw earlier—sometimes much earlier—in a CEO's career. Every year, we assess an additional 250 CEOs who are added to the data set. We are unaware of any other firm that knows as much about what CEOs do, how they got the role, and how they manage the daily grind, sweat, and tears.

chapter 2

Decide: Speed Over Precision

I've missed more than nine thousand shots in my career.
I've lost almost three hundred games.
Twenty-six times, I've been trusted to take the game-winning shot and missed.
I've failed over and over again, and that is why I succeed.
—Michael Jordan

SO MANY STORIES AND LEGENDS AROUND CEOs INVOLVE WHAT WE call the "big decision." This is the "bet the company" moment, where everything is on the line and the CEO must choose. If she (or he) is wrong, the company implodes, people lose their jobs, and sometimes the company disappears entirely. And, of course, the CEO's career is over. So she gathers the facts, runs scenarios, deliberates. She confers with her colleagues and the board, wrestles with self-doubt. Finally, she calls on her experience and instinct, looks into the future, ignores the naysayers, and makes the call that saves the company and propels it into an even more profitable future.

These moments exist. We've watched them unfold. So our first instinct as consultants was to focus on this big decision—making the right call. We focus our advisory work on CEOs in large part because their decisions have such outsize impact. The livelihood of thousands of families may hang in the balance. At that level of impact, surely nothing could be more important than the quality of each and every decision. But, as it turns out, something *is* more important—dramatically more important.

When we dug into the behaviors that differentiated high-performing CEOs, the behavior that stood out wasn't thoughtfulness, analytical rigor, or any other trait you might link to quality decision making. *Successful CEOs stood out for* decisiveness *itself*—the ability to make decisions with speed and conviction. *Decisive CEOs in our study are twelve times more likely to be high performers.*[1]

Decisive CEOs are driven by a unique sense of responsibility: "It's on me to handle this," they realize. While the rest of us may tie ourselves into knots, wanting to get each decision right, they make calls they know could be wrong, operating in a sea of uncertainty. What makes all this possible: deciding with speed and conviction. Knowing which decisions require nine minutes of deliberation, which require two weeks, and which don't require your attention at all. And, above all, conscientiously learning from every call—good or bad.

"A potentially bad decision is better than a lack of direction," said Steve Gorman, a CEO we assessed a few years back. When he led the bus company Greyhound Lines, his ability to decide with speed and conviction saved the company.

Greyhound was Steve's first job as CEO. Taking this job was more a marriage of convenience than a dream. Reeling from an unwise career move that had taken him to North Carolina, Steve and his family were eager to relocate back to Dallas. At Greyhound, Steve inherited a company on dwindling life support. It had been years since the company had made enough money to cover the operating costs and capital investments necessary to be consistently profitable. The parent company, Laidlaw, was coming out of bankruptcy and creditors would not allow investment of more than $10 million per year into Greyhound—they felt it would be wasting money. Steve was operating on a knife's edge, and he knew it. If he missed his targets, the creditors were ready to shut the doors on the business. And after a short and unsuccessful previous career chapter, Steve needed this new one to be a win. The stakes were high for everyone involved.

Not one to shy away from a challenge, Steve dug in to learn the business and define the path forward. It soon became clear that the biggest problem facing Greyhound was that the company had too many unprofitable routes. Company executives had lots of different ideas about how to fix the carrier's network. Some thought they should chop up some of the regions. Others wanted to raise ticket prices on long-haul routes.

For four months, Steve listened as his executive team came up with and dismissed a growing list of options. Any change was going to be hard, and there were plenty of reasons why any approach could fail. Finally, enough was enough. Among the piles of data was a satellite map of the United States and Canada at night showing where all the nation's lights were concentrated, a reflection of population density. Looking at that map, Steve decided Greyhound's fate: "We cannot have miles where there are no lights." No lights, no people. He imagined reshaping Greyhound's service routes around high-yield regional networks, connected with a few long-haul routes. Would it work? He couldn't know for sure. What he did know was that the company was hemorrhaging money and that people were relying on him to fix things. The network had to be reduced to profitable routes.

With the company's future and his career on the line and with success uncertain, Steve moved forward quickly and with total commitment. The plan worked. When Steve came on as the CEO, the bus operator had lost $140 million over the previous two years. When he left four years later, in 2007, Greyhound reported $30 million earnings, leading to a successful sale of the company for more than four times its 2003 value.

Steve had pushed forward decisively—not because he knew he was right. He did it because he understood that *a potentially bad decision was better than no decision,* especially when decisions on the route structure could be modified if needed.

What differentiates CEOs like Steve Gorman is their recognition, their firm belief, that when you need to get somewhere, even having the wrong map is better than no map at all. Art Collins, the former CEO of Medtronic and board member at Boeing, U.S. Bancorp, and several other leading corporations, told us, "It's like calling a play. I was a quarterback when I played football. You didn't always call the right play, but, boy, once you called the play, you'd better have all your teammates execute against it."

Success here rests on action more than pure intellect. Often CEOs with the highest IQs struggle with "decisiveness."[2] They can get bogged down in analysis paralysis and struggle to set clear priorities. Their teams and their shareholders pay the price for their generally earnest desire to get it right.

So if you hope to make it to the corner office, stop sweating every decision. Instead, like Gorman, choose your map and press forward with speed and conviction. Become **Decisive**. As you strengthen those **Decisive** muscles, focus on three things: make decisions *faster,* make *fewer* decisions, and put in place practices to *get better at decision making every time.*

Make Decisions Faster

Ninety-four percent of the executives who rated poorly on the **Decisive** competency decided *too slowly,* not too quickly.[3] Their desire to get it right can even prevent them from making any decision at all. High-performing executives make decisions faster. The unique challenge of decision making as a CEO often isn't the intellectual challenge of the calls you make, it's the volume and speed at which they're coming at you. There are two principles that we see employed over and over again that enable high-velocity decision makers to act quickly:

1. Make the complex simple.

Effective CEOs—and high performers at all levels of their careers—move faster by finding ways to make the complex simple. They develop mental models specific to their industry and their company that they can use to box in uncertainty, distill new information, screen out noise, and pull the trigger quickly. These mental models serve to focus decisions on the most important drivers of business performance.

When Doug Peterson arrived at his first day on the job as CEO of McGraw Hill Financial, he was asked to decide on a sizeable acquisition. Executives at the company presented the plan almost as a fait accompli. The team passionately advocated the idea, believing it was the only way to save a stagnant division of the business.

Doug knew he didn't know everything—he was new to the business and new to being a CEO. But he also knew he had to decide quickly. The deal was about to go to a binding bid, and this was the last opportunity for the company to walk away. He'd studied the CEOs he'd worked with in the past and had detected a pattern that he wanted to emulate. "I noticed that the successful CEOs were willing to make decisions with only eighty percent of the information. They didn't need to wait around. It wasn't intuitive; they weren't gambling. It was about quick judgment based on listening to lots of viewpoints very quickly," he said.

He ultimately simplified the various viewpoints by framing the decision in the very simple terms that legendary GE CEO Jack Welch had made famous: *Can we become number one or number two in that sector?*[4] He had enough information to know that the answer to that question was no. So he made the call to walk away from the deal. People were shocked, even furious, but Doug stood firm.

Using a framework adds speed to decision making by simplifying complexity. Such a framework makes it clear to the entire organization what is important, so that not only the CEO but everyone can make better decisions. You can also bet that your team will model your own approach to decision making: If you move fast, within clear decision principles, so will they. It was a point Jack Krol, the former chairman and CEO of DuPont, drove home with us. Jack, who started at DuPont as a chemist, told us about the transformation he made at DuPont Agricultural Products in the 1980s.

When he arrived as senior vice president, most people within his business were focused on innovation. "Great, we've got new products coming," he said. "But no one was thinking about profitability and shareholder value." So Jack introduced a simple framework centered on return on investment. Return on investment became the new standard for decision making: Could a given plan or innovation initiative meet our threshold for return on investment? A decision on any plan that crossed his desk was judged by that equation. As Jack recalls, "I needed to break down what goes into each part of the equation so people understood the pieces they controlled that contributed to the return on investment." His senior management started calling this the Krol Equation and vetted their decisions using the framework he'd applied.

By understanding what drives value in your business, in your job, or on your team, you too can make the complex simple. Reade Fahs, CEO of National Vision, Inc., aims for a simple decision-making framework that is aligned with his business's objectives. Reade told us, "We create one formula that works, and we replicate it over and over again. It can be hard to find a winning formula. But once you find it, you need to stick to it."

Early in his career when he was at Vision Express in the United Kingdom, he determined there were a set of key levers to improving profitability for the retail eyewear business, and every decision the team made had to revolve around those—and only those—levers. "I got there, and I thought, " 'Oh, my God, this place needs a lot of work.' I went in the next day and asked, 'Hey, guys, could you tell me when was the last time this business was doing well?' We identified what had changed, like incentive structures in the store, displays in the front window, and on and on. Through that process we honed a clear model of what works, and of the thousands of specific areas we could focus on, we distilled the list down to twelve things that mattered." Then they focused all their decisions and actions in those areas, training store leadership and assessing those areas every time any leader walked into a store: Were the front window displays set up correctly? Was the bonus program getting paid out? And so on.

The business doubled its profits and grew sales by 15 percent in fewer than two years under Reade's leadership. With that same decision-making framework, he would later go on to lead a similar turnaround at United States–based National Vision, which went from a $5 million market cap when he took over to being sold for over $1.1 billion to KKR ten years later. Reade delivered sixty consecutive quarters of same-store sales growth, unmatched in the U.S. retail industry. As experts predict the demolition of the traditional retail industry by Amazon and Google,[5] Reade's advice about cutting through complexity to focus on what matters the most appears all the more prescient.

2. Give a voice, not a vote.

It would be a mistake to see CEO decisiveness in a vacuum—the lonely executive sitting atop a kind of ivory tower in perfect control of everything. In fact, CEOs and decision makers at all levels live in the same chaotic world as the rest of us. New variables come up that change the system all the time. A huge web of people, inside and outside the company, informs and affects every move the chief executive makes. Effective decision makers actively involve others in their decision process. They do that for two reasons. First, to get multiple inputs to improve the quality of the decision. And second, to pave the path to smooth execution by building ownership and buy-in for the decision with relevant stakeholders. So when the time comes to execute, those who have to carry out the decision become champions and willing volunteers, not chain-gang prisoners. We will come back to this second point in the next chapter.

Here we will tackle one nagging question: How does a CEO move fast and yet still engage others in the process? The participative mantra of decisive CEOs is this: *Everyone has a voice but not a vote.* Top CEOs recognize that there is an art to gathering input as part of the decision-making process. Yet they do not wait for consensus.

Christophe Weber, now the CEO of Takeda Pharmaceutical Company Ltd., provides a case in point. When Christophe was regional director of GlaxoSmithKline Asia Pacific (GSK), he took a chance on a new strategic direction for the division. The idea had come from a group that he had noticed lacked a voice in the organization: high-potential midlevel employees in each country in the region. He saw them as potential innovators, and it was a good instinct. When Christophe was in the Philippines, one of these employees came forward with an idea for a new model of access for drugs that would require GSK to lower pricing and increase its marketing and sales force reach while increasing volume. Some quick research suggested that the plan could work, but they couldn't do it alone. Adopting a new model would require a series of changes that needed solid buy-in. Christophe collaborated with the team to develop a plan—but stopped short of seeking consensus. "Being consensus-driven can be too slow and often pushes toward least-common-denominator solutions," Christophe told us. "But that doesn't mean you can't be collaborative. Allow people to speak out and express a different point of view, then make a decision and communicate."

Madeline Bell, CEO of the Children's Hospital of Philadelphia (CHOP), has a clear process in place to gather information and input from a variety of sources. She is incredibly inclusive when it comes to getting input from those around her. The information contributes to her decision. But often it has another purpose: to help her *communicate* the decision in a way that will bring all the parties into alignment. During those discussions, she learns the pushback and sources of hesitation and can then build the rationale to address the sources of concern. Participative, yes—but consensus driven? Not at all. Every decision she makes is unpopular with some contingent of stakeholders. But once she's made a decision, she doesn't look back unless material new information emerges.

Make Fewer Decisions

A powerful additional benefit of simple decision frameworks is that once they are embraced by the organization, CEOs can step back from the vast majority of the decisions that now can be made by their employees. And that is true of many of the best CEOs we see. Whatever their business, they are adept at triage. As problems and decisions cross their desk, they know which deserve real deliberation, which they should make a call and move forward on, and which should be passed to someone else to handle. They make fewer decisions.

The "gel versus foam debate" at CHOP was one of those moments for Madeline Bell. Passions ran high over the question of whether gel or foam in the hospital's hundreds of soap dispensers was the better choice to keep patients safe from infection. While it seems like a simple decision, hand hygiene is regarded as one of the most important elements of infection control within hospitals.[6] As Madeline says, "I was stepping into a minefield, and I very quickly recognized that if I was sucked into pacifying and placating people's emotions, this could bog down the organization and set the wrong precedent for decision making." The leaders were divided into two warring camps: gel people and foam people. They wanted Madeline to referee the decision.

"Absolutely not," she told them. "I'm not up to speed on the issues involved." She suggested that to answer the question, they look *down* the chain of command instead of up. "People closest to the day-to-day operations should be the ones to debate and decide it. This is not my decision."

Gel versus foam was an important decision given its potential impact on the hospital infection rate, to be sure, but it was one that should be decided by others in the organization. Madeline was employing one helpful tactic: *Do not step in when the decision rights reside with others in the organization who have the information and experience to make the decision.* It is a tactic that can be incorporated by leaders at every level.

Another tactic we've seen CEOs deploy to lighten their decision-making load is to screen decisions for those that can really hurt the business. Under the daily pressures, it's often hard for any leader to find the time to step back to define the clarifying framework that we talked about in the previous section. Ironically, leaders are often mired in a reactive, day-to-day churn exactly because they haven't stepped back to define the most critical "business killer" issues that should shape their decision making and screen for what they do and don't jump into. With the number of issues crossing a CEO's desk, if every problem carries equal weight, so do the decisions. It's a recipe for overload.

Steve Kaufman, former CEO of Arrow Electronics and a lecturer at Harvard Business School, shared three questions he uses to triage decisions:

1. **Does this decision need to be made now, or can we wait a week or a month without causing irreparable harm?** Not *all* decisions require immediate action. What is the cost of waiting? How important is this decision to the goals and priorities of the business? Understanding the levers behind the business and being crystal clear about what matters most allow leaders to figure out the right time line for each decision.

2. **Will waiting bring some additional insight and information that can help make the decision?** What is the benefit of waiting? If additional information is attainable and could significantly shift a high-impact de-

cision, it may be worth waiting. If, on the other hand, it is unlikely you will know more in three months or six months, then what is the benefit of continued analysis?

3. **Could the issue resolve itself?** Many CEOs told us that there were countless instances where time solved a problem better than they ever could have. But we suggest you proceed with caution on this one.

Intuit's CEO Brad Smith once wrote, "A major adjustment I needed to make when becoming CEO was getting used to the change in altitude. I didn't grasp this concept initially, and in my first year as CEO I found myself straying into decisions and offering recommendations that were more appropriate for the leaders closer to the action."[7] Brad learned what all the best CEOs do: Your job is to decide on the *what* and empower others to decide the *how*.

Get Better Every Time

It would be cavalier to say, "Just make a decision, any decision." Clearly, CEOs wouldn't be where they are if the majority of their calls weren't good ones. The best CEOs make decisions quickly, and they stick to them—yet, over time, they develop a track record that's better than that of most. How do they do it? They put into place practices to get better every time. *Decisive leaders don't belabor the decision in search of evasive perfection. They recognize that there is a cost to perfectionism. Instead, they move forward and continually improve.* Reid Hoffman, the serial entrepreneur who sold his company LinkedIn to Microsoft for $26.2 billion, is aware that in startups, speed of execution often determines success. He has coined the antiperfectionist manifesto in Silicon Valley: "If you aren't embarrassed by the first version of your product, you shipped too late."[8]

During the thousands of CEO and executive assessments and interviews that we conducted, we asked about his or her mistakes. The future CEOs' answers roughly followed a pattern that we discovered in one of our early interviews with Andy Silvernail, the CEO of IDEX Corporation, an industrial company. He was promoted internally in 2011, shortly after making one of the largest acquisitions in the history of his company. A year later, the acquisition was in meltdown. The acquired company had missed bottom-line targets by 40 percent—and now, as CEO, Andy had inherited his own mess. He had to tell the board to expect a greater than $200 million writedown. Worse, he had to convince his leadership team to stick around when he reduced their compensation (and his own) to absorb some of the loss.

Here was a classic bad decision. It hurt his standing with the board and led to pain for a lot of people. It was a very difficult six months— and yet when Andy talked about his mistake, it was as if he was recounting a particularly eventful trip to the mechanic to fix his car, or a disaster that had happened to someone else. He never once used the word *failure*. He calmly dissected what had happened, detailing not just the mistake itself but the "aftershock" challenges that followed. How he reacted *after* the disastrous acquisition was telling. He took ownership. He collected facts. And he took a controversial stance to reflect the cost of that mistake in both his pocketbook as well as his team's. And, even more important, with time and distance from the decision, he had a list of things he had learned from the experience that he took with him into every decision to come. He went on to outpace his industry in Total Shareholder Return over the following four years.

What follows is the series of practices we've distilled from Andy and the other CEOs we have encountered over the years who have learned to use their decisions as a platform for growth and evolution.

1. Look back. Make mistakes your laboratory.

Avoidance of the word *failure* isn't spin for these CEOs. It reflects their true attitude: Errors aren't fearsome embarrassments but *inevitabilities* that provide the most reliable laboratory for future improvement. SAS research pointed to a tangible benefit of not dwelling on the concept of failure: CEO candidates who used the word *failure* in talking about their mistakes were half as likely to deliver a strong performance in the seat as CEOs who did not.[9] Successful CEOs learned to take mistakes in stride and take ownership for them as the necessary scars of battle. Another interesting point: These CEOs somehow learned intuitively what we saw in the data, that having a career blowup doesn't obstruct your future performance as a CEO but, rather, prepares you.

Jean Hoffman sold her company, Putney, Inc., a generic pharmaceutical company for pets, in 2016 for $200 million. Reflecting on the journey, she told us: "One of the keys to success is, you have to be comfortable making decisions in ambiguous situations and learn from those decisions and get better each day. Those mistakes are part of the success. They aren't really mistakes."

Successful CEOs build a system to learn from their past decisions—good or bad. One CEO we interviewed showed up with a folder cataloguing every mistake he had ever made and what he had learned from them. Others told us they gathered their teams for postmortems to measure results against specific criteria, and they put together a list of learnings when things went wrong. Earlier in their careers, before they had teams, they applied the same rigor in the wake of decisions about school, career forks, and even their personal life.

Building consistent practices to learn from failure helps leaders get better at the two modes of decision making described by the Nobel Prize–winning psychologist Daniel Kahneman in his book *Thinking, Fast and Slow*: "System 2" thinking—the rational, deliberative, and slow kind of decision making—and "System 1" thinking, or what most of us think of as intuition, where decisions are made quickly and often unconsciously, based on what we already know.[10] Successful CEOs, with their relentless focus on postmortem analysis to determine which decisions worked out well and which did not, used System 2 thinking to "train" their System 1 thinking, to improve their "gut instinct." Strengthened by experience, that gut instinct became far more reliable.

The Art of Apology

We have yet to encounter a leader who hasn't made costly mistakes. When you are a leader, *most things that go wrong are not directly your fault, but they are always your responsibility.* The art of apology can make the difference between lost trust and ruined reputations and emerging stronger than ever. Art Collins, the former CEO of Medtronic and board member at Boeing, U.S. Bancorp, and several other leading corporations, has seen a lot of mistakes in his day. Below is his advice on the art of apology, which is instantly applicable whether you aspire to be a great CEO or simply a good partner and friend:

1. **Be personal.** Assume personal responsibility rather than simply act as a spokesperson for the institution you represent.
2. **Be focused.** Address specific acts or mistakes as well as impacted parties, so it is clear that you understand the ramifications of what went wrong.
3. **Be genuine.** Convey in both words and tone honest remorse and atonement for mistakes made and any resulting damage caused.
4. **Make no excuses.** Avoid shifting blame, minimizing harm, or whitewashing a bad situation.

5. **Act swiftly.** The sooner an apology is given, the better the chance the apology will be accepted by those who count.

6. **Be comprehensive.** Get all the facts out, admit all known shortcomings, and clearly articulate what has yet to be determined.

7. **Prevent recurrences.** Articulate an action plan to correct what went wrong and to make sure the same problem doesn't recur.

2. Look inward. Condition your mind for decisiveness.

We found that maintaining emotional distance from their decisions helps leaders learn from mistakes. So how does one create the required emotional distance to flex and build that **Decisiveness** muscle? Too many leaders don't realize the degree to which their physical state—whether they are rested, exhausted, or overcaffeinated—affects their emotional state and therefore their ability to perform when it comes to making decisions. Effective leaders recognize that under physical or emotional stress or fatigue, they tend to default to their natural behavioral biases related to decision making. They are aware of their natural default tendencies and put in place habits, people, and processes to support them even in the most trying moments. Even the most effective decision makers may fall into counterproductive extremes when their mental and emotional resources are depleted. They may become pedantically analytical, get dragged down a rabbit hole by a trivial issue, or find themselves tempted to pull the trigger too quickly without sufficiently exploring contrarian points of view. As General George S. Patton said, "Fatigue makes cowards of all of us."[11] A leader showing up to work without attending to her physical and emotional state is akin to an athlete entering a competition wearing the wrong-size shoes.

As president of the College Board, David Coleman led the organization through a difficult period of reexamination, including a redesign of the SAT in response to new evidence that the cornerstone assessment used in college admissions was widely perceived to favor more affluent students. He told us that his biggest insight as a first-time CEO was the importance of getting enough rest—he discovered it was key in terms of his ability to be decisive. "I had to be extremely well-rested to be my best self," he told us. "The more tired and exhausted I was, the more vulnerable I was to pettier emotions. Keeping myself physically balanced and healthy allowed me to be steady and strong."

3. Look to the future.

Some leaders apply a different frame of reference to improve their decision making: getting into a time machine. They think forward to the future they want to see and reason back to the type of decisions they need to make to get there. One of the most steely decision makers we've worked with isn't a Fortune 500 CEO. It is Ashley Wheater, the artistic director of The Joffrey Ballet in Chicago, only the third person to hold this position since its creation in 1956. Founder Robert Joffrey created an innovative ballet company, perhaps the first truly American dance troupe. Upon his death in 1988, the Joffrey lost much of its maverick spirit. Ashley didn't let the past glory of the Joffrey blind him to its present and future needs. His mandate was to put the Joffrey back on the map as one of the top dance companies in America. When Ashley became director, the organization was, by his description, in "a precarious state," in terms of both its funding and the quality of its work. The Joffrey had stopped "creating." Audiences dwindled. Finances were tight. Ashley understood that the Joffrey should honor its original vision and expand upon it. The Joffrey had always embraced risk, discovered new talent, and celebrated the spirit of the times and built a dance company as diverse as America. The Joffrey needed to stand for inclusion and for elevating all lives through art. It wasn't about elitism or inaccessible luxury. Ashley restored the Joffrey brand, breaking down the stigma of classical ballet as an elitist art form. "We're not Louis Vuitton," he told us. "We should be for everyone."

To turn the ship, Ashley had to make choices that weren't popular, either in the organization or in the press. But he never backed down. Today he credits his resolve to two behaviors. First, he came to every decision with a clear mind. And second, whenever critics unsettled him, he reminded himself that they were focused on the present, not the future. He believed the benefits would become clear in time. "People who were really angry with me the first two years now understand our journey," he told us recently. "Time is the greatest leveler." (Of course, that's especially true when you've made the right decision.)

Ashley's use of a forward-looking view to stay the course reminded us of the "10/10/10 technique" that Chip and Dan Heath recount in their book *Decisive: How to Make Better Choices in Life and Work.* "Imagine how you will feel about a decision in 10 minutes, 10 months, and 10 years," they write.[12] Gaining distance from the pressing decision at hand helps you approach it more rationally.

4. Look around. Seek contrarian perspectives.

The great "gel versus foam" debate at CHOP we mentioned earlier points to another truth: CEOs routinely have to depend on others for answers when delegating or when seeking input for the decisions they'll own. Many or even most of the decisions they have to make lie outside their own expertise. The best CEOs are extremely intentional in whom they reach out to. They realize early on that not all input is created equal. Through what lens is an advisor or division head viewing the issue? What personal biases affect their point of view? Do they have an agenda? Are they able to think beyond historical approaches?

Even when a leader does have the necessary experience, his own involvement creates a natural bias. Dan Ariely, a professor of psychology and behavioral economics at Duke, conducted a fascinating experiment showcasing the creator's bias.[13] He provided participants with paper and instructions to make origami. After completion, the origami was put up for sale to two groups—the origami makers and the observers, people who were brought in just to view the finished pieces. Perhaps not surprisingly, the builders were willing to pay five times more than the observers. Whether we recognize it or not, when our fingerprints are on a decision, we are inherently biased.

Smart decision makers get help to counter their own bias while carefully screening their sources. We saw a few common strategies among high-scorers in the "decisive" competency. CEOs often rely on what we call Multiple Outsider Perspectives (or MOPs). Kim has worked closely with Doug Shipman, the president and CEO of The Woodruff Arts Center in Atlanta, who has earned a reputation for changing the game with counterintuitive calls that somehow always turn out to be right. He told Kim that most of his "truth tellers" were not just outside the company, but outside his industry.

Doug told us three ways that MOPs helped advise him in ways that his employees couldn't. First, because they were outsiders, he had to bring them up to speed on the issue at hand in simple, clear language. Sometimes just that step of the process revealed to him a new answer or a flaw in his logic. Second, despite being outsiders, they often had information or perspective that offered insights to the issue at hand. And finally, because these outsiders knew him personally, they were terrific sources of "soft" advice. They asked questions that most colleagues would never dare to ask, such as, "Is this direction in line with your values?"

Geoff Smart, the chairman and founder of ghSMART, introduced us to a process called 3D-ing that he uses to ensure a variety of inputs and perspectives in situations where company executives are too close to an issue. The three Ds stand for Discuss, Debate, and Decide. Let's say you are making a hiring decision, and, for whatever reason, you have an easy and immediate consensus. But this could be an example of groupthink, so you turn to the 3D-ing process. First, the team

Discusses: The information and case are presented, and everyone can ask questions to fully understand the information. Then comes the *Debate:* The hiring candidate is assigned a champion who has to make the pitch for hiring that candidate to everybody in the room. A second person is asked to play devil's advocate, arguing the opposite point of view and listing reasons the candidate shouldn't be hired. Once the committee has heard from both sides for the candidate, it *Decides.*

The process helps managers get a fresh point of view. But there's an important secondary effect too. Once each stage is completed, commitment increases. The executives never go back. This prevents them from questioning matters that have already been decided. The team moves relentlessly—*decisively*—forward.

. . .

Reaching a decision only solves half the problem. You have to get the organization to act on the decision, or it is no decision at all. So how do you create clarity, momentum, and motivation to enlist others to carry it out? When the VC firm Andreessen Horowitz evaluates CEOs, one of their primary questions is, *Can the CEO get the company to do what she knows is right?*[14] This is critical to understand, not just for CEOs, but for any leader.

Each CEO and leader has his own unique way to compel others to action. They become skilled envoys not just of the "what" but also the "why." Veteran CEO Bill Amelio is one of the best we know at motivating his teams to action. When we asked him how he does it, he said, "The leader needs to paint the picture very clearly of what the reality is that you're in and then how tomorrow could be better than today. If you do that in a compelling way, you can get a lot of people to follow you pretty quickly."

Decisiveness is inextricably linked with your ability to engage with others in a way that drives results. How best to do that as a leader is the focus of our next chapter.

KEY TAKEAWAYS

1. Make faster decisions.

2. Make fewer decisions.

3. Look back. Learn from your past decisions.

4. Look inward. Ensure you are physically and mentally ready to make clearheaded decisions.

5. Look forward. Gain distance from the decision at hand. Consciously apply a "future" lens to the current decision.

6. Look around. Ensure the diversity and robustness of your information in an effort to screen out bias.

7. When things go poorly, take full ownership and mine the mistakes for learnings.

chapter 3

Engage for Impact: Orchestrate Stakeholders to Drive Results

A conductor is nothing without an orchestra.
—Gustavo Dudamel, music director of the Los Angeles Philharmonic

AT THEIR BEST, LEADERS HAVE THE POWER TO CREATE A NEW AND better reality. But the only way this new reality will emerge is by leaders enlisting others around them to do something different and often seemingly impossible. This is especially true for a CEO. *Despite their power and authority, CEOs are almost entirely dependent on the actions of others for their success. Interdependence—not independence—wins the game.* SAS analysis of our assessments shows this statistically: Two out of every three highly independent CEOs are likely to underperform expectations.[1]

CEOs have always had to be masters of relationships and influence. Today, the challenge is especially daunting, and the stakes are higher than ever. The range of stakeholders that CEOs deal with is vast and their interests ever changing and often divergent. Customers whose needs and tastes can shift faster than the wind. Millennial employees who want unprecedented levels of autonomy, transparency, and frequent positive reinforcement. Shareholders who want a strong long-term growth trajectory but are unwilling to sacrifice earnings and dividends today. Media who are hungry for a big story. Retirees who want a say on benefits. The list goes on. A CEO's day may start with a call to Asian investors at six in the morning and end with a customer visit at a farm in Kansas later in the day. There is little margin for error, as any CEO today is just one tweet or bad-news story away from public disgrace.

You'd imagine that navigating this dizzying parade of people and often-conflicting agendas must take the stamina of a marathoner and the likeability of "Miss Congeniality." While stamina is always an asset, the story with likeability is more intriguing. When Kaplan and Sørenson analyzed 2,600 ghSMART assessments of C-suite executives, it became clear that *the odds of being hired are indeed higher for "likeable" executives. Yet when it comes to performance in the CEO role, likeability alone leads to suboptimal results. CEOs who engaged others with a results orientation were 75 percent more successful than those who simply excelled at interpersonal skills or being likeable.*[2]

Meanwhile, Cambridge University professor Sucheta Nadkarni and her collaborators analyzed CEO profiles and results in 195 Indian companies in the business process outsourcing industry. Nadkarni uncovered a bell-curved relationship between CEOs' "agreeableness" (psychologists' term for what is colloquially referred to as "likeable" or "nice") and business performance.[3] Up to a certain point, having the ability to engage well with others translates into better performance. But past a "sweet spot" at the top of the bell curve, being too agreeable (too nice) can backfire as CEOs hesitate to make the tough calls out of fear of upsetting the apple cart.

Research by Kaplan and Nadkarni highlighted analytically what we have observed in our experience. *Successful CEOs engage with others for impact rather than affinity.* They balance keen insight into their stakeholders' priorities with an unrelenting focus on delivering business results. They deeply understand others' needs without falling into the temptation to pander to them. They are aware of the discomfort or even pain a tough decision may impose on others, but ultimately they subordinate their own and others' needs to the demands of the business. In contrast, CEOs who engage for affinity are driven by their desire to be liked and are concerned about causing discomfort to others. Nadkarni's analysis and our experience point out that both extremes—"too nice" and "not nice enough"—lead to disappointing results and can get a CEO fired. So, how do successful CEOs hit the sweet spot at the top of the bell curve?

NICENESS BELL CURVE

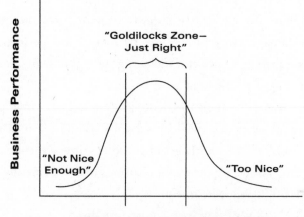

Being Too "Nice" Can Get You Fired

"Gary" is a CEO who prides himself on being a consensus-building leader. He cares deeply about his employees and is eager to please. When he was first hired a couple of years ago, the board was impressed with Gary's values and trustworthy demeanor. But Gary's desire to be a "good guy" had led to an ever-growing list of priorities with no strategic focus. If his marketing leader proposed targeting a new customer segment,

Gary agreed—even if previously he'd decided to focus on core customers. If his real estate director advocated leasing new facilities in Europe, he said yes—despite Europe not being a priority market. Gary's attempts to please everyone led to major dysfunction on the team. Conflicting priorities and initiatives caused friction among his leaders. Conflict avoidance led to backdoor politicking and tolerance of mediocrity. With the team distracted, competitors started to gain share and the company fell behind plan. Before long, the board decided to change its CEO.

Skewing *too nice* can be a devastating problem for leaders. It can damage every one of the trifecta of key performance drivers—managing priorities, picking the right talent, and creating the right relationships.

Nice leaders struggle to say no, leading to ever growing and shifting priorities, followed by suboptimal and often slow results. Decisions constantly get revisited anytime someone raises a concern, paralyzing the team. Cautious to avoid creating "losers," these CEOs create no winners.

"Nice" CEOs allow subpar performers to remain in the organization, creating a huge drag on morale and results. While the organization pays lip service to upgrading talent, the toughest personnel decisions go unaddressed, leaving strong performers frustrated.

Conflict aversion is among the hallmarks of "nice" CEOs, who misinterpret *collaborative* to mean *frictionless*. Their team meetings are the business equivalent of a group hug, with no in-depth discussion of real issues. Invariably, this soft touch gets interpreted as an absence of candor and, over time, can lead to a loss of trust and credibility as well as an organizational addiction to groupthink.

CEOs who **Engage for Impact** are akin to great orchestra conductors. *The only member of the orchestra who doesn't produce any music directly, the conductor, like a CEO, is entirely dependent on others to deliver results.* To better understand parallels between great orchestra conductors and great leaders, we turned to Robert Spano, the celebrated conductor and music director of the Atlanta Symphony Orchestra. In addition to his artistic mastery, Spano is recognized for his distinctive communicative abilities, creating a sense of alignment, inclusion, and warmth among musicians and audiences that is unique among American orchestras. According to Spano, "A conductor's purpose is to set the musical vision, to elicit orchestra members to buy into that vision, and to establish the pulse for the group to perform that vision. A great conductor does a lot of listening to deeply understand his performers: what they think, what their concerns are, what's motivating and disappointing them. The conductor does all of that with the sole purpose of serving the vision of the music."

Even the conductor's relationship to the audience is instructive. The conductor stands with his back to the audience—seemingly the ultimate arbiter for his art—undistracted by immediate reactions and entirely focused on fulfilling his vision of the score. It is much the same reason that Warren Buffett advocates that publicly traded companies not be required to provide quarterly earnings guidance to Wall Street analysts: to avoid the temptation to cater to short-term reactions of the market.[4] *Great conductors and great leaders alike conduct without pandering.*

Tom Monahan, former CEO of business information services company CEB, is keenly aware of the need to artfully "conduct" across multiple and often conflicting stakeholders. "As a CEO, I've always worked hard to understand the needs of all my stakeholders—customers, employees, board, shareholders . . . and keep them all *constructively dissatisfied* so that we could move the business forward in order to deliver for all of them. If you did what it takes to fully satisfy any of your stakeholder groups, you would bankrupt the company in a hurry. At their most extreme, each group's needs put real pressure on the company. Customers want everything better and cheaper. Employees would ideally want to get paid more for less work. Shareholders want maximum profit and growth, often at the same time, in perpetuity. So you need to keep all of them at a point of constructive dissatisfaction where they are not getting all of what they want but enough to continue to support the company, so that you can grow and innovate the business to deliver for all of them." Tom essentially advocates for leading a company with one's back toward the audience.

A tour of the pantheon of the world's greatest orchestra conductors would reveal a colorful array of styles, personalities, and philosophies. Yet these diverse conductors share a common language of gestures and approaches. Similarly, we see common principles among CEOs who **Engage for Impact:**

- *They lead with intent.* These CEOs translate their vision, goals, and acute awareness of context into commercial intent for the business overall and for every interaction they engage in.

- *They understand the players.* They tune in to understand the unique needs—emotional, financial, physical, or otherwise—of the full multitude of players who impact realization of the intent.

- *They build routines* to enlist these players to support the intent.

How they do it—and how you can engage for impact in your own career—is the focus of this chapter. We will offer the most important "conducting" practices we have uncovered to help you engage for impact like a CEO, no matter where you are in your career.

Lead with Intent

Crafting strategy comes readily to many who reach the corner office. The harder challenge is constantly translating that strategy day in, day out, in different ways and for different audiences, so that all participants, in every interaction, clearly understand what they need to do and why it's so important. Good CEOs have a clear vision; great CEOs can enlist everyone from the janitor to the largest customer behind the vision and explain how and why the smallest details of that individual's role are critical to success. Their secret? *They lead, in every interaction, with intent.* Leading with intent requires a leader to a) clearly articulate the intent to herself, b) consistently align her daily actions with her intent, and c) act on her intent in each interaction based on deep understanding of her audience and context.

There's nothing inspiring about showing up with a "to do" list and doling out tasks. People want to know where you're taking them and *why,* particularly if you're asking them to do something difficult or different from what they're used to doing. When they understand the why, they can improvise, straying from the plan as needed to fulfill your original intent. They will trust and enlist behind your intent when your own daily actions and even small habits are consistent with it.

Often we find that communicating intent to others is hardest when leaders haven't explicitly articulated it for themselves. We recently coached a CEO of an investment firm (we will call him Nick) who was painfully aware of his need to delegate more. A brilliant investor, this CEO was admired for his commercial insights, analytical prowess, and deal instincts. He naturally played "principal violinist" in any important meeting ever since he'd started the firm.

Until the nineteenth century, orchestras were led by principal violinists.[5] All the other members took their cue from them. That worked initially but did not scale. As orchestras got larger, it took too long for the signal to travel from the front of the orchestra to the back. The lag between what the violins and the timpani were playing became noticeable. Thus dawned the era of professional conductors.

Nick didn't have centuries to make the transition. He wanted to move faster. Nick's firm has been so successful that it has grown very quickly and now needed him to be a conductor, not a performer. Easier said than done. "I'm really frustrated," Nick told us. "I feel like I'm still running the investment meetings. No one is stepping up. We have smart people, but they rely on me too much."

"Well, if you want others to lead, why are you still attending the meetings?" we asked. Nick, who typically left no space for a breath, paused to think for a few seconds before he responded. He hadn't considered this simple question of intent.

"I'm there so that I can listen and coach them into being good stewards of our firm's capital. I should be mainly taking notes and asking questions occasionally, but they keep turning to me to lead," he said.

We observed, "If you weren't clear with yourself or with them about why you were attending, *they* probably aren't clear either. You're their boss, and they are used to you driving the discussions, so it's natural for them to turn to you. You need to communicate your intent."

By taking just a few moments at the beginning to express his intent, Nick changed the effectiveness of these meetings. Once he was clear with himself about why he was attending, he found it easy to communicate that intent to others. And once his team understood his intent, they were emboldened to step up. Nick and his team didn't change their old habits overnight, but their explicit shared intent became the catalyst they needed to shift from a frustrating stalemate to gradual positive change.

If the first challenge is to clearly articulate the intent, an even greater test is a leader's commitment to carry out that intent in every action, decision, and interaction, no matter how small. A conductor's and a leader's actions speak louder than words. If a conductor's gestures fall out of sync with the musical vision he expressed in rehearsals, cacophony and confusion ensue.

Leaders (and, really, all of us) operate on two levels of intent: aspirational and transactional. Aspirational intent is born in the answers to questions such as: *What is the one thing that matters most? When this company is successful, what will others say about it?* Transactional intent is our underlying goal in a specific situation. In the example of Nick his aspirational intent was to grow the next generation of investors in order to ensure the lasting success of his firm. When it came to investment committee meetings, however, he was stuck in his old, habitual, transactional intent of driving towards the right investment decisions on individual deals. His transactional intent was misaligned with his broader aspirational intent, resulting in frustration and ineffectiveness. We see costly and sometimes even tragic misalignments between aspirational and transactional intent all around us.

In the early evening of Sunday, April 9, 2017, Dr. David Dao boarded United Airlines Flight 3411 to get home to Louisville, Kentucky, from Chicago's O'Hare International Airport. The flight was two hours delayed and overbooked—an inconvenience, but hardly out of the ordinary. What happened next became front-page news all over the world. As the *New York Times* reported, "The disturbing scene captured on cellphones . . . went beyond the typical nightmares of travelers on an overbooked flight. An unidentified man [Dao] who refused to be bumped from a plane screamed as a security officer wrestled him out of his seat and dragged him down the aisle by his arms. His glasses slid down his face, and his shirt rose above his midriff as uniformed officers followed."

The Kentucky doctor suffered a concussion, a broken nose, and two lost teeth. United Airlines shareholders suffered a loss of as much as $1.4 billion as stock dropped 4 to 6 percent by Tuesday morning.[6] CEO Oscar Munoz suffered a huge reputational crisis and lost his shot at becoming chairman. Testifying in front of the House Transportation Committee, Munoz summarized: "Our policies got ahead of our values."[7] After the CEO apologized to the public, the company reached a settlement with Dao.

This was a painful case of transactional intent being woefully out of line with aspirational intent. The United flight attendant who called security was acting under the *transactional* pressure to avoid further costly delays—she needed to get the plane on its way to Louisville. The security officer was acting under the *transactional* pressure to stop the conflict reported by the crew. Munoz (who, ironically, had been named communicator of the year by *PRWeek* just weeks earlier) was acting under the *transactional* pressure to support his employees and save face. Trouble was, none of these served the *aspirational* intent that can be glimpsed in the "United Customer Commitment" featured on the corporate website: "We are committed to providing a level of service to our customers that makes us a leader in the airline industry. We understand that to do this we need to have a product we are proud of and employees who like coming to work every day. Our goal is to make every flight a positive experience for our customers."

While the United debacle represents an extreme case, misalignment between aspirational and transactional intent is always costly. The cost may not be immediately obvious, but over time it is corrosive to a leader's effectiveness and ultimately to his or her credibility. When aspirational and transactional intent are misaligned, a leader can come across as manipulative, advancing his own agenda at the expense of others—one hardly worth following. To the contrary, leaders who act with alignment of aspirational and transactional intent are better able to enlist others. Perhaps that's why our data shows that the strongest persuaders don't sacrifice respect for others when they engage. In fact, they are more likely to treat people with respect than are underperforming CEOs.[8]

Finally, to translate intent into actions effectively, ask yourself the following questions before each interaction: What is my *one* most important goal? [Your aspirational intent.] How does this interaction fit within that goal? What is the outcome in this interaction that would best contribute to that one most important goal? What do I want this person or this team to think, feel, and do? [Your transactional intent.] What will it take to deliver that outcome? The best CEOs learn to ask these questions habitually before every important interaction. Those who do it well find it has a dramatic, sometimes surprising, effect on how they engage with others.

We were recently prepping a new CEO for his first big meeting with his extended leadership team. We invited him to explore each individual and functional area in the room, asking, "What do you want each of them to think, feel, and do as the result of stepping out of that meeting with you?" For example, the sales function was in the midst of introducing a new approach to selling solutions (instead of discrete products). As a result of recent misses in key customer deals, we got agreement from the CEO that the intent for the sales leaders coming out of the meeting would be that those sales leaders:

- **Think:** the recent lost deals were sizeable, critical misses and a sign of a concerning pattern, not just the normal course of business

- **Feel:** responsible for those misses and motivated to try a new way of approaching these deals, as their bonuses are tied to meeting quota

- **Do:** proactively bring services leaders into future big deals early on to engage customers with solutions rather than isolated products—the key reason they lost out versus their competition.

Taking this clear intent, the CEO then tailored his messages to achieve those goals. As we've heard several CEOs say, "Sell the people, not the concept." Skilled persuasion is a consistent differentiator of successful CEOs. These CEOs are clear about their intent. They deliberately influence stakeholders around them. To do that, they develop deep insights into their stakeholders.

Understand the Players

Once you are clear about your intent, you need to understand your stakeholders in order to rally them behind your decisions. Going back to the metaphor of the conductor, you have to be able to translate the score equally well for the oboist and the violinist.

When it comes to connecting to myriad stakeholders, Neil Fiske is a master. In his first CEO job, at Bath & Body Works from 2003 to 2007, he reversed twenty-six months of negative comparable store growth and grew sales from $1.8 to $2.5 billion, all without opening new stores. When Billabong called in 2013, the Australian surf sportswear maker had just posted $860 million in losses, triple the previous year's. Despite market headwinds and a lot of challenges under Neil's leadership, in 2015, Billabong posted its first full-year profit since 2001.

You might think that Neil was a hatchet man, a guy who only cared about numbers in a ledger. But that was not the case. The progress he drove had everything to do with his well-honed ability to hear what others—consumers, bosses, and employees—needed and pull it all together in service of a vision.

Neil attributes his success to being a good listener and "translator." "I remember one story from my time working with Neil," says Kim. "We were leading a focus group for a specialty women's clothing company. In one room, there were a dozen women in their midtwenties. In another room, behind a one-way mirror, sat Neil and I and a team of [marketing] executives. Some guys would have shied away from that conversation, saying, 'This isn't for me. I'm not going to sit here to learn how women feel about their clothing,'" says Kim. "And yet Neil was 100 percent laser focused on learning what really made a difference for these women. He somehow pulled off being able to listen and watch the customers, extract from them what made them really feel good, and then, through a moderator, reflect it back at them, in their own language. And on top of that, he was absolutely fluid, switching from their language to the language he needed to speak with the marketing executives, and back again to asking questions of the women in the focus group." Neil didn't know what it's like to be a woman feeling sexy in her clothes—he couldn't know that. So he didn't presume to guess. Instead, he became a detective. He paid careful attention to the women's each and every word and gesture. He asked questions, drilling down, coming at the topic from every possible angle. In trying to get into these women's heads and hearts, he didn't rely on empathy or try to connect emotionally. Instead, he engaged intellectually to listen and gather information to understand, and then harness what mattered to these women. Results speak for themselves. Neil's efforts became the cornerstone of what became a $1 billion business for this specialty women's clothing company, the biggest launch in the company's history.

Whether a male leader seeking to glean insights on how women feel in particular clothes or a CEO understanding why a major shareholder is disgruntled about a new revenue recognition method, as you rise through the ranks you face an increasingly complex set of stakeholders, many of whom have needs, assumptions, and feelings very different from yours.

CEOs in our sample who **Engage for Impact** focus on understanding exactly who their stakeholders are and what they want. Successful understanding of another's point of view comes from asking and listening—not imagining. Chicago Business School professor Nicholas Epley calls this more accurate approach *perspective getting*.[9] Epley comments that actively trying to imagine being in another person's circumstance is no guarantee that you'll be able to imagine it correctly. If you've ever had a doctor with an incredible bedside manner, you've already experienced this firsthand. A great doctor doesn't take one look at you and tell you what's wrong. He (or she) gently interviews you—not just about your physical state, but probably about your mood, too. As he sits beside you, you think, "What a great doctor. I trust that guy." In your relaxed state, you tell him everything. And so, not only are you more confident in his diagnosis, it's also more likely to be right. Not all of us are gifted in the ability to connect with diverse stakeholders. As Epley points out, we are often overconfident in our ability to infer what's going on in another's mind, what they think, feel, and want; and even further, we have difficulty feeling what they feel. Luckily, the good news for all of us is, *perspective getting* is something that can be learned, practiced, and applied.

One CEO we've worked with, whom we will call Devon, is a charismatic leader who openly admits that he struggles with empathy. And yet he's an expert at *perspective getting*. He learns everything he can about a person before a meeting and listens intently in the room. He picks up on subtle cues using active listening and pattern recognition. Preparing for a recent meeting with a prospective customer, he observed: "You know what? I think this guy likes to be smart, and he is risk averse. If we want him to add us to his roster of suppliers, we need to get him to see it as a low-risk move." Then in the meeting he will drop casually: "A leading player in this space partnered with multiple suppliers rather than single sourcing this component. It proved to be a smart strategy—many of the competitors experienced stock-outs and they picked up share," and you can see this customer's eyes light up with insight that perhaps maintaining multiple suppliers is the most prudent strategy. What Devon lacks in empathy he makes up for in insight and analytics, helping him understand and engage his audience.

Introverts are often gifted at *perspective getting*. They are naturally predisposed to listen more than talk, and they deliberately process and prepare for interpersonal interactions.[10] This likely contributes to the fact that in our data set, self-described introverts were slightly more likely to outperform expectations than were extroverts.[11] Fred Hassan is a good example of an introvert who wildly exceeded expectations.

Fred is a legendary CEO and deal maker who ran Pharmacia, Schering-Plough (growing the value of the company 62 percent while a comparable peer set dropped 21 percent), and Bausch + Lomb. "Early on you may not have seen it in me. I was rather shy growing up. Most people would've said 'nice guy but not the most extroverted among the people out there.' I wouldn't have said I was a natural leader early on, but I've always had a genuine interest in people. I wanted to do what I could to help them, taking a lot of enjoyment and pleasure out of that. I wasn't into my agenda—I was much more into understanding others."

Perspective getters recognize the need to go straight to the source to find out what people think and feel, whether board members, customers, or employees. Scott Cook, founder of Intuit, built an over $5 billion business on the power of *perspective getting*. Intuit teams regularly spend a day watching their customers work to understand firsthand the problems and pains they encounter. "In 2002, I looked at every new product that we made, trying to understand successes and failures. Winners shared two characteristics. First, was there a really important and painful unsolved customer problem? Second, did we solve it better than anyone else? And generally, if we got those two right, we had a successful business. Businesses are here to improve people's lives. Our mistakes all seemed to err on one or both, so we created a process to really immerse ourselves in customer experience to better identify unsolved customer problems."

Instead of *perspective getting*, we often see executives fall into the opposite trap—projecting their experience or feelings onto others. That leads to mistaken assumptions and misguided expectations, alienating others and ultimately eroding the willingness of people to follow you as a leader.

Steve Kaufman grew Arrow Electronics from $500 million to $12 billion as a CEO from 1986 to 2000. By all accounts, Steve is a successful CEO. Yet early in his CEO tenure, Steve learned a painful lesson on **Engaging for Impact**. As a distributor, Arrow's relationship with its suppliers was critical, and there was a large organization responsible for managing those relationships. Steve decided to split the marketing and purchasing activities into two separate organizations. "The numerate geeks will run inventories and purchasing, while the smooth-talking guys who don't love numbers will do marketing programs. It made all the sense in the world! Everyone will love it," he assumed, without digging deeply into his team's motivations. To Steve, this was an obviously superior approach.

Everyone did not love it. "Our most senior people lost the power to spread purchasing dollars among the suppliers, so they just refused to go along. They started telling the suppliers that this Kaufman is crazy. He doesn't understand the industry. This thing is terrible." Major suppliers such as Intel and Texas Instruments quickly lashed out at Steve: "What the hell are you doing? You're destroying your company! Your people are gonna leave! You just don't get how this business works!"

"My own people turned adamantly against this initiative," Steve told us. Although it meant losing face, he had to back off his plan. And he never forgot the lesson—to be sure to get into the heads of his stakeholders and thoroughly understand relevant context (*perspective getting*) before acting. As he reflected, "I became more sensitive to the need to get buy-in from the organizational thought leaders. I learned I needed to have people who knew how the business ran involved during the design phase." Just because something made sense to him didn't mean it would make sense to the people who had to carry it out.

Whether you're motivating your team to take the hill, bringing a new product to market, or winning over a prickly board of directors, *perspective getting* can make the difference between success and failure.

Typically, every CEO candidate we meet is good at relating to others in some domains, but few have mastered all of them. We might see someone who's listening closely to the customer but is anxious dealing with board members. Someone else might be perfectly in sync with her direct reports but jarringly out of tune when it comes to peers. At every level of our careers, we are part of a web. And each of us benefits from developing connections across that web—asking enough questions and listening closely enough to develop strong *perspective getting* muscles.

A Surprising Tool for *Perspective Getting*

The importance of finding powerful and supportive mentors is among the mainstays of your typical "Career Management 101" instruction. However, when we had SAS crunch our assessment data, we found that the *weaker* CEO candidates talked about the importance of mentors to *their* careers. The *stronger* candidates talked about *offering* mentorship to others more than about the mentorship they received themselves.[12] While completely contrary to conventional wisdom, this is consistent with everything we know about engaging for impact.

Mentoring others is a powerful laboratory for *perspective getting*—it's hard to help someone without understanding his needs. Those who mentor others become the men and women who have the team, the network, and the resources to get things done. Growing as a leader is a lot easier when there are people eager to follow you. And corporate boards know that when they hire a CEO, they hire her network too.

Jim Donald summed up his success across his CEO roles at Starbucks, Pathmark, and Extended Stay Hotels this way: "The secret of rising in your career is taking care of everybody in the organization first, by giving people credit when they do it correctly, and then by forming relationships on the front line. That's so critical because, as you climb, it's easier to have a base of support underneath you that pushes you up, rather than trying to pull yourself up as an individual."

Build Your Relationships Through Routines

Much of an orchestra conductor's job is done during rehearsals, well before the musicians get onstage. Similarly, for a leader, aligning effectively across an entire organization requires more than mere intention, more than a mere understanding of stakeholders' motivations and needs. It requires everyday habits and routines to build those relationships and to translate relationships into actions that advance business results. In fact, it requires rising stars and CEOs alike to adopt the very same deliberative practice that makes an orchestra great. Set routines and methods, repeated day in day out, ultimately make the complex act of prompting an orchestra of diverse musicians to play in concert seem effortless and invisible. What follows are the four critical routines for achieving that level of performance mastery in how you **Engage for Impact:**

1. Communicate. Communicate. Communicate.

Repetition matters. At Billabong, Neil Fiske created a five-year, seven-stage turnaround strategy. He made sure people always knew where they were in the strategy and whether they were ahead or behind. "Every conference call we have, every internal meeting, we come back to that in some way, shape, or form."

How do you make sure your message gets through? Neil suggests what he calls the rule of sevens: Any message has to be repeated seven times in seven different ways before an organization has any hope of hearing it. Formal memo. Videotape. A blog. Posting a printed memo on the bulletin board. A town hall meeting. Parking lot talk as you're walking. Chat around the water cooler. You've got to push. You can't overcommunicate.

Without this constant push, messages simply don't land with enough consistency to engage everyone, as Steve Kaufman found at Arrow Electronics, to his great frustration. When Steve visited local offices, he'd spend the first half of the day going through the office, talking to the operations people, and sitting with the general manager. Then in the afternoon he'd go out and ride with the sales reps. "Hey, you know, what do you think of the marketing program with Texas Instruments? Is it working or not?" he might ask. A third of the time the rep might say, "It's a great program. It's working. I'm getting a lot of sales." A third of the time, the person would say, "You know, it doesn't work here, and we've just adjusted it because our market is different." "And I can live with that," says Steve. "The real trouble are the last third, who'd say, 'What program?'"

2. Break down the sound barrier.

Most executives we work with severely underestimate the sound barrier around their office. In their minds, they are still "Mary" or "Randy"— one of the team. Whereas for others in the organization, they became the big boss the moment they got promoted. It takes extra effort to continue unfettered communication. CEOs must proactively take steps so that people feel comfortable opening up and sharing critical information, whether it be early-warning indicators, opportunities to improve, or even great wins.

Robert Hanson, the current CEO of John Hardy, used this tactic earlier in his career to turn around the decline of Levi's Europe when he was the brand's president. At the time, the general manager in each European country was running his or her own fiefdom. This created expensive inefficiency and a Levi's 501 product that varied significantly from country to country, a problem for an "iconic" look. The general managers were decades older than the then-young and inexperienced Hanson, and they were wary of giving up their autonomy. Calling them to his office would have been seen as an immediate power play. Instead, he showed them the respect of a personal visit to build common ground. By showing respect and learning their needs, Hanson got them on board with the changes. By the time he left Levi's, revenue was growing again, reversing a double-digit decline.

3. Marry corporate, date the field.

A concept in Kaizen methodology suggests managers "go to where work is done." Effective CEOs get out of their office to meet their teams in their own comfort zones, where the work is being done. Some of the best CEOs—for example, Jim Donald, the former CEO of Extended Stay Hotels, Starbucks, and Pathmark—have told us they spend up to half of their time out of the office and in the field. Think about that: *Half* of Jim Donald's week was spent with receptionists, housekeepers, and guests—far afield of the image of the jet-setting, tycoon-greeting CEO. From his former boss Sam Walton, the founder of Walmart, Jim had learned early that leaders belong out on the floor, ever persistent in their quest to learn from customers and employees and, in turn, improve.

When it came to management, Jim used e-mail to create a powerful feedback loop. At Extended Stay, he sent two handwritten letters (which were then scanned and e-mailed) to hundreds of district and regional managers every week. The letters closed with a call to action: "Please e-mail me." Every week he got flooded with responses, and every week he answered every single e-mail. Property managers for the company received a daily voice mail from their CEO. The time invested paid off: Jim frequently heard about issues even before his executives did.

. . .

We often see talented professionals flatline midcareer because they fall too far to either extreme on the **Engage for Impact** bell curve. Some drive toward results with urgency but leave behind a trail of broken glass. Others are so concerned about how everyone feels that they struggle to move the business forward. In both cases, it can be daunting and even unnatural to shift the approach. As Jim told us, "It's not glamorous. It's not sexy. It's not fancy suits. You have to actually roll your sleeves up and put on the company shirt and go get your hands dirty."

Engaging for Impact is the deliberate application of intent, perspective getting, and broad and consistent outreach carefully tuned to the climate of the organization and its people. It's actively probing and assessing what matters to whom and why.

Eventually, this muscle building develops into what feels like natural instinct, enabling you to engage with everyone from a marketing intern to an engineering executive without the need for specialized expertise. The path to CEO is an endless education in human nature. Those who rise from the pack are, quite simply, the most devoted students.

Test Your Ability to Engage for Impact

Whether you are managing others for the first time or are already well along in your career, we challenge you to assess whether or not you've fallen into the niceness trap. Rate yourself using the questions below; get feedback from trusted colleagues. If you have answered yes to more than three questions below, you may be falling into the niceness trap. You may find that changing your behavior will pay outsize dividends in business performance:

1. Do your teams feel that your organization has too many priorities?
2. Do people leave performance review meetings you conduct with them unable to clearly articulate their strengths, gaps, and what's expected of them?
3. Do you move slowly to determine how to handle a loyal team member who is unlikely to fit with the company's future?

4. Is the word *nice* in the top three adjectives used to describe you?
5. When considering a decision, is your first thought about how it will impact relationships?
6. Do those around you (your team, your boss) say you avoid or minimize conflict?

KEY TAKEAWAYS

1. Define your intent. Align your aspirational intent (your most important big-picture goals) with your transactional intent (your goal for any one interaction).
2. Deploy perspective getting to understand various stakeholders.
3. Build routines to enlist stakeholders behind your intent.

chapter 4

Relentless Reliability: Deliver Consistently

We are what we repeatedly do.
Excellence, then, is not an act, but a habit.
—Aristotle

ONE OF OUR MOST SURPRISING DISCOVERIES CONCERNED AN ATTRI-
bute considered so mundane, it's generally ignored. In fact, you'll
never see it celebrated in CEO profiles or the business press. And yet
of all the behaviors that lead to executive success, it is the only one that
both increases a candidate's odds of getting hired *and* his or her odds
of excelling in the job.

What is that quality? It's not confidence or experience or even decisiveness. The killer behavior behind both hiring and performance
success is **Reliability.** *CEOs who are known for being reliable are fifteen
times more likely to be high performing, and their odds of getting hired are
double those of everyone else.*[1]

While reliability sounds obvious, we see leaders struggle every day
trying to get themselves and their organizations to consistently execute
on their commitments. A case in point—over nine thousand leaders have taken our diagnostic on the CEO Genome Behaviors, and

reliability continues to score the lowest. Why? Often, leaders rising up through the ranks in large companies are reliant on management systems that already exist. They are users of reliable systems but haven't had to build them. When faced with a situation where reliable systems and processes are lacking, they struggle. For leaders who have come up through the ranks in small companies, too often the experience is "all-hands-on-deck" all the time—addressing crushing problems and putting out fires. The executives fighting those fires feel that they are accomplishing a lot—and they are—but in the heat of constant firefighting, little attention is spent on putting processes in place to prevent the next fire. When they are thrust into CEO roles with high expectations, immense pressure, and short time lines, it is very difficult for them to make the case to invest time and money to build a strong business management system.

Why is reliability so powerful? Leaders who are reliable create the assumption among their customers, board members, and staff that they will get things done. Boards love "a safe pair of hands." So do fellow senior executives. And the data suggests that these candidates go on to create high-performance organizations.[2]

Take Bill Amelio. He's a veteran three-time CEO and currently the CEO of electronics distributor Avnet. Bill is high-energy, decisive, always pushing forward. He is an activity junkie who cannot sit still. There's nothing he loves more than winning and nothing he hates more than losing. He is the sort of person who almost never fails to keep a commitment, as his high school wrestling team learned when he competed through an entire wrestling season while recovering from a dislocated elbow. He ended up placing a close second in a tough Pennsylvania State finals match, losing the championship 6–4.

As a CEO, Bill exudes reliability. Everything about his MO says to those around him, "We're going to get this done." In each of his five executive roles since the late '90s, Bill established a calendar of communications—from weekly team meetings to quarterly town halls—and didn't deviate from that. In the words of one of Bill's direct reports, "You can't help but get the sense with the cadence of meetings that there is a strong management discipline. Bill has a systematic approach for succinct meetings, takeaways, accountabilities, and a sense for the rhythm of how the organization is run." Everyone knows exactly what's expected and is held accountable to it.

When we first met Bill Amelio, he had recently become the CEO of CHC Helicopter. CHC operates the largest fleet of medium to large helicopters in the world. Their metal birds transport oil rig workers offshore and fly search-and-rescue and emergency medical missions from Nigeria to Azerbaijan to the North Sea. Lives depend on CHC delivering reliable performance. But while the company kept customers safe, it was doing so at great expense. The billion-dollar-plus global enterprise with five thousand employees in thirty countries had been run like a mom-and-pop shop. The management team hadn't met its budgets in years. Helicopters sat idle. Getting spare parts was a mess. Bill was tasked with turning things around. A year into Bill's CEO tenure, CHC started meeting its budgets, and beating them, despite severe market pressure and a large debt burden.

When Bill takes the helm of an organization, he rebuilds like an engineer, creating business systems that find and address root problems. He redesigned the structure of CHC, making accountability a top priority. He wanted one person clearly accountable for each and every business priority. He quickly upgraded the management team, bringing on board a world-class CFO, head of operations, and other executives. With his executive team, he tracked action items relentlessly. The list had 347 items at its peak, which Bill thinned out to 35 as he led the team to more solid footing.

As part of advising Bill, we conducted an annual 360 feedback process for him and his executive team. Twenty-one feedback providers we interviewed for Bill were unanimous in reporting that his

Reliability was the key factor driving the company's success. They spoke admiringly of "Bill's diabolical follow-through." After CHC, Bill went on to become CEO of electronics distributor Avnet. Here too he quickly implemented his playbook of building a strong team and a robust business management system.

A hallmark of reliability is following through on commitments. In the sample we studied, 94 percent of the strongest CEO candidates followed through consistently on their commitments.[3] Research in the field of organizational psychology has found that people who are organized, disciplined, and thorough—that is, people who score high in conscientiousness, one of the five basic personality dimensions—have an increased probability of success in management roles.[4]

Bill Amelio may be one of the toughest bosses you are likely to encounter. But, tellingly, strong people follow him from company to company. The reason is simple: With Bill at the helm, they consistently win. And winning employees are engaged employees. Harvard Business School's Teresa Amabile, who studies the science of engagement, has found that nothing makes employees more satisfied and fulfilled and enthusiastic about their work than making progress.[5]

In business, reliable and competent people are cherished. Employers and clients are more apt to take risks on them and more apt to give them opportunities. They know instinctively that their determination to follow through is a huge factor in terms of career and company success. Moreover, being known for reliability gets you recognized. Mary Berner, today the CEO of Cumulus Media, told us that she got her first CEO gig at Fairchild Publications as the publisher of *Glamour* magazine because of her reputation for "delivery without drama."

The pillars of **Reliability** are personal consistency, setting realistic expectations, practicing radical personal accountability, and embedding consistency into the organization.

Discover the Thrill of Personal Consistency

Boards and shareholders place great value on consistency of results. Consistency leads them to believe that they can count on continued strong performance in the future. For example, we recently advised a board on CEO succession that was considering two strong internal CEO candidates—call them Peter and Mike. Peter often delivers way beyond his targets, pulling rabbits out of hats right and left. The trouble is that he's erratic. His wins look more like wild luck than repeatable behavior. There's a fine line between visionary thinking and harebrained schemes, and with Peter, the board isn't sure which they're getting.

Then there's Mike. Mike, on the other hand, rarely exceeds expectations, but he always meets them. You could set a clock by his performance. He's consistent and as solid and reliable as a rock. The board feels that they can trust him to deliver year in, year out.

Most boards, we find, choose a predictable performer over a mercurial genius. Life is full of surprises, but in their way of thinking, none should come from the CEO. Understandably so. In the boardroom, reliability consistently trumps exceptionalism as an individual character trait.

The fact is, people can anticipate and control for consistent if unusual behavior. But managing or working for an inconsistent boss or partner is like trying to do good work while running through a minefield.

Of the hundreds of 360 reviews we've conducted of underperforming CEOs, almost without exception, each one displayed destructive inconsistency in countless arenas. Here are a few archetypes that stuck out:

- **The Seagull:** "She is hands off until she has a flight to catch that will take her away from the office for a few days. Suddenly you get a million e-mails, and every-thing you've been doing for three months is wrong."

- **The Fireman:** "He waits to act until things become a crisis, and we don't know when or if or how he will step in."

- **The Dilettante:** "I never know what he'll dive into on any given day. Today it's China, tomorrow it's lean man-ufacturing, the next is how big data affects our business. His limited attention span whipsaws the organization, and we end up mastering nothing."

- **The Hothead:** "His reaction to anything depends on whether you catch him in a good mood or a bad mood. He has a new measuring stick to judge our work every day. None of us can figure out what puts him in a bad mood."

Doug Shipman, the founder and former CEO of the Center for Civil and Human Rights and current president and CEO of The Woodruff Arts Center in Atlanta, said to us: "Being consistent creates clear expectations. You want your team to be able to anticipate the first and second questions you ask and have already thought through the answers. You are teaching what you want them to pay attention to. If the budget numbers come back out of whack, you want them to dig into the critical levers on their own. The moment you are inconsistent twice, there is a new pattern." Jeff Swartz, the former CEO of Tim-berland, echoed this sentiment. "If you want to be serious, then you have to be serious all the time. Because if you're serious one day and happy the next, people will be confused. They won't be able to figure out where you're coming from, and that'll be threatening."[6]

Personal consistency creates a powerful, compelling rhythm that allows people to perform at their best.

The Habits of Highly Reliable Leaders

The successful CEOs we meet who understand the critical importance of reliability know that the little stuff matters. They work hard at being reliable in everything they do:

- They are on time for meetings, for planes, for phone calls.

- They make individual commitments (who is taking what actions by when) clear in meetings.

- They follow up on agreed-upon actions religiously.

- They make lists (to do, to read, mistakes, people to keep in touch with, useful resources, etc.)—and put those lists into action.

- They are aware of their mood, words, and actions in their interactions with their teams—are their actions and words having the desired effect?

- They keep the people who need to know in the loop, so that no one drops the ball.

Set Realistic Expectations

The belief that you are reliable, that you will do exactly what you say you're going to do, is the force that moves others to action. As Elisa Villanueva Beard, the CEO of Teach For America, put it, "Everyone is watching a chessboard, and each move you make speaks about who you are as a person, your values, your expectations, and how you care about and steward the work." So how do you create the perception of reliability when you are in the early stages of your career and may not yet have a track record you can point to? Here's what we've learned from studying the best: They proactively shape their commitments to create a situation where they can reliably deliver.

There are plenty of workers, from deliverymen to desk jockeys, who do what they say they're going to do. The superstars who transform reliability into a core leadership trait take this a step further. Just the "doing" isn't enough. They actively shape expectations for themselves and their teams. They don't wait until their pay grade or title gives them the authority. Jason Blessing, the CEO of the software company Plex Systems, told us that he owed his success on a global software implementation project—"the most challenging project of my life"—to his ability to seize and reset expectations.

He was only twenty-six and working at PeopleSoft at the time. A senior partner was in way over her head on a $10 million global software implementation. People on the project were calling it a "train wreck." Jason was asked to step into what was, indeed, a mess, initially working alongside the partner who was in over her head. While he brought strong project-management skills, the real difference maker was how he reset expectations with his client. The expectation was to use PeopleSoft resources, but Jason saw that they had staffed the project all wrong. For the project to be successful long-term, they needed a different approach. He had to sell the client not just on taking the partner (his boss!) off the project, a politically tricky move, but on staffing more of the project in-house, instead of relying on consultants. In short, he needed to sell them on a new set of expectations on how to best accomplish the job. Jason and his team ultimately crushed their goals. And the success he achieved put him on the map throughout the company as the guy who delivers, and the doors to opportunity flew open.

Reliable leaders look beyond the commitments that have been established explicitly. They watch carefully for signs of *implicit* expectations that are in play. Boards and bosses can often be spectacularly unclear in their communication. We recently saw a CEO trip up, even though he had not only met but even exceeded established revenue targets. His company, an Internet security services firm with around $50 million in revenue, had been acquired by a midmarket private equity firm. Based on market conditions at the time of the acquisition, they set revenue targets.

Now, the CEO was no slouch. He was working nonstop and had his team moving at a rapid clip. But busy as he was, he wasn't staying abreast of his communication with the board—constantly taking their temperature, monitoring their feedback and comments for signs that the expectations they had made explicit had changed. As the year went on, the economic climate for the industry improved. The owners got excited. And although they didn't explicitly ask for it, they assumed they'd see a corresponding boost in revenue beyond their agreed-upon goals.

When the CEO finally showed up to present the numbers, he thought they would be pleased with his performance. He'd hit all the targets. But the board was unimpressed. They wanted a lot more than he'd delivered. He felt blindsided, which caused frustration on his part and strained relationships with the board.

Attempting to set expectations with your boss or, in the case of a CEO, the board isn't about believing you have the right to set your own terms and agenda. It's having the skills to sense what others want—but may not say—as well as the ability to persuade them to see the future as you intend to shape it.

Wherever you are in your career, you too can shape expectations to ensure reliable delivery. When you're handed a project, your response shouldn't be, "Okay, I'll get to work on it." Say instead: "Here's what I'm going to deliver by when. And consider it done." And then make sure you follow through.

Stand Up and Be Counted On

Getting others to move to your drumbeat requires more than clear expectations and relentless follow-up. You need to become a leader who makes his or her employees *want* to hit the target. There are two ways we've seen such exacting leaders as Bill Amelio buy themselves the latitude to be as tough as they are and still win the undying loyalty—and reliability—of their teams.

CEOs who excel in **Reliability** practice *radical personal accountability* with their stakeholders—employees, customers, clients, partners, and the board. They earn the right to hold others accountable by holding themselves accountable to the highest standards.

Mary Berner, the "delivery without drama" CEO we mentioned earlier, told us how she held herself accountable to her team—and her entire organization. At one of her tougher CEO gigs, a few years after she joined, Mary steered *Reader's Digest* through a prearranged bankruptcy. Mary realized she needed to quickly embed a fresh, twenty-first-century notion of personal accountability and transparency while enacting some very tough decisions, such as cutting 8 percent of the workforce. So what did she do? She let every single one of her five thousand employees grade her personally every six months. And she posted every comment without filter on the company intranet for everyone to see. "People thought that I would filter them, but they could tell by what was up there that I didn't. Because the good, bad, and ugly were all out there, it created credibility. What happens as a CEO is that you live in your own little world, and CEOs spew out a lot of rhetoric. Every CEO out there talks about accountability, but if you are not personally accountable to your people, they don't buy it."

The second behavioral pattern we recognized was deeply rooted in the motivations of these high-rising leaders. Underneath the customary ambition and drive, we witnessed a core desire to be someone whom others can truly depend on. In their personal and professional lives, highly reliable CEOs want to stand up and be counted on.

We saw this trait while interviewing Jason Blessing, the Plex Systems CEO we mentioned earlier. When he stepped into that early career-defining project we described earlier, professional ambition wasn't on his mind, and he wanted us to understand that. He wasn't jockeying for power or looking for renown. His drive was much simpler: He just wanted to help. "I was trying to act with integrity to make our customer successful and the team successful," he told us.

Earlier on in our work with CEOs, we would have naïvely told you that Blessing must be an outlier. What trait other than hard-driving ambition would cause someone to take on such a difficult project with such a low chance of success? Now, having interviewed hundreds of CEOs, we know that this motivation—the desire to be someone others can always count on—isn't an anomaly. In fact, it's a dominant theme. Bill Amelio may have said it most clearly: "One of the best reasons [to want to be CEO] is that you really love managing and leading people. It's something that just turns you on. The fact is, you care about others." The last time we saw Bill, he had just spent the better part of his weekend helping one of his executives navigate a family crisis.

"Leaders are there when it counts," said former USC professor and leadership guru Warren Bennis. "They are ready to support their co-workers in the moments that matter."[7] Early in our careers, we tend to be task oriented. It is the desire to achieve individually that leads many of us to become high-performers. For those of you who are young and hungry, words like *dependable* and *steady* may still feel foreign in a professional context. That's normal at this stage of life. Not many begin their careers with a natural focus on responsibility to others. But with experience over time, those who aspire to senior leadership develop in that direction.

There is a simple reason: Those who don't focus outward find that their careers hit a brick wall. To become a successful manager and leader, you need to be able to transition from being focused on individual achievement to collective achievement. One scales, and the other doesn't. Those focused primarily on themselves stop delivering when they begin managing others. The more senior you become, the more attention and energy you have to invest in your team. Those who move up start asking themselves, "What are my boss/colleagues/clients trying to do, and how can I help them get there?"

Adopt the Drills of Highly Reliable Organizations

Our final insights on reliability come from some unlikely places: nuclear reactors, aircraft carriers, and oil rigs, high-risk workplaces where reliability isn't a matter of meeting quarterly targets but, literally, a matter of life and death. Every aspect of these organizations' culture and process has to be fine-tuned to minimize failure, ensure safety, and avert catastrophe. They're confronting head-on the challenge that we've heard hangs on a sign posted at the Navy's "Top Gun" fighter pilot academy: "Under pressure, you do not rise to the occasion; you sink to your level of training."

Organizational psychologists call these High-Reliability Organizations.[8] In comparing practices in them to the habits of reliable leaders in our own data, we saw parallels that can help people perform in complex, high-pressure systems—basically, every modern corporation.

Of course, bringing these practices to life will require some tailoring to your business, industry, objectives, and context. For companies in turnaround, for example, we've seen CEOs go so far as to personally sign off on every check, because successfully managing cash flow carries "life or death" implications. Yet this same tactic would amount to harmful micromanagement in a highly innovative business in growth mode.

1. Make mistakes safe.

We've spoken before about the importance of learning from failure to fine-tune your decisiveness muscle. In high-risk environments, leaders recognize that a minor "slipup" is a precious opportunity to prevent a future major catastrophe. Then they work to build better procedures. For this to work, of course, employees are encouraged to *uncover* those tiny slipups. The more mistakes are shared, the faster conditions improve. They create an environment in which employees willingly draw attention to mistakes instead of sweeping them under the rug.

An estimated 440,000 hospital patients in the United States die annually because of preventable errors—that is over 1,000 people every day![9] At the Children's Hospital of Philadelphia (CHOP), CEO Madeline Bell hired Health Performance Improvement, a consulting firm founded by former nuclear plant managers and naval aviators, to train CHOP's staff. When the consultants interviewed her staff, they spotted an immediate red flag: Employees reported that management had a "punitive response to errors."

A punitive culture is not one where employees rush to tell managers about mistakes. Leaders focused on increasing reliability need to destigmatize mistakes. At CHOP, the solution was a program to celebrate rather than criticize staff who reported "near misses"—for example, when a patient was about to receive the wrong medication. CHOP implemented a critical change in language as well: Today, *near misses* are called *good catches*. As CEO, Madeline meets everyone who has had a "good catch" on a monthly basis and sometimes meets them at the bedside. And the hospital also offers an annual "Good Catch of the Year" award. Three years after Madeline's retraining effort, serious safety events had decreased by 80 percent.

2. Level the playing field.

These leaders create the expectation that everyone—workers, managers, and leaders—are equally qualified for and responsible for calling out problems and identifying solutions. All employees are encouraged to raise issues, even when it means ignoring hierarchy.

In a hospital's operating room, for example, lives are on the line. But this is also a place where a strong hierarchy is very natural; the surgeon is king, and a nurse is far down on the totem pole. Atul Gawande, a renowned surgeon, bestselling author, and health policy expert, set out to discover the most powerful ways to save lives and reduce suffering. Our colleague Alan Foster has been working with Atul as his leadership advisor for over seven years. Atul has found that crushing the barriers of hierarchy is critical to reducing the number of patients who die on the operating table. Atul's colleagues trained surgical teams to introduce themselves to one another by name. It's a seemingly superficial icebreaker, yet Atul's team found that it instantly opened the channels of communication. It announces to each person on the team: "Your voice is unique and valued. You have a responsibility to speak up." This empowers the nurses and technicians with the confidence to tell the surgeon if they have doubts whether the doctor is operating on the correct leg.

Similarly, great CEOs empower all their employees to raise their voices—and, equally important, they make sure they stay close enough to the field to listen. CEOs often tell us that the ideas that moved the needle didn't come from their senior team but from the cashiers, the customer-service reps, the drivers, and the button pushers. As Bill Amelio put it, "You just gotta get out there. Kick the tires. Lo and behold, things always come out on the table that you hadn't known before. In general, people want to tell you the truth." Bill will respond to an e-mail from *anyone* in the company within twenty-four hours.

3. Create a precise shared vocabulary.

Leaders of reliable cultures recognize that successful execution requires seamless communication. They invest in creating a shared precise vocabulary to speed up alignment and reduce the risk of mistakes.

Our former ghSMART partner David Works knows a thing or two about precise language. He was an engineer at a semiconductor manufacturing plant at Motorola and was CHRO at Sears and Windstream after leaving ghSMART. He spent his early career in the Navy on a nuclear submarine, where a reliability failure could easily cost lives. Precise language was drilled into the culture. Everyone on the sub knew that "Watch Team Backup" meant that everyone was accountable for double- and triple-checking that a mission-critical process was followed correctly. "Every time the quartermaster plotted a fix on the chart," David recounted, "the officer of the deck double-checked it. Every time. It is very much a part of the nuclear submarine force. I can remember that a friend of mine realized a critical chart was mislabeled as he was diligently rechecking. The submarine was at risk of being submerged in water they were not authorized for. This risks friendly collision, which is almost certain death on a submarine. Employing 'Watch Team Backup' resulted in a successful good catch."

David carried this forward as the CHRO and then business unit president at Windstream. He realized that the organization needed to focus more on becoming operationally excellent and improving collaboration across functional areas. One step he took was developing a common language so that everyone understood what it meant to be accountable. One example was the concept "Own It!" David led a team to mutually define and adopt "Own It!" as committing to find a way to win instead of getting bogged down in finger-pointing. This specific shared vocabulary helped build a stronger execution-oriented culture, which contributed to improvement in customer satisfaction (Net Promoter Score or NPS) of roughly 20 percent in the installation of new services.

How do you know that you have adequately embedded a shared vocabulary to ensure reliability? If you ask fifty people in your organization about the meaning of a particular term, everyone describes it the same way and acts consistently. Language is one of the ways a culture signals what is important.[10]

4. Build the machinery of consistent process.

Reliable leaders at all levels aren't just personally consistent. They build consistency into their organizations by engineering reliable processes. While outsize results are revered and celebrated, sometimes they are the result of herculean efforts (or market tailwinds) that aren't sustainable in the long run. Inefficient and poorly designed work processes create ambiguity, confusion, and, ultimately, errors and failure. To sustain reliable results over time requires a thoughtful management system, complete with process, metrics, and a predictable cadence that architects for discipline. Of the strong CEO candidates we studied, 75 percent scored high on organization and planning skills.[11]

Will Powell, the CEO of Sears Hometown and Outlet Stores, learned this when he hired the wrong leader for one of his businesses. "They got me a year of good results, but I could sense, underlying it, [the head of the business] structurally couldn't replicate it," he told us. "He had flash and pizzazz to push ideas out there but wasn't putting in place a foundation that was replicable. It started to unravel in year two and I had to let [him] go."

The magic comes from the fact that the system itself—the clear steps, deadlines, and measurable outcomes—makes it possible to hold people accountable for results. In our research, CEOs are almost twice as likely to be strong in holding people accountable than the average senior leader.[12]

Scorecard: Simple Reliability Tool

One way leaders at every level create personal accountability for themselves and each team member is by completing and sharing what we call a scorecard. Boards, CEOs, and senior executives and their teams use scorecards to make the implicit goals explicit and align around individual and collective accountabilities. This ensures all are clear about what they need to deliver. Scorecards can be used in the hiring process to articulate what success looks like in the role or as an ongoing alignment and performance management tool.

A scorecard forces you to write explicit expectations on paper for each responsibility you have, asking you to define:

- **Your mission and vision:** A mission is a short statement of the immediate purpose of your work. A vision looks further out: What accomplishments and values will your company be known for in the future?

- **Your top five priorities to accomplish them:** What will move the needle—and what needs to change so that your calendar going forward reflects those priorities?

- **What would thrilling success look like for you and your organization three years out?** What accomplishments would fulfill your vision? How do you quantify and measure those accomplishments?

- **How will success be delivered?**

Simon Castellanos, CEO of Advanced Infusion Solutions, a leading provider of home infusion solutions, was one of many CEOs who told us that learning to build processes for consistency was one of the most important steps he took as an executive to prepare himself to be a CEO. Simon is yet another seemingly unlikely CEO. Simon immigrated to the United States from Ecuador in 1985 and started out his adult life in the United States walking forty-five minutes to his carpenter's job in an abandoned building in Harlem so he could put the ninety-cent bus fare he saved toward English classes. As soon as he learned the basics of English, he got a job as a late-night doorman that allowed him to attend college during the day. For the next four years, Simon worked all night and attended City University of New York full-time, graduating with a bachelor's degree in accounting. His first professional job was as a staff accountant at Parrish Leasing, a small local company. It was his ability to reliably deliver that led him to be pulled into new, more challenging assignments. Bigger assignments led to bigger roles, bigger roles to bigger companies, and in 2014—three decades after he'd arrived nearly penniless in America—his improbable résumé of success landed him the title of CEO of Western Dental, a $500 million company providing affordable dental care to underserved populations in the Southwest of the United States.

Earlier in his career, Simon arrived at Fresenius Medical Care as a vice president of operations and was soon promoted to president of the central business unit, a $470 million dialysis services unit based in Chicago. Simon walked into a severely underperforming division that was failing at every quality metric. Staff turnover was well above industry benchmarks. "The company was a revolving door," Simon told us, and the turnover was hurting their ability to deliver quality. He had to find a way to engage the staff. What he did first was to create a clockwork-like system of reporting, on a weekly and even daily level. This included not only rear-view financial numbers for the prior time period, but also leading indicators that could show something might be going off the rails, such as patient satisfaction or clinic staff engagement levels. At first, people were reluctant and mistrustful. "We've had three or four guys in and out of the President position; why should we take you seriously?" was their attitude.

But Simon pushed forward. He implemented a consistent drumbeat of meetings and communications. He met with his team weekly to review reporting results across the regions. Regions that fell below industry benchmarks on operating metrics or financials had to put remedial plans in place. Simon was personally on top of the metrics and on top of the team in a cadence of: *Meet, measure, tweak. Meet, measure, tweak.* Employees' ideas were sought, and good ideas were implemented. And over time, what was initially onerous and rote began to take on a different character. Consistency became *momentum*. It became commitment—among the team and to Simon. After two years under Simon's leadership, the central division moved up from being the last to second of five business units on quality and became the most profitable division in the company. Employee turnover decreased from an abysmal 30 percent to the industry average of 19 percent. As Simon's team started to reliably deliver for customers and employees, the revenue decline turned into 3 percent annual growth in a market that was virtually stagnant. Simon credits the consistency of his actions with setting progress in motion. His team was crystal clear on what to expect and where to focus and had a consistent process in place to ensure quality. Strong financial results followed.

. . .

As we've discussed, reliable leaders build consistent practices personally, and they embed consistent routines into their organization. One counterargument we have heard from some executives is that in an era of uncertainty, process and routine can constrain an organization's ability to improvise and adapt. Not so, says Atul Gawande, the surgeon we introduced earlier. Atul's work has proven that the best way to help doctors and nurses manage the complexity and unpredictability of health care is to create a process in its simplest, most rote form: the checklist. In the book *The Checklist Manifesto: How to Get Things Right,* he writes: "The fear people have about the idea of adherence to a protocol is rigidity or bureaucracy. They imagine mindless automatons, heads down in a checklist, incapable of looking out their windshield and coping with the real world in front of them. *What you find, when a checklist is well made, is exactly the opposite. The checklist gets the dumb stuff out of the way.*"[13] In other words, by freeing ourselves of the cognitive burden of the "dumb stuff," we can better take on the hard stuff—especially the relentless change that requires leaders to be nimble, capable of adjusting to surprises and functioning in disaster. Which brings us to the next chapter and our fourth and final core CEO Genome Behavior: **Adapt Boldly.**

Assess your reliability. Ask yourself:

- How consistent was I this week in my interactions with customers, colleagues, senior management, and the people who work for me?

- When am I thrown off my game? Is it situation specific? How do I manage those situations?

- Does everyone on my team understand what is expected of them? Do they own their results? Do they embrace responsibility and hold themselves accountable?

- What are my boss/colleagues/clients trying to do? And how can I help them get there?

- What expectations do my stakeholders have of me that aren't being openly discussed?

- What am I expected to deliver? Have I written it down? Have I shared it with my boss, peers, and team?

- How often was I on time for meetings in the last week?

KEY TAKEAWAYS

1. Operate with personal consistency.
2. Take a mind-set of radical accountability.
3. Proactively shape expectations in the first weeks on the job and revisit as conditions change.
4. Build a business management system to drive repeatable results.

chapter 5

Adapt Boldly: Ride the Discomfort
of the Unknown

Most of the time I spend when I get up
every morning is trying to figure out what is going to happen.
—Madeleine Albright

KODAK. BLOCKBUSTER. BORDERS. WHAT DO THESE NAMES HAVE IN common? They were all once hugely successful companies that failed to adapt. The average life span of today's leading companies in the United States has decreased over the last century from sixty-five years to just twenty-three years, according to Richard Foster at Yale.[1] To paraphrase H. G. Wells, "Adapt or perish, now as ever, is today's inexorable imperative."

We spend most of our careers being rewarded and recognized for knowing more than do those around us. And yet every senior leader faces a turning point in her or his career when knowledge is no longer enough. It tends to coincide with the moment these leaders are given far more people to manage than they've managed previously and when they are confronted with challenges that have no one right answer. Suddenly, or so it seems, they find themselves in uncharted waters beyond the boundaries of their competence. To get to the top, aspiring leaders have to learn to navigate the uncharted. And it is in these unknown waters that they, as senior leaders, will likely spend the rest of their career.

What does it mean to be good at navigating the unknown?

We asked a Navy SEAL senior officer who has experience in both operational and training environments, what separated a good SEAL leader from one who was great. We expected to hear such adjectives as *bravery, toughness, extreme confidence*. The officer's unequivocal answer: *humility*.

Every person who achieves the status of a Navy SEAL has shown himself, through years of experience and months of harsh and demanding training, to be exemplary. That is the cost of entry. What distinguishes a great leader, according to this SEAL officer, was the humility that allowed him to recognize what lay before him and his team for what it really was—responding to the unknowable. Theaters of operations in which our military operate are dangerous, ambiguous, and constantly changing environments. Humility enables leaders to understand that they do not have it all figured out and that "what they know" is less important than how quickly they learn and adapt. The great leaders are the ones who are willing and able to learn from those from different services, units, ranks, and experiences.

The parallels to the CEO journey, and specifically that moment in which aspiring executives come to see their jobs as daily acts of adaptation and agility, are uncanny.

Jean Hoffman, founder of the vet pharma company Putney, Inc., compared life as a CEO to leading people in a foxhole every day. Ali Jameel, the CEO of the Pakistani firm TPL Trakker, told us that in fifteen years as an entrepreneur and CEO, he'd never had a plan that worked from start to finish. We would argue that most of the issues that are known should be addressed by those below the CEO level, freeing the CEO to focus on navigating the unknown.

No matter how broad and deep your expertise, whether you're hired from the outside or promoted from within, your job as CEO is to turn the relentless, unending uncertainty the organization will face into opportunity and growth. Most of the leaders we interviewed in this research talked about having to adapt to unexpected challenges or crises.[2] The best leaders thrive in a condition of relentless discomfort, adapting their organizations and themselves. These CEOs chart new paths *before* they have to, not when there's no other choice.

In other words, these leaders reap the benefits of **Adapting Boldly.** *Our research shows that CEOs who adapt boldly are roughly seven times more likely to be successful than those who wait for change to confront them.*[3] If **Reliability** in our data showed up as the strongest differentiator of performance, **Adaptability** is the behavior that is rapidly growing in importance. In our discussions on the four CEO Genome Behaviors with boards and investors, adaptability gets the highest attention as the increasingly important behavior for success at the top—where playbooks often do not exist.

The CEOs who are best at adapting themselves and their organizations to changing conditions have learned to welcome discomfort, conflict, and change. They take the attitude, *If I am not uncomfortable, then I am probably not learning or changing fast enough.* Being uncomfortable in leading the organization is actually a goal. The role of the CEO is about navigating that pressure and change. This chapter will highlight the key instruments—*letting go of the past* and *building an antenna for the future*—to use when sailing through the uncharted waters of the unknown.

Let Go of the Past

Jim Smith, CEO of Thomson Reuters, is one of those rare CEOs who seem to revel in the uncertainty that causes discomfort for so many. He grew up on a farm in Kentucky and boasts no special pedigree. Jim graduated from Marshall University in West Virginia. He didn't attend an Ivy League school or launch his career at a big-name firm such as GE, P&G, or Google. He started out as a journalist, working for the company that years later he would lead as its CEO. (Journalism isn't a field commonly associated with the CEO track, but as you'll see later in this chapter, maybe it should be.) Even among our diverse CEO pool, Jim Smith is unusually kind, open, and seemingly without affectation.

Perhaps more than any other CEO we've met, Jim came into his role prepared for an endless cycle of change.

"I came to realize early on that if I was going to be successful, then the only thing to build is a culture and an organization and a team of people that would be capable of morphing and changing long after I had left," Jim told us. "I can't draw organizational charts fast enough to keep up with the changes in the external market."

If you look deeply at the details of his early career, it becomes clear that he had been honing his uncanny comfort with discomfort all along. Hardscrabble beginnings built a foundational expectation that nothing comes easy. One particular story from his early career jumped out at us as a defining moment.

Jim was in his first publishing role at Thomson, many years before the company would acquire Reuters to become the world's largest financial news provider. For the first time, his business unit wasn't going to make its monthly targets for ad revenue. He and his team tried everything they could think of to sell more ads. They looked outside their industry practices for ideas, leading to the paper's first department-store-style buy-one-get-one-free "white sale."

But their out-of-the-box thinking didn't work.

"We still didn't make our number!" Jim said, laughing easily.

Jim didn't give up. He went into the next month with even greater resolve that the executive team would find a way. Instead of fearing failure or shame for the weak prior month, he became enthralled by the challenge. They kept hitting the phones, working relationships, tossing out new ideas—and before too long, they were back above targets. "Let's be clear, the white sale never worked," Jim told us. "But something else did. And what mattered was that we came back to fight another day."

The lesson Jim took from the experience: *You're not going to win every time. You might not even win most of the time.* "There's a lot of stuff that's not within your control, so how do you bounce back? Do you learn from it? Do you get better? Do you get stronger?"

Even in an average week, the CEOs we know are uncomfortable about something. Every CEO we meet comes to us carrying a portfolio of near disasters. Like Jim Smith, who now is at the helm of a global media conglomerate, these leaders learn to face the uncertainty of change. They turn fear into courage and curiosity.

Recently Elena was coaching a newly appointed CEO facing a very challenging situation. The CEO said, "I need to remind myself that I've been uncomfortable before and I've succeeded anyway. And knowing that, I can relax and know that it's uncomfortable right now because it's new." We have worked with countless successful leaders who have learned how to strengthen their **Adapt** muscle and embrace the discomfort of the unknown. So what are they doing differently? How do they strengthen that mind-set of adaptability and resilience?

1. They actively seek out novelty.

If you are not quite ready to be an adaptation black belt in your day job just yet, there are safer and even fun ways to practice. Taking on new habits, skills, and experiences in your personal life could be a safer laboratory for building your adaptation muscles. For example, Nancy Phillips, the CEO of ViaWest, told us that some of her best training to be CEO didn't take place while she was wearing a suit. She spent three years traveling the world, including a month in China during which she never met another Westerner. "I had to learn how to survive every day," she said. Discomfort was the only constant, and every new experience required an improvised response. The expense and time required for a global adventure may not be for you. Learning to play an instrument, to speak a new language, or simply picking up a new hobby are all simple and low-risk ways to raise your adaptation game. It won't make you a bold adapter in a business context overnight, but it will help you grow.

2. They weigh jobs as much by their learning potential as by their pay grade.

Dozens of CEOs we've interviewed—and in particular, many of those who have shot to the top faster than average, as you will learn in Chapter 6—have made lateral, unconventional, and even risky career moves. Susan Cameron, the retired CEO of Reynolds American, Inc., was one of many who told us that taking a "lesser" role—moving from global brand director to senior vice president of marketing—was the decision that catapulted her to the CEO suite. Stepping into new, unfamiliar roles that broaden their experience or require leadership amid crises are two of the hallmarks of successful CEOs we saw in our research. When Susan coaches her own employees, the number one skill she focuses on is openness to experience—taking on new challenges and soliciting feedback to improve along the way.

3. They acquire the skills they don't have.

Rob Wenger, CEO and co-founder of the SaaS (Software as a Service) company Higher Logic, told us his favorite thing to do is write software. But after two years as CEO, he realized he had to engage more actively with his customers. "Growing up, I couldn't stand in front of a group and talk. I purposefully changed just by doing what I dreaded over and over. I even surprised myself how much the practice itself changed me. Ten years ago, I'd dread dinner parties, and now I walk in and talk to everyone. So now I pick traits I want, and I take action." Rob also forced himself to practice by surrounding himself with people who enjoyed the activities he dreaded: "My best friend, Rico, was very extroverted. He'd make me go to social things, and I'd give myself a job, like setting up the music." Rob continued to flex and strengthen that "social" muscle until it became strong and natural. Under his leadership, his company has grown at a 44 percent average annual rate over five years and received a substantial private-equity investment. Adaptable leaders work to acquire the skills they don't have; they get in the ring and practice them, no matter how awkward or uncomfortable they feel at first.

4. They are willing to let go of approaches that have worked before.

Most of us imagine that when faced with uncertainty, the biggest challenge is setting the right strategy. *In fact, most failures to adapt are the result of a leader's failure to let go of what has made him successful in the past.* An engineer at Kodak invented the world's first digital camera, but company executives threw it into the proverbial broom closet for eighteen years. Blockbuster had three chances to buy Netflix.

In 1983, Intel faced a truly dramatic "evolve or die" challenge. The company had single-handedly created the market for memory chips. It was all they did. And yet between 1984 and 1985, their profits dove from $198 million to $2 million.[4] Japanese companies had turned chips into commodities and were now beating Intel blind. Their entire identity was memory. This wasn't just a financial crisis but also an existential one.

Andy Grove, Intel's founder and president at the time, tells the story in *Only the Paranoid Survive: How to Exploit the Crisis Points That Challenge Every Company.*[5] After weeks of paralyzing angst, he found himself standing at a window, gazing out at a Ferris wheel in the distance. In that moment, he rose above the details, above the panic of crisis, even above his own ego. From that height, he was able to ask his CEO Gordon Moore the clearheaded question that would change

Intel forever: "If we got kicked out, and the board brought in a new CEO, what would that man do?" Grove asked. Moore didn't miss a beat: "A new CEO would get Intel out of the memory chip business." Grove stared at him, numb. "Why shouldn't you and I walk out the door, come back, and do it ourselves?" he replied. That's exactly what they did. They shut down Intel's memory chip business and pioneered a new market, manufacturing microprocessors, that would increase Intel's market cap from $4 billion to $197 billion.

The most successful CEOs we know, like Grove, become experts at letting go, whether that means letting go of past company strategies, business models, or their own personal habits. Craig Barnes, president of the Princeton Theological Seminary (PTS) since 2012, spent many years as a pastor before heading to Princeton. As a pastor, his calling was to be available and present to his people at their time of need. When he joined the seminary as president, he started out with the same one-on-one leadership approach he had enjoyed so much with his parishioners. His passion to be present and available drove him to keep his office door always open, and people flooded through it. But he soon came to realize that he would never accomplish his mandate—rebuilding the seminary to serve an increasingly global, diverse, and digital world—by spending all his time in one-on-one meetings. Those intimate personal interactions had been in his comfort zone. They fueled his passion and his calling as a pastor. But once he was president, they left little time for Craig to think and set the vision that the institution sorely needed. He finally sat down with his assistant and blocked time on his calendar for the strategic and administrative work that needed to be done. And he stuck to it.

Many of us who start our careers as craftsmen of sorts and who are passionate about our craft must let go of the very practices that drove our success in order to take on leadership roles. If this sounds trivial, it isn't. Changing any habit is difficult, but changing habits we love, that give us energy and fuel our passions, is almost impossible. We've seen many leaders who are eager to transform their organizations yet vehemently resist letting go of meetings they like to attend or making other seemingly minor shifts in how they spend their time and energy. Craig's willingness to let go and change his habits paid off both for him and for PTS. Under his leadership, the seminary has thrived: The student body has grown by 30 percent, morale has improved dramatically, and several new academic programs have been launched.

Great leaders, whatever their titles, are constantly *becoming*— becoming better, different, more informed. In this act of constant learning, they are becoming more comfortable with discomfort.

Red Flag: The Control Freak

"Sam," a president who's on the CEO succession list for a retail manufacturer, received a 360 review. Kim asked him, "Have you shared the results with your direct reports?" The exec responded, "Well, no. That would show that I'm weak or not in control." We would argue that if you're not willing to get vulnerable and honest around your own needs for continued learning, or what you need to let go, you're not ready to be CEO. Being open about your learning goals shows that you are willing to learn and grow and encourages your team to do so as well.

Build an Antenna for the Future

Many employees and managers spend the bulk of their time focusing on near-term delivery and do just fine. But when one becomes a CEO, that goal no longer suffices. To keep the organization on a solid course, CEOs need to orient their focus to the future.

The time leaders spend thinking beyond the next year into the future doubles *when they become CEOs.*[6] Sucheta Nadkarni at Cambridge

University has led research which studied the effect of temporal focus on adaptability.[7] Looking at 221 firms in 19 industries over a 7-year period, the research showed that in dynamic industries, those firms with CEOs who focused mostly on the future (not the past or the present) were the ones that introduced new products faster, a litmus test for their ability to help their companies adapt.

A meaningful glimpse of the future requires more than a three-year strategy document. Brad Smith, the CEO of Intuit, describes an exercise that helped him stretch his time horizon further. Brad and fellow leaders were asked to reflect on a decision or a strategy they wished their predecessors had executed differently ten years earlier to put the company in a better position today. "Everyone had a field day with this portion of the exercise, quickly identifying the 'would have, could have, and should haves.' Oh, the benefit of hindsight is a magnificent thing!" recalls Brad.[8] But it was the second part of the exercise that brought the lesson home. They were asked to fast-forward ten years and think about what their successors might wish *they* had done differently. "That shifted my perspective and made me realize that as CEO, things were now different. Beyond the short-term goals of delivering business results, and even the three- to five-year plans, came the responsibility to consider the longer-term implications of everything I was doing today," says Brad.

Most CEOs know they have to divide their attention between short- and long-term perspectives. The CEOs we interviewed spent significantly more of their time—over 40 percent, the equivalent of two days a week—thinking about the long term. Other executives, by contrast, devoted an average of a day a week, or roughly 20 percent of their time, to long-term thinking.[9]

CEOs with the most effective future orientation have built an antenna for change. This "antenna" is the time and resources they commit to trawling the future. Certainly, there are CEOs who seem naturally gifted at keeping their eyes on the future. But for the rest of us, we offer what has worked for the most adaptable CEOs we have encountered.

1. Build diverse information networks.

To see into the future, your own market data isn't enough. Those who are best at spotting potential train wrecks and seizing opportunities look outside their own business, and often outside their industry, for signs of shifts. Actively curious, they assume that everything is relevant to their business in some way. The best CEOs plug into broad and seemingly unrelated information flows. Then they take all the information they gather and make creative connections to get out in front of the competition. Nadkarni found that CEOs who rated highly on openness to experience were more effective at initiating strategic change. They tap into broader networks and information sources and as a result are able to sense changes earlier and make strategic moves to take advantage of the changes.

Jean Hoffman, who sold the pet pharmaceutical company she founded for $200 million, told us she was able to see where vet pharma was going to be in thirty years by looking at trends in human pharma. She didn't rely on what existing vet players were saying or writing. Looking at the data trends herself, as well as being able to see what pet owners wanted and then thinking through how the vet sector would change, allowed her to get ahead of her market. As Tom Bell, former chairman and CEO of Young & Rubicam and Cousins Properties, told us, "In today's world, by the time you hear the words 'we all know,' the next thing they say is likely wrong or at least disputable. The world has moved beyond it."

One way these CEOs have proactively adapted is by expanding the definition of who their competitors are. They think beyond their own market boundaries. Disney World isn't competing against other theme parks; it competes against anything that vies for the attention and entertainment of parents and kids. The Naval Special Warfare Center (the Navy SEAL training center)—arguably where they train the most adaptable warriors—lists "outreach" as one of its operating principles. For anything they do, they seek out the best experts across far-reaching disciplines. One of their officers told us: "Sometimes just having a conversation with people [who] do similar things but in very different contexts can open your mind. When they ask questions of you, they open up your blind spots, and you're, like, 'Wow, I didn't even think about that.'"

To build a diverse network, encourage regular interactions with bright, engaged people outside your company and outside your field. Assemble an "Inspiration Cabinet" who inspire you to consider new, unexpected ideas and help you see things from new angles. Share challenges, bounce ideas off them. You might be surprised by what you learn. It's not hard to do. Highly adaptable leaders do it daily because they see it as vital. Others bury it on the bottom of the to-do list.

2. Use the power of questions.

The best CEOs don't think of themselves as the ones with all the answers. Instead, they tend to ask the best questions. When Tom Bell was CEO and chairman of the real estate investment trust Cousins Properties, he asked what turned out to be a well over a billion-dollar question.

Cousins owned a large amount of premium office space, including Atlanta's Bank of America building. But in early 2004, as real estate values were continuing to rise, one of Tom's direct reports told him that a key tenant intended to negotiate a lower lease rate. They looked into it and discovered that in many of Cousins' markets, lease rates in real dollars were trending down. Tom's question, "What do leasing prices look like for premium office space in other markets?" led them to dig into the data. What they found was that the downswing wasn't just taking place in Cousins' markets—it was nearly nationwide. Tom considered what this news meant and came back with an unorthodox idea: "Let's sell the assets."

His team was aghast. But Tom convinced them to move forward, and they sold a little over a billion dollars in office assets at the height of the market. Cousins' shareholders were rewarded with incredible dividends—something that had never been done at that point in the public REIT world. Tom says, "I remember getting calls from other REIT CEOs asking what the hell was I thinking. I certainly wondered if I made the wrong call." Then the U.S. real estate bubble burst. Vacancies soared, and property values and rents plummeted following the economic collapse in the United States. The Bank of America building that Tom sold for $436 million in 2006 was foreclosed upon in the wake of the real estate meltdown in 2012. It traded in 2016 for roughly $180 million.

In hindsight, Tom's call seems blindingly obvious. But it was not so at the time. How did he decide to make that controversial call? He started by asking questions. He paused when he heard something that caused him to second-guess his assumptions. Then he built a fact base. And he acted.

Asking good questions was an approach Tom Bell learned at a young age. Early in his career he had been promoted far beyond his experience level. A mentor pulled him into his office and warned him he'd be in many conversations he wouldn't understand. "You must get underneath what they are telling you. Here's what you do," he said. "First, pay attention. Let them get about halfway into something they really think is important and then interrupt. Ask: 'Wait, tell me why you think that is important?' That forces them to back up and describe the assumptions, the facts, and the logic. Second, beware the declarative statement. When someone makes a point as if it [is] a fact, by saying: 'Everyone knows that . . . ' or 'We all agree that . . . ' stop them and say, 'Wait, do you have data to back that up?'"

Being curious is a hallmark of adaptable CEOs. And it can start with a question as simple as: *What? How?* or *Tell me more!* Hal Gregersen at MIT is a world renowned expert on innovation who invites every leader to set aside 4 minutes every 24 hours (totaling one full day each year) to ask better questions.[10] Earlier, in discussing Jim Smith of Thomson Reuters, we claimed that journalism was a promising path to the C-suite. Why did we suggest that? Well, who is more expert at asking probing, insightful questions than a journalist? Jim told us that his curiosity—both his natural curiosity about the way the world worked as well as the sense of curiosity he developed professionally—was one of the most important contributors to his success as a CEO. When the going gets tough, the tough open their reporter's notebook. They ask questions, and they learn.

3. Tackle "premortems" before postmortems.

With infinite available data and so many directions to look in, how does someone who aspires to reach the corner office separate signal from noise? Gene Wade is the co-founder and CEO of OneUni, Inc., which builds apps that allow students around the world to get a college education via their mobile phone. He is no stranger to the pains of adapting in a quickly changing environment. "At my prior company Platform Learning, we built this really great business that grew like a rocket ship, but it was built on quicksand," he told us. The regulatory environment shifted so fast that they often didn't see new changes coming.

Looking back, Gene realized that he wasn't blindsided because there were no signals. The problem was that his antenna was down. "I was so busy scaling up the business that I didn't really keep my eye on the regulations." Today he actively leads teams in a practice that he calls the "premortem" to keep his antenna tuned to finding the signals amid the noise. He explores with his team: "Let's say it's eighteen months out, and we've failed. What are all the plausible reasons? Now imagine we were wildly successful. Tell me what happened." Once they've created failure scenarios—and to Gene, there are no givens in business, only potential scenarios—they develop a signal list for each issue: What data, news, or trends need to be tracked to stay on top of the issue? What steps can be taken today to increase the odds that the success scenario becomes reality?

Beware Cognitive Overload

The economist Herbert Simon suggested that the human brain has hard "cognitive limits." He came up with the incredibly prescient dictum, "A wealth of information creates a poverty of attention."[11] We have found that when it comes to effectively adapting to change, one differentiator between mediocre managers and those who rise to the top is the ability to insulate themselves from cognitive overload. CEO Dawn Zier is a star in striking this balance. Dawn has been the CEO of Nutrisystem since late 2012, when she embarked on an ambitious four-point turnaround and growth plan. The overall result is a resurgence at Nutrisystem under Dawn's leadership.

An MIT engineer by training, Dawn is a naturally analytical thinker. When she arrived at Nutrisystem, an e-commerce company by trade, she was surprised by how many decisions were not fact based, especially given how much data was available. "In those early days, the team would show up and literally do a data dump. They delivered spreadsheets and spreadsheets of so much data, but hadn't identified the data points that mattered. They couldn't tell the story of what was happening or what the key insights were for the decision at hand. As the team matured, we began developing data dashboards that focused on what mattered. And that's when it got exciting and the data went from potentially overwhelming to quite powerful." Data, placed in a clear context and shaped by critical questions, began to deliver real knowledge and a road map for the future for Nutrisystem.

4. Look into the crystal ball of customer experience.

The successful CEOs we studied spend roughly 20 percent of their time with customers, even with the burden of so many new demands on their time.[12] We did not see them decrease the amount of time they spent with customers when they moved into the CEO role. They realize that there's no replacement for personal contact with the market. Customers don't always know exactly what they need or how to articulate it. For this reason, the CEOs who get the best insights from the market pay the most attention to what customers are *experiencing*; then they search for solutions from there.

In 2005, a CEO we worked with, Marcus, took the helm of a family-owned business that is a leading supplier to the construction industry in Europe. Marcus discovered some of his best ideas by walking the construction sites of his customers. On one such tour, a problem and possibility hit him simultaneously: "There were so many nails lying everywhere. They were running out of high-volume supplies way faster than planners had anticipated. For low-cost items like nails, it was hard for them to accurately forecast when they would need the product and how much. Suppliers of these products were fiercely competing on price. Right then I saw the customer's chief problem *wasn't* pricing. Their chief problem was getting the right quantity of the right supplies exactly when they needed it to ensure their staff was productive." The cost of idle workers at construction sites, Marcus realized, was far more expensive to builders than the price of a box of nails.

Marcus's solution was to *adapt* their business model to set up shop right at the construction site of his customers, who could then get whatever they needed whenever they needed it. In doing so, he provided immediate access and drove better margins for himself at a time when his competitors were focused on pricing. By walking the customer site and seeing what was and wasn't working firsthand, Marcus uncovered a significant opportunity to improve profits.

Assess your **Adapt** behavior.
Ask yourself:

- *Am I uncomfortable now? What is driving that? What am I working on improving personally?*

- *When is the last time I shed something—product, process, practice—that had made me or my business successful in the past?*

- *Am I doing this simply because I'm comfortable doing it this way or because this is what is needed in this situation?*

- *Am I approaching divergent points of view with an open mind?*

KEY TAKEAWAYS

1. Train your adaptation muscles: Pick up a new skill or hobby; immerse yourself in an experience or place that you find uncomfortable; take on a job or volunteer assignment in a completely new area.

2. Let go of the past: Conduct annual "spring cleaning." Ask yourself and your team which habits, practices, and assumptions hold you back today or in the future. Pick the one that feels easiest or most valuable to let go. Let it go.

3. Build your antenna for the future:
   - Assemble an "Inspiration Cabinet": a network of people in different fields who expose you to new unexpected ideas and information and help you see things from new angles
   - Schedule "Foresight" time at least twice a month: actually block time on your calendar to consider the

big picture view and future scenarios. Pick a location, time, and conditions that put your mind in the best state for insight.

- Conduct full immersion into customer experience: regularly spend time walking in the shoes of your customers
- Get curious and ask questions.

Adding It All Up

EACH OF THE FOUR CEO GENOME BEHAVIORS DISCUSSED IN SEC-
tion I of this book is treated as distinct, self-contained, and equally important. In reality, they are interconnected. For example, it might be
easy to build a business management system in the spirit of delivering
relentless reliability and then become a slave to process. However, with
an equally strong "adapt" muscle, you will be actively seeking to leave
behind processes that no longer work in the face of changing customer
needs or competitive context. Jeff Bezos, in his 2016 shareholder letter,
said it best: "If you're not watchful, the process can become the thing.
You stop looking at outcomes and just make sure you're doing the
process right. A more experienced leader will use a bad outcome as an
opportunity to investigate and improve the process."[1] In the desire to
decide with conviction and speed, it might seem easy to railroad your
decision through the organization, resulting in a lack of alignment and
failed execution. Yet with strong **Engage for Impact** muscles, you will
understand the needs of the key stakeholders and thoughtfully align
their actions with your intent.

The second reality is that context matters. The relative importance
of each of the four CEO Genome Behaviors varies widely, depending
on the industry, company, and point in time. It is hard to imagine a
technology startup, for example, that thrives with a CEO who lacks
the ability to adapt. On the other hand, you wouldn't want to be a

patient in a hospital where the CEO isn't personally committed to reliability in everything the hospital does.

To be highly successful, your strongest behaviors should match the behaviors most needed to drive value in the business. And even if you have weaknesses, you can learn to thrive by building your strengths over time as well as by proactively harnessing the strengths of others. Surround yourself with people who bring complementary skills and experience to the table. For example, Matt Kramer, the former co-CEO of Teach For America, shared with us that while he is strong on delivering reliably and being decisive, he depends on other people to support his ability to reflect on the future, a key element of the **Adapt** behavior: "I have to be in regular conversation with people who have well-developed antennae. I cannot be surrounded by people who are heads down."

The bottom line is that you do not have to be a superman or superwoman to be a successful CEO or to grow to your potential. There is no perfect, all-weather leader at any level who excels at all four of the behaviors we discussed. However, the CEO position does require a baseline level of proficiency in all four behaviors and a pronounced strength in one or more. The strongest CEOs in our data set are ten times more likely to be skilled in more than one of these behaviors than the weaker CEOs we analyzed.[2] Many of the strong CEOs got there by identifying where they were weak and working to build strength over time. *Most important, it's never too early or too late to strengthen your muscles on any of the four behaviors.*

To help you measure where you are today on your path to the top, and to suggest ideas on how to improve, we have created a diagnostic online at www.ceogenome.com.

GET TO THE TOP

WIN YOUR DREAM JOB

1
GET
STRONG

2
GET
TO THE
TOP

3
GET
RESULTS

CAREER CATAPULTS

STAND OUT

CLOSE THE DEAL

chapter 6

Career Catapults: Fast-Track Your Future

Life can only be understood backwards; but it must be lived forwards.
—Søren Kierkegaard

AT THE AGE OF FOURTEEN, SCOTT CLAWSON SET A GOAL OF BECOMING a CEO one day. Surrounded with plenty of CEOs in the family—his father, grandfather, and later on his brother were all CEOs—for Scott, taking the helm of a company was a natural career destination. Since childhood, Scott had stood out for his hard work and competitiveness. He charted a bulletproof path to the top, following in his family's footsteps. With a 3.96 GPA from Brigham Young University, Scott spent two years at his father's business gaining the work experience required to qualify for admission to Harvard's MBA program. Graduating from Harvard in the top 15 percent of his class gave him a strong platform for a steady rise through the ranks, as he took on roles of increasing scope and authority, first at Alcoa and later at Danaher. At the age of forty-two, Scott stepped into his first CEO role at GSI, a role that seemed almost predestined. Scott went on to deliver a home run for GSI investors, selling the company only four years later at 3.8

times the original investment. His second CEO role, at the helm of the water treatment company Culligan, ended in a successful sale to a private equity firm.

If you're scratching your head, saying, "That's not me," you're not alone. While Scott's trajectory looks picture-perfect, it is not nearly as common as you might have thought before reading this book. The reality is that *over 70 percent of the CEOs we have interviewed had no idea they wanted to be a CEO until they reached senior executive roles late in their career.*[1] In other words, they didn't plan their career as a set of steps to become CEO. Most didn't work at academy companies like GE or P&G. Most didn't get an MBA at an elite business school. Yet, as these future CEOs advanced in their careers, their aspirations grew. In 2014, Korn Ferry did a study of just over a thousand senior executives, and an astounding 87 percent wanted to achieve the top job.[2]

Even armed with the CEO Genome Behaviors you have learned in Section I of this book, you might still find career choices daunting. How do you know which paths lead to the top and which end in blind alleys? We have analyzed almost a thousand career journeys to the CEO suite to give you the inside track to the top.

Here's the punch line: *Your career trajectory is the output of two factors that have a multiplying effect: getting results in the right roles and getting noticed for those results.* This chapter will show how their career choices positioned future CEOs to hone their skills and demonstrate CEO-worthy results. In Chapter 7, we will demystify the art of getting noticed to help you achieve full recognition and professional growth for your results.

Launching Your Career to the Top

Most CEOs don't start out their careers with the goal of becoming a CEO. Nevertheless, we saw patterns emerge in the routes to the top.

Take "Christine," a first-time CEO we recommended several years ago to run a health and wellness company. She went on to move the company from a crisis to profitability in fewer than twelve months.

Christine was the daughter of horse trainers and was brought up working seven days a week next to her boss, her dad. She worked full-time while in college and lived at home. Her résumé looks nothing like the typical Fortune 500 career path, adroitly described in a *Forbes* magazine article: "After graduation, grab a few years of related work experience before heading back to school for an MBA at a top university, and then follow that up with a stint at Bain or McKinsey. Finally, make the jump to the company you hope to lead one day, and be sure to get some operational experience and international exposure."[3]

Christine never received an MBA, never joined a management consulting firm, and was an external recruit when she became CEO. Yet her career story is right in line with an experiential trajectory that we identified across almost a thousand journeys to the CEO suite. On average, CEOs we have analyzed took twenty-four years to get from day one in their first job to the CEO role. There is no one-size-fits-all prescription. Each journey is unique. However, we have uncovered several common patterns on the way to the top that can help guide your choices.[4]

CEOs' careers are roughly divided into three stages. Each stage has a role to play in preparing one for the top. Many of the insights below are helpful to anyone looking for professional growth at any stage in one's career, whether or not the C-suite is the ultimate goal.

Stage 1: Go broad (years 0 to 8). The position of CEO requires one to be the ultimate generalist. We see roots of that profile early in future CEOs' career trajectories. They build a wide breadth of skills and experiences early on by moving across functions, industries, companies, and geographies. Making unconventional moves is both easiest and least risky at this stage.

For those starting out their careers in large companies, this diversity of early experiences often comes from rotational programs that offer new recruits opportunities to try their hand at different parts of the business. In professional services companies, working on projects solving different types of problems for clients across a wide range of industries delivers similar exposure. Small or startup companies also afford an opportunity to wear multiple hats at the same time. Some future CEOs accelerate their progress at this stage with an MBA—either a full-time program or part-time around a demanding work schedule.

As for Christine, she started as a horse trainer, later taught financial literacy classes, and then shifted into corporate training before opening new retail stores for a fitness company.

No matter your starting point, the key priority guiding choices in this first stage is to maximize the breadth and pace of your learning, ideally in direct contact with role models for high professional standards. Much like early life experiences, early professional experiences form a powerful imprint that influences one's views on what is possible. This makes it even more important to learn from a broad range of people, styles, and situations. This is also a time to build valuable foundational skills that will be harder to master later, particularly problem-solving, financial analysis, and oral and written communications skills.

Stage 2: Go deep (years 9 to 16). If stage 1 is about learning above all, stage 2 is about measurable results above all. Years 9 to 16 are typically spent building leadership ability, depth of industry experience, and a track record of results. The CEOs in our sample had on average 13 to 16 years of experience in the same industry as the company they were seeking to lead. In these years, future CEOs work toward general management roles that directly drive topline and/or bottom-line revenue or profits. That might mean running a P&L, or it might mean being a functional leader in sales, marketing, or operations. Most important, *future CEOs are demonstrating that they can lead others to produce outsize measurable results.* Over 90 percent of our CEOs had general management experience prior to becoming CEO. On average, CEOs have 11 years of general management experience under their belt before stepping into their first CEO role.

Christine eventually held a North American general management role, responsible for a $400 million portfolio of retail stores for a company within the fitness industry. According to Kaplan and Sørensen's research on our data, divisional P&L roles are the most common stepping stone to CEO.

In this second stage, career stories of leaders who go on to become strong CEOs are peppered with examples such as: "I took the Southwest region from the worst performing to top quartile across the company" or "I turned marketing from a dusty department producing PowerPoint charts into a generator of 90 percent of new million-dollar leads in the company" or "I built the plant in Mexico in record time and on budget—unprecedented for our company." Stage 2 is the time to show measurable impact and value as a result of your leadership.

Stage 3: Go high (years 17 to 24). Stage 3 is where we see careers of future CEOs take a dramatically different turn. While many will remain effective functional leaders, middle managers, or even P&L operators, *future CEOs differentiate themselves as enterprise leaders.* As enterprise leaders, they make decisions taking into account the context and impact on the entire business rather than confining their view only to their own area, and they impact results beyond their immediate scope of authority. At this stage, future CEOs impact success of the entire company.

By the time they finish this third stage, roughly 24 years into their career, future CEOs have typically held 8 to 11 positions, which translates to between 2 to 3 years of tenure per role. They also have been exposed to between 4 and 6 companies. When appointing CEOs, boards look for them to have roughly a ten-year runway in the role. Approximately three quarters of finalist candidates for CEO positions fall between the ages of 40 and 54, and only 5 percent are over 58 years old. Many cross the finish line into the CEO role through placement by executive recruiters. In our analysis of 91 midmarket first-time CEO hirings, 30 percent were sourced through recruiters, as was Christine.

More important, leaders start to look like future CEOs in this final period when they succeed in growing influence and demonstrating initiative beyond the formal authority of any given role. For example, a vice president might lead a company-wide initiative that requires him to influence peers and other senior players who don't report to him. Christine, for example, initiated discussion about, advocated the business case for, and ultimately led the implementation of a company-wide ERP, the company's largest investment for that year, which impacted every function and commercial team. This is also the time in which future CEOs expand their reach beyond the walls of their company. They build a brand within their industry, taking visible, conversation-defining positions on the driving questions of the day and communicating them through speaking opportunities, the media, and by convening other CEOs and leaders.

There are no ready-made maps to the top, especially for those in the first two stages of their career. No matter where you are today, the real takeaway is this: *Don't look at your career as a succession of jobs to land; instead, look at your decisions as a portfolio of experiences to build.*

Is your career portfolio CEO-ready?

Below are the common requirements we have seen in hundreds of CEO selection processes we've supported. It is rare that a single candidate meets all the requirements, but building a portfolio of experiences that covers at least five of these areas makes it easier to get on the slate of final candidates.

- Industry experience

- P&L leadership on a similar scale

- Evidence of strong people leadership—signs that you can attract and develop talent (people look at your Glassdoor ratings!)

- Proven success in a relevant context; e.g., M&A if the company needs to grow through acquisition, growth if that's the primary goal, etc.

- Breadth of experience across different types of business problems and roles; e.g., delivering growth and improving operational efficiencies

- Strategic vision and ability to set direction and champion change

- Operational and financial acumen

- Ability to work with the board and external stakeholders

- International experience (where relevant)

To help you make the smartest choices in building your portfolio of experiences, we closely investigated a sample of sixty leaders who made it to the CEO seat faster than the average twenty-four years. We call these CEOs "Sprinters." Our research team analyzed Sprinters' career histories in great depth to understand patterns of choices and experiences shared among them. Not surprisingly, we found that nearly a quarter of Sprinters benefited from an elite MBA program.[5] But a much bigger discovery was that that 97 percent of Sprinters (virtually all of them!) undertook what we came to call Career Catapults. *Career Catapults are inflection points that accelerated strong performers to top-level leadership, both in terms of their capabilities and in terms of how others saw their potential.* Whether or not you have an MBA from an elite business school or work with a marquee company, you can actively seek out and create Career Catapults to accelerate your trajectory at any stage in your career. By spotting catapult opportunities, seizing them, and ultimately building your leadership capabilities, you will increase your odds of becoming a CEO candidate more quickly and will accelerate your career no matter where you are headed.

Career Catapult #1: The Big Leap

When it comes to proving CEO mettle, there is no more powerful catapult than what we call the "big leap." What do we mean by that? Accepting the challenge of a role that is a big stretch from what you have done previously—either because the role is much larger than anything you've done before or because it takes you into unfamiliar territory. With a big leap you may find yourself overnight managing a hundred times more people than you ever have before or taking on roles for which you don't have the required experience. A big leap, when successful, demonstrates you have the ability to thrive in a new, uncertain environment. It demonstrates your ability to scale your leadership skills and deliver results even amid a new and much more complex terrain. Your success with a big leap suggests that you have the skills, acumen, and temperament to make the biggest leap of all, to the highest levels of senior management and even to CEO.

Over a third of the Sprinters had made big leaps. Roughly half of those leaps occurred during the first eight years of their career.[6] *These leaders proactively sought out opportunities to take on a new large challenge before they felt fully prepared or ready.*

Christine's experience included two big leaps. The fitness company that she joined in an entry-level training role was growing quickly and opening up new centers. She first moved from an entry-level training role, where she was teaching existing store employees how to sell customer memberships, to running the Midwestern region P&L, leapfrogging the next natural promotional step as a district manager to run a small cluster of city-wide centers. She got the job running a region thanks to her own initiative. At an annual meeting, she had met the VP of Operations, whom she admired. And she thought, *That's who I'm going to be.* She sought the woman out and told her of her career aspirations.

Once the division head learned that, as a trainer, Christine had already gone beyond her formal duties to support the opening of new centers, the head of operations decided to give her the chance to run a regional P&L when a role opened up. Christine shared, "I said to myself, what have I got[ten] myself into? Our mission was to grow revenue per center. Customer conversion and retention were low, and costs were high. I was scared. But I learn well on the fly. And I went in and said we are going to be the top-performing market at the conference next year. I actually made my team role-play walking onstage to get the award." Christine's region ended up as the second-highest-performing market in terms of revenue per center. And they did get to walk across the stage and collect an award. Her success during the leap paved the way to her becoming a field vice president.

Then, in another leap four years later, she took on a CIO role without having any technology background. As Christine recalled, "I learned that the business speaks a different language from the technology group, and you don't really realize it until you are in it." One of the benefits of leaping to new functional places is a deepened appreciation of the broader set of functions that any future CEO will need to manage.

Robert Hanson, the CEO of the jewelry company John Hardy, also credits a big leap for fueling his career success. Robert came from humble beginnings: "My lack of economic security was a real driver for me. I didn't want to struggle." He won a scholarship to St. Mary's College, a small liberal arts college in California, but his liberal arts degree wasn't enough to attract offers from the top consulting companies. So he took a job as a research analyst at a small regional firm. His big leap came later, working for Levi Strauss. He was "overpromoted," as he put it, to run the Levi's brand in Europe as its president. His promotion was the result of a conversation he initiated with his boss about how he could have a greater impact on the organization.

The European brand was Levi Strauss's marquee division, and Robert was surprised when he received the job. But he took on the challenge. "To run it at such a young age was surprising and terrifying," he told us. "There were nine country clusters, twenty-two countries and cultures, and even more languages. That moment was one of the most transformational experiences I've had as a professional. . . . There were parallels to the CEO role. It was lonely. There were fewer advisors. The business was oriented more externally. All of which were new to me and great preparation for later." Honing his **Decisiveness** and ability to **Engage for Impact**, he tapped mentors and stakeholders to make up for his lack of experience. And he delivered. In three years, he moved the brand from an 11 percent decline in revenue to low-digit growth.

Krista Endsley, the former CEO of the software firm Abila, has a career arc built largely from a series of big leaps. Krista is one of those rare CEOs who plotted every move of her career with her ultimate destination in mind. At the age of twelve she had announced her intention to become a CEO someday.

She attributes making her biggest leaps to having the guts to ask questions and confront being uncomfortable: "I have this theory that everyone should always feel a little bit outside their comfort zone, because it means you're growing. That discomfort is completely natural." Moving out of her comfort zone included an early shift from marketing to leading product management ("I pushed and I pushed and I pushed"). "Moving out of that marketing role, into product management and owning something, really set my career into the trajectory that it went in." The product management job prepared her to run a small $23 million division selling financial software systems to non-profit organizations. When the company decided to spin off the division, Krista was the natural choice to lead it as CEO. She was up to the challenge. She raised capital from private investors and added an acquisition of a similar-sized competitor, improving market position and doubling the employee head count. As CEO, she tripled the business.

Our point? If you see a big leap opportunity, seize it, whatever your experience or fears. Better yet, don't sit around waiting for it to appear—go seek it out.

DIY Big Leaps

It doesn't take a promotion or luck to practice your "stretch" potential. Here are ways you can make your own luck:

- Seek out cross-functional projects at your company to learn more about departments such as sales, marketing, IT, accounting, etc.

- Get involved in the integration of a merger.

- Volunteer to lead or participate in a top-priority business initiative.

- Ask how you could best contribute to the business.

- Ask your boss for additional responsibilities, especially those that will add to your skill set.

- Proactively look for and solve problems before you are asked.

- Make a habit of saying yes to greater opportunity, even if you don't feel ready.

- Seek out relationships that are broader or more senior in your customer organizations than what is customary for someone at your level.

- Look at your personal life as a way to practice big leaps and build new skills: Take on civic leadership roles, from city government to the school board; volunteer in a leadership role or even form a new nonprofit; look for public speaking opportunities if that's a big development area for you.

Career Catapult #2: The Big Mess

Often the best opportunity to accelerate your career comes in a seemingly unattractive package: what we call the "big mess." About 30 percent of the Sprinters we studied had led the way through a big mess.[7] It could be an underperforming business unit, a failed IT implementation, or a recalled product. It's a big problem, and the person who solves it will prove her ability to **Reliably Deliver** where someone else failed. To clean up a big mess, an executive must have the ability to figure out what's broken, decide how to fix it, and then flex her **Engage**

for Impact muscles to rally others to deliver results. Often, there's significant time pressure to fix the problem—the company, or the part of the company she is responsible for, is in crisis. Decisions must be made quickly and under pressure. Learning to lead through the uncertainty of such chaos requires the courage to take risks, persevere in the face of adversity, and set a path without a clear playbook to follow.

When we asked our interviewees about how to develop the behaviors critical to CEO success, a majority of them mentioned leading during a crisis. As Elisa Villanueva Beard, CEO of Teach For America, put it, "I don't think people know what they are capable of unless they have put themselves in the toughest situation. You have to dig deep to figure out, ultimately, what am I about, what are my values?"

Large companies known for grooming strong leaders, such as GE, Pepsi, or Danaher, deliberately use big messes as an opportunity to develop future executives. They give relatively inexperienced but talented executives underperforming or broken business units to see what they can do. Many of the CEOs we advise recall handling a big mess as a big turning point in their career. Strong CEOs, it turns out, are forged under pressure.

You don't need to wait to be tapped to take advantage of a big mess opportunity. Go find it. A CEO we'll call Bruce found such an opportunity from an unusual source: a newspaper ad. A large metropolitan county on the West Coast had posted an ad searching for a chief administrative officer for the city—the city government version of a CEO. This was a $4 billion county with 20,000 employees, and it was bankrupt.

Bruce smelled an opportunity to make a mark. At the time, the former Marine was on the executive track at an aerospace and defense company. He had job offers within the company to move up, and recruiters were calling as well. But Bruce felt that the VP jobs he was being offered would move him much too slowly toward his ultimate goal of running an enterprise. So he applied for and was offered the job as the county's chief administrative officer.

While there, Bruce engineered a total financial turnaround, adapting the playbook as he went, under the intense scrutiny of the local press. To generate the much-needed cash, he privatized trash-hauling services despite fierce political blowback and even death threats. Bruce redirected funds from administrative costs to programs benefiting taxpayers. For example, keeping middle schools open in the afternoon to provide safe spaces for kids and quintupling the budget for initiatives to combat infant mortality. Over two years, Bruce took the county from junk-bond rating to a respectable A–, enabling it to borrow money on much better terms. His success won him a spot in the county Taxpayers Association Hall of Fame as well as C-level employment offers. Today Bruce is the CEO of a Fortune 500 technology services company.

Navigating a big mess is a good testing ground for all four CEO Genome Behaviors. It is an especially great way to hone **Decisiveness**. No one knows this better than Shanti Atkins, a litigator-turned-CEO. Shanti was eking it out as an employment lawyer, when the firm chairman, knowing her interest in technology, asked her to help build a related business, ELT, a technology company focused on compliance e-learning. Shanti dove headfirst into product development and market positioning while doing her day job as a lawyer. In 2000, the bottom fell out of the market, as it did for so many companies during the economic meltdown. ELT lost its last round of funding and went through three rounds of layoffs. The company was on life support. As Shanti recalls, "I was one of twelve people left when I was offered the CEO role. It was an environment of extreme volatility and stress, but I was young and naïve. My answer was an unwavering 'yes!'" The task was to find a buyer for the assets of the business and essentially wind it down. "But I became obsessed with the product and the potential. You should have seen my apartment. Storyboards and ideas on the product were everywhere. I was consumed by the idea that we did not have to close this down, that the product was good and the market was there—we had just suffered some execution errors."

Ultimately, she did a complete restart of the company and grew the business from almost nothing to more than $100 million. Looking back, she says, "I like to make decisions quickly. Which is funny, being a former lawyer. But it comes back to the crisis. Being early on in a crisis gave me an opportunity to practice that skill of rapid decision making." Shanti applied a decision-making rule, "If I had to decide in thirty seconds, what would I do?" The pressure of a crisis changes the perceived cost of getting any one decision wrong. Plus, there's no time for indecision.

One tactic for those who feel they've been overlooked for the most plum assignments: *Take the job no one wants.* This is the job that no one considers important—until you see and realize the potential to make it amazing. It's the tough job that no one wants to risk his or her career on. Often during a big mess, management hierarchy gives way to those who step up—opening up opportunities that otherwise wouldn't present themselves.

Career Catapult #3: Go Small to Go Big

Smaller companies often offer opportunities for a faster career trajectory. Incoming CEOs at large public companies on average have had four to six more years of experience than those coming in to run midsize and small businesses. "Going small" as a Career Catapult can also mean starting something new within an existing company. *Roughly 60 percent of the Sprinters we analyzed had taken a smaller role at some point in their career.*[8] Many of these were starting something new within their company or, in some cases, stepping out to join a new business. It is an invaluable opportunity to build a product, division, or company from the ground up and show a transformative difference in performance. In this environment, one often gets responsibilities much faster than in a more stable environment. And later, this gives these CEO candidates an edge over executives and managers who have worked only within a predictable hierarchy or structure and never had to build a business system and process.

Damien McDonald was a rising star at Johnson & Johnson. As VP of global marketing for Ethicon (the world's leading surgical supplies business), he reenergized growth of the business from a tepid 1–2 percent to the industry-leading 3–5 percent. He had a great boss who was also on the fast track and was respected by the most senior executives. Life was good and getting better. Impressed with Damien's performance, his boss saw him as the likely successor and had explicitly told him he was in the running for his job. Who wouldn't be happy to hear that? The trouble was, Damien didn't want to succeed his boss: "I looked at his general management role and knew that was not what I wanted." A $50 billion company, Johnson & Johnson was a sprawl of divisions, departments, and stakeholders weaved into a corporate matrix of byzantine complexity. Damien wanted to be CEO of a $300–500 million business that could move and change direction with the agility of a race car rather than that of a transatlantic cruise ship. Damien left Johnson & Johnson for Zimmer, a company that was a fraction of the former's size with none of the prestige. He took over a struggling $250 million spine division, which delivers surgical solutions to enhance the quality of life for spine patients. It was a chance to learn how to be a general manager and to show that he could deliver. Which he did: His division achieved 12 percent year-on-year growth, performance good enough to win him a position as a group executive and corporate vice president leading a $1.5 billion group of dental consumables companies at Danaher, widely regarded as a training ground for future CEOs.[9] Ultimately, Damien's willingness to take a job with a smaller company paid big dividends: In 2016, he was made CEO of the medical technology company LivaNova, headquartered in London.

Christine's Go Small catapult came when she asked for the opportunity to run an online business within her fitness company. Many competitors were beginning to build a strong online presence to sell fitness products, but the online business at her company was unprofitable. "I was making a decision to go to something smaller," she told us. "It was scary. I didn't know the space well, and I had to learn it." Christine became a master of building performance metrics, repeatable processes, and standard operating procedures—the machinery of **Reliability.** "I knew immediately we had to find a way to make the business scalable," she said. "I needed some sort of system. And I had to create it." Because she was learning a new online business model, she strengthened her ability to **Adapt** by reaching out broadly for input and advice. She consulted functions outside her organization, such as the corporate finance team or the marketing department, earning a reputation for being more inclusive and outward-looking than her peers. She called colleagues in similar industries who were already selling online. "I just reached out. I picked up the phone and called Boston Market and the Gap and learned by visiting their call centers. I learned from other industries. I had to force myself to look at it differently," she says. "We got it profitable." In fact, she'd *quadrupled* the business's revenue by the time she moved on.

Vyomesh (VJ) Joshi, president and CEO of 3D Systems since 2016, kick-started his career by going small in his early years at Hewlett Packard. In 1993, he was a well-regarded R&D manager running large labs in San Diego and Barcelona with over two hundred R&D engineers focused on large format printers. At that point, an expected and "safe" trajectory would take VJ to run a larger team. Instead, his boss, Antonio Pérez, then a senior general manager at HP (and later CEO at Eastman Kodak) offered him an opportunity to build a business from scratch as the operations manager for multifunction printers. "All-in-one" printers are commonplace now (you might have one at home), but in the early '90s they represented new territory for HP. The role had barely anyone reporting to it and offered no guarantees of success. VJ thought hard about this risky step, which on the surface looked like a demotion or at least a side step. He ultimately took the role, attracted by the opportunity to build something new and to make an important contribution to HP.

VJ was no stranger to taking risks. In his early twenties he'd sold everything he owned and come to the United States to get a master's in engineering, despite the vehement disapproval of his family. VJ recalls his first minutes in the new country: "I landed at the JFK airport in New York City. I was thirsty. I see a water fountain, and I have no idea how to operate it. A woman showed me how to operate it." Much like the risk of coming to a new country, the risk of taking on this off-the-beaten-path assignment paid off for VJ. He built the multifunction printer business from scratch to $100 million. He repeated this success by building out a home imaging division for HP—again, from scratch.

On the heels of these successes, in 1999 VJ took a big leap with a promotion to run the $9 billion Inkjet business. By 2001, he became executive vice president in charge of the entire $19 billion Imaging and Printing Group. His professional ascent culminated with his appointment as CEO of 3D Systems (pioneer in 3-D printing) in 2016. The small risky role launching multifunction printers back in 1993 became a powerful catapult for VJ's rise to the top.

Blowups: Curse or Crucible?

Career Catapults can be risky, to be sure. Careers that elevate one to senior ranks often come with big blowups—a failure that goes beyond a meaningful mistake. Typical blowups that we came across ran the gamut from getting fired to overseeing a financially disastrous new initiative to making a high-profile bad call. Slightly fewer than half of the CEOs in our sample experienced a blowup in their careers. *Surprisingly, these blowups had no apparent negative effect on their likelihood of being hired or their eventual performance as a CEO.*[10]

Inspirational speeches extolling the virtues of risk-taking are a staple feature in university commencement addresses, career advice columns, and mentoring conversations. We have all heard successful people decades older than we are cheerfully recall their painful experiences in the rearview mirror from the safety of their present-day successes. We also often hear nightmare stories from our friends living through the anguish of career disasters. *How does one know which risks to take and how to handle blowups to ensure they become a valuable "learning experience" and not a career disaster?* Here are a few guideposts. First, having several different kinds of blowups in a career does not disqualify you as a potential CEO. Having the same blowup over and over does. Second, the earlier a blowup comes in your career, the lower its cost. And, most important, when it comes to acquiring leadership skills and getting selected as a CEO, it's not so much the blowups themselves that matter, but how you handle them.

How you handle blowups is critical to your success in any leadership role. CEO assessments we have analyzed reveal two common mistakes. First, CEO candidates who talk about a blowup as a failure are half as likely to deliver a strong performance compared to leaders who see setbacks as opportunities to learn.[11] As we described in Chapter 2, avoidance of the word *failure* isn't spin for these CEOs. It reflects their genuine attitude: Errors aren't fearsome embarrassments but *inevitabilities* that provide the most reliable laboratory for future improvement.

The second mistake we see too many potential CEOs make is hesitance to take ownership for a blowup. In our interviews, they deflect ownership and instead point to external factors or blame others for failures on their watch. Our data shows that candidates who blamed others reduced their chances of being recommended for hire by a third.[12]

So what do the best candidates and CEOs do? They look facts in the face, they own their mistakes, and they reflect actively on what they have learned and how they adjusted their behavior and decision making to minimize the chances of a blowup occurring in the future.

Anne Williams-Isom is the CEO of Harlem Children's Zone, a nonprofit committed to ending generational poverty in Central Harlem. She's won praise for her leadership—no easy task, given that she followed the organization's much-loved, iconic founder Geoffrey Canada into the role.

Anne is genuine and straightforward. When you sit down with her, you quickly sense that she cares deeply about what she does. Her childhood was chaotic but guided by a courageous single parent. Her mother was the first African American immigrant nurse at Long Island Jewish Medical Center. The family endured a lot of setbacks. Can we pay the oil bill? Can we get the kids to school? Anne has lived through some tough moments and difficult circumstances. She didn't hesitate to share her biggest blowup with us.

While reporting to Geoffrey Canada as COO, Anne was the person in charge for what could have turned into a tragedy. It began simply with a conflict between two seventh graders. Normally, an incident like this would be handled by the principal and after-school workers. After getting an early update from the principal, Anne had assumed the situation was being properly handled by the staff and left for the day.

Unfortunately, this time Anne's team was unable to de-escalate the conflict. Adults who knew the girls showed up at the school ready to fight, turning the situation from stressful to dangerous. Anne wasn't on site when it escalated. Shortly after, she got a tense call from the CEO telling her the situation hadn't been resolved. Anne went back immediately and was able to contain and ultimately resolve the crisis. It all ended well, but to Anne it felt like a very close call. Anne felt the children's safety was unnecessarily jeopardized because the staff had encountered a situation for which they were unprepared.

In hindsight, she saw that she severely underestimated the risks in that moment. Instead of letting this mistake hold her back, Anne seized the anguish of the moment to learn valuable lessons that made her a stronger leader. First, it was a lesson in contingency planning and risk mitigation. Going forward, she became obsessed with asking questions to anticipate risk. Second, she learned a lesson in ownership: There are certain moments—safety risks being chief among them—when a leader needs to be on the ground. Today, these lessons are embedded in her leadership and in the operating rules she has set up for her team.

Anne is the perfect demonstration of how a blowup, approached with a learning mind-set, becomes not a blemish to be hidden but an important leadership building block. Extracting lessons from even the toughest experiences has made Anne the leader who earned promotion to CEO of this lauded institution, one that is successfully transforming nearly one hundred blocks of Central Harlem.

How to Catapult Without Crash Landing

Catapults are a high-risk, high-reward approach to career choices. So how do you ensure a catapult propels you up, not out?

- **Align supporters:** Taking risks with people who have witnessed and invested in your success improves the odds that if you fail in a risky assignment, it will be interpreted as an outlier and a valuable learning experience on an otherwise strong trajectory.

- **Align senior management on the risk involved:** Get multiple perspectives on the probability of success. Make sure it's clear to key senior people, including one to two levels above your direct boss, that you are taking an extraordinary risk for the benefit of the business. You've agreed to take on a big challenge, and there will be value even in the lessons learned from potential failure.

- **Ensure you have the resources you need:** Assess and secure the budget and talent you need to deliver, and ensure you have authority to make the decisions necessary to drive results.

- **Stay connected:** Stay actively engaged with your network, even if it isn't immediately relevant in your current role. Regular communication and consultation with senior players will help ensure there are no surprises and help you identify the next role when you are ready to move on.

Making the right career choices is only half the battle in terms of career advancement. You can excel on the CEO Genome Behaviors and achieve every Career Catapult, but if no one notices, it doesn't count for much. The relationships and visibility you build with the right people in the right way matter as much as the results you achieve. In the next chapter, we break down the mechanics of how future CEOs got noticed.

KEY TAKEAWAYS

1. Optimize your career choices at each stage:
   - Stage 1 (first 8 years of your career): Achieve breadth and rapid pace of learning
   - Stage 2 (years 9–16): Demonstrate measurable results
   - Stage 3 (years 16–24): Become an enterprise leader

2. Deploy Career Catapults to accelerate your trajectory:
   - Big Leap
   - Big Mess
   - Go Small to Go Big

3. Own your blowups and turn them into learning opportunities. Stay connected to your supporters as you undertake the Career Catapults

4. Conduct an annual CEO-readiness assessment looking at:
   - your mastery of Four CEO Genome Behaviors
   - your portfolio of experiences against typical CEO re-quirements (see p. 113)
   - catapults that can help you accelerate your path

chapter 7

Stand Out: How to Become Known

LIEUTENANT GEORGE: *"I don't like blowing my own trumpet."*
CAPTAIN BLACKADDER: *"You might at least have told us you had a trumpet."*

—*Blackadder Goes Forth* (BBC comedy)

WE DIDN'T WANT TO WRITE THIS CHAPTER. THE CORNERSTONE OF our work is a focus on performance and outcomes, not on claiming credit or working your network. But the data and our own experience forced us to be honest with ourselves and with you. The formula for getting on the CEO short list is not "get great things done and hope somebody hears about them." Instead, the key is "get great things done, and get noticed for them."

Getting to the top seat is the output of two mutually reinforcing factors: getting results in the right roles and getting noticed for those results. This is true for any coveted position. We live in a crowded world. There are likely five other qualified people standing next to you for any prized job opportunity. Performance is a necessary but not sufficient ingredient to getting on the short list of finalists for a CEO position or most other leadership roles.

One of Elena's favorite stories about reaching the CEO seat is the journey of an Australian executive she met three years ago, whom we'll call Christopher. Elena assessed Christopher for a CEO role in 2014 and was impressed with his well-rounded profile across the four CEO Genome Behaviors. Having spent his career in product businesses, he wasn't the right guy to lead the turnaround in a services business Elena assessed him for, but she walked away convinced that Christopher was ready to become a CEO in a business that was a better fit with his strengths.

That CEO search had been Christopher's first experience on the short list—and for a while, to his great frustration, it seemed as if it might be his last. Like everyone who is a stone's throw from the top, he's a driven high-performer with a wealth of experience. Christopher had started in sales at a leading global consumer products company and then made a big leap to running a P&L at another firm. He moved his family to Europe for more international experience. Finally, he moved to a company with a reputation for its business management systems, where he led a division with more than $1 billion in revenue.

Christopher had delivered impressive results, mastered the CEO Genome Behaviors, and made a lot of the right career moves. Yet he was stuck, and his shelf life as an attractive CEO candidate was nearing its expiration date. (Boards are wary of candidates who have been in striking distance for more than a handful of years but never got the position.) At his current employer, Christopher was viewed as a high-potential leader, but the current CEO was about his age and had no plans to retire. His wife, who was his biggest supporter and co-strategist, started thinking the problem might be that he didn't look the part. She pressured him to get his teeth fixed and straighten up his posture.

At breakfast in New York one day—surrounded, Elena will admit, by attractive, well-groomed men and women in expensive suits—Christopher somewhat bashfully asked Elena what she thought: Was his wife right? Were his teeth really to blame? Did he simply not look the part?

Elena shook her head.

"Good teeth are not your problem," she told him. His relief was palpable, until she told him he had a bigger, harder problem but one that was equally fixable.

"You've built a strong track record. But how much time are you spending getting to know people who could actually hire you for a CEO job?"

Christopher, like so many talented midcareer executives we see get stuck (and many who get stuck even earlier), was working double time on one part of the equation: getting results in the right roles. He had underinvested, however, in getting known by the people who could get him to the next job. Even straight white teeth weren't going to solve that.

At this stage of Christopher's career, he was still lacking what we found to be a key bridge between senior executive and CEO. All of the CEO candidates we meet who are on the short list were visible to the right people (those who are making the CEO decisions) in the right way. We'll return to Christopher later.

Interestingly, we didn't find any sign that they were *overtly* working to get noticed. In other words, these people weren't aggressive self-promoters, seeking attention for its own sake. They weren't name-dropping or bragging about thousands of LinkedIn endorsements. They were building relationships to deliver results *for the good of the company—not their own self-interest.* They created visibility with the right people in the right way. We have distilled a set of tactics that, with time and intentional practice, deliver that one-two punch.

Visibility with the Right People

1. Pick your boss.

No one has more control over your visibility and success in an organization than your boss. "Glenn," a COO we met several years ago, learned this the hard way. When he learned he was on the short list to succeed the CEO of his company, he stopped nurturing his relationship with his boss—the incumbent CEO—and shifted his attention to the company's executive board. Eager to show that he deserved the top job, Glenn began to operate unilaterally and often openly criticized his boss's decisions.

The CEO, as you might expect, noticed and eventually lost faith in him. "You have the talent to be the next CEO," he told Glenn, exasperated. "It is unfortunate that you are always breathing down my neck. You are so ambitious that I feel like you are my rival—not my successor." Instead of the nod from the board, Glenn got the boot and was out of the company in a year. He saw himself as a corporate hero hamstrung by an insecure leader. He might have been right—but being right didn't get him any closer to his dream job.

Obviously, across the arc of a future CEO's career, not all relationships with one's boss will necessarily be strong. On the other hand, when we look at those successful in attaining executive roles, they tend to have positive relationships with many of their bosses. These leaders are able to avoid the two most common pitfalls of the employee-boss relationship. One, they hold their own—even engage in conflict—without their bosses feeling attacked. And two, they distinguish themselves in the organization without leaving their bosses feeling upstaged.

Your best protection from both of these pitfalls is simple: Do your diligence up front, and, to the extent you can, pick the right boss. When that's not an option, make sure that every suggestion you make mirrors the language of the organization's goals and, better yet, your boss's goals too. Make your boss your collaborator. Of course, this can be difficult when dealing with a boss who is ineffective, is mean, or has a strong need to control. Below we share the best tactics deployed by successful rising leaders who have made the most out of even the toughest boss situations.

- **Understand your boss's goals.** What does success look like to her? How does your role fit into that? How can you best support her? What are her career goals? What motivates her? Know which individuals in the organization are most important to your boss, and look for ways to get her noticed by them.

- **Don't guess his or her expectations and preferences.** *Ask.* What are her top goals for your work? How does she prefer you communicate with her? And don't just ask once; priorities shift over time. For example, you might turn in a project a day late to double-check the numbers, assuming she expects perfection, while she needed to make a quick decision, even if the data wasn't perfect yet. A good way to make this conversation less abstract is to ask about the best direct report your boss ever had: What made him or her so great?

- **Let your boss help you.** Keep your boss looped into your career goals, and connect your interests to the organization's. You want to keep these at the top of your boss's mind so that when your boss is in a meeting and your dream assignment is mentioned, your boss has both the knowledge and the motivation to say, "You know who would be great for that . . ." and name you. On the other hand, if your boss hears you're considering a job opportunity in another division without consulting her first, you can turn a fan into a critic overnight. People who see themselves as being invested in your success want to be consulted and involved in your important career moves.

- **Master the regular update on the things that matter.** Send a focused update on where you are on your boss's top priorities with respect to your work. The appropriate time frame and medium for these updates will vary depending on your boss, company, role, etc., but the consistency shouldn't. The message to get across is: *I understand what's important to you and to the business. I'm on top of it. You can count on me.*

Some people go to work to please their boss. Others show up at work to get the job done. Neither of those is the same as saying, "How do I help this individual above me achieve the goals for the enterprise?" That's the secret to making your superior your sponsor—someone who can introduce you to opportunities or pull you up with him as his star rises in the organization.

We are not advocating that you become a sycophant or a political operator. We are suggesting that you genuinely seek to support and collaborate with your boss to achieve her objectives, yours, and the organization's. If you find yourself in a situation where your boss is intractable and not aligned with the goals of the enterprise, the best medicine is to actively make a move to another role.

In assessing candidates, getting "pulled" by bosses into bigger and bigger roles is a common sign of high performers that we look for in making a strong recommendation. It tells us as much about a candidate's ability to engage and manage relationships as it does about his ability to perform.

2. Build your tribe.

We found that in addition to strong relationships with bosses, almost half of the Sprinters we studied had powerful sponsors throughout their career.[1] Sponsors are those individuals, often people more senior than your own boss or residing in other parts of the organization, who have the influence and the access to open doors and introduce you to valuable opportunities. Support from an influential sponsor can help accelerate you in an organization. Why? Sponsors take action, provide valuable access, and effectively lend you their credibility.

And therein lies the challenge. We know we need sponsors. The importance of sponsorship has become a perennial topic of leadership development articles and career advice blogs. But the advice typically has limited value for those who need it most, because not everyone can access a sponsor with equal dexterity.

However, sponsors often throw their weight behind the people they see as "one of us." What does all this mean for anyone looking to break into an opportunity where they find themselves in the minority? Some might advise that they cloak themselves in the clothes or hobbies of the in-crowd. We are more intrigued by the CEO candidates who have creatively and proactively created sponsorship on their own terms. Instead of trying to become what they are not, they are resourceful and deliberate in their quest to connect in ways that are true to who they are.

Nataly Kogan, CEO of the wellness company Happier, attributes a fair part of her success to creating sponsorship on her own terms. Nataly emigrated to the United States from Russia at age fourteen. With barely any English, she survived the terrifying social and academic challenges of American high school thanks to an adroit ability to read people and her environment quickly and to find points of connection. In the suburbs of Detroit, she had to walk into the cafeteria her first day as a student and figure out "which kids were going to be the least mean."

Identifying the "friendlies" was half her strategy. The other half was to adapt her approach to the audience. Telling teachers, "My English isn't so good; can you help me?" had a reasonable success rate. Telling teenagers the same thing? Crash and burn. She found she had more success bartering: "I'll give you my math notes if you'll give me your English notes." With high school students, notes had currency. Humility did not. Later in her career, as the only female managing director at the New York–based VC firm Hudson Ventures, Nataly realized she could cut through with humor to build bridges with her sports-talking colleagues. She told us that, earlier in her career, her husband would prep her on sports news so that she could go in on Monday morning and have something to say. But she woke up one day and said, "This is not me. This is fake. This is not what I want to do. And I realized that I connect with humor, and it works for me."

Younger and midcareer professionals often lament that they haven't been lucky to find powerful sponsors in their career. *Rather than passively waiting for your luck, you can proactively create sponsors.* First and foremost, sponsorships get created by great performance. Beyond that, we offer a few tactics to help you get noticed and cultivate sponsors. An important word of caution before you try these at home. The tactics below bear fruit when they are grounded in real performance and genuine attitudes. If you try to fake your way to getting noticed, it will cause flameouts instead of fireworks:

- Share your aspirations—not problems or issues—with potential sponsors. This creates positive energy and demonstrates that your goals are aligned with the business's and the sponsor's objectives.

- Ask a potential sponsor for advice on topics relevant to her. If you want someone to feel invested in your success, give her easy opportunities to contribute to it. Advice is a powerful sponsorship-building approach. Most people enjoy giving advice, and the very act of doing that encourages them to be more invested in your success. Not to mention the value of the advice itself! Close the loop later by letting the sponsor know how the situation played out and how her advice helped you.

- Make clear, specific requests that are easy for your sponsor to fulfill. For example, if you want to get more exposure to senior clients, asking the head of sales is a lot more fruitful than going to the head of manufacturing.

- Give sponsors your genuine gratitude. Acknowledge anything they did that helped you—no matter how small. Thank them for advice or an opportunity and share how that's made a difference. People tend to do more of what earns them positive recognition; senior people are no exception.

- When you ask for a sponsor's help, don't drop the ball. Follow through. For example, if she makes a requested introduction, don't let the e-mail sit. Take the ball and run with it.

- Bring rare goods. One way to break into closed networks and attract sponsorship is to offer new, needed skills. One of our investment clients works primarily with people the firm has known for decades. However, as they look to infuse cutting-edge digital practices into their business, they are beginning to court new partners, purely because these individuals bring a needed skill. Invest in building valuable expertise and become known as the expert.

3. Build a bonfire.

One of Elena's mentors at McKinsey, Kurt Strovink, once sat her down for a talk: "You are doing good work but not getting the reputation you deserve. You are working with a partner in media, then for another partner in financial services, then on to London, then back to work on a consumer project. It's like moving to a new town every few months—you are not going to build a strong support network that way." Kurt told Elena to imagine that she was looking at her career from a spaceship: "You're setting a million little fires in different places, and who cares? Instead, what you need to do is build a really large fire that can be seen from space—then you'll get [a] real return on your efforts."

Pick a village and build a bonfire, Strovink was saying. *Stop flitting from place to place throwing off sparks.* At some point in your career, intentionally focusing your relationship-building efforts is critical. The key is to decide where to invest your time and energy to build a critical mass of relationships that help you stand out.

A great way to gain exposure well above your pay grade is to take on a staff role with a senior person several levels above you. This can be an effective early-career visibility booster. Often, operational leaders eager to run their own P&L overlook corporate roles, such as chief-of-staff roles or director of strategy. Yet those roles can provide both built-in visibility to senior leaders and unparalleled insight into how successful leaders operate at the top. Even if you are in a smaller company that might not have "staff roles," volunteering for important cross-functional projects outside the boundaries of your job can increase your exposure.

Christopher, the CEO aspirant we mentioned earlier, was told he was crazy when he left marketing early in his career at Merck in order to take a staff job as a business improvement manager. High fliers wanted to move up the ranks in marketing and sales. The business improvement function was part of the much less glamorous operations team. But he guessed correctly that it would broaden his view on the business, his skills, and his network. "As a business improvement manager, I had the ability to roam around the company to help fix things. Thanks to this role, I learned the business and all of its different functions much better than did any of my peers. Because I was leading improvement initiatives that were important for the business, I got to know my boss's boss." Christopher discovered it gave him instant visibility within a very influential village: "That job gave me more visibility to senior leadership than anyone thought," he says.

You have much more oxygen to feed the flame when you're working at an intersection where you can add the most value and contribute what the organization values most. If you give a heroic effort to some IT project in the basement—or twenty IT projects in the basement—in an organization that lives and dies on sales, no one's going to care. Getting known organization-wide is much harder when you're working in a function that's considered an "also-ran" rather than a primary driver of the company's success. If you find yourself in an also-ran function within an organization, you've got to take the risk to make a lateral move to broaden horizons, or you may even need to leave the company for one where your expertise will be more central to the company's priorities.

Vyomesh (VJ) Joshi, whom we met earlier, president and CEO of 3D systems, learned this the hard way early on in his career. VJ was eager to get a promotion from R&D section manager to R&D manager in the Imaging and Printing group at Hewlett Packard. VJ had met all of his goals and was known as a good colleague. Going in for his performance review, he assumed he'd receive the promotion. To his shock, he was passed over. Disappointed, he went to the head of his business unit to better understand what had happened and to learn from his career hiccup. "My boss gave me incredible advice that I share with others to this day. He said to me, *'At your level, to get promoted, it's not enough just to check the boxes and meet expectations. You need to make a contribution that moves the needle for the company. Something that is visibly and meaningfully core to what drives value.'*"

This led VJ to embrace a thorny challenge within the "crown jewel" at Hewlett Packard at the time, the Printing and Imaging business. The market for printers was stagnant. Despite the counsel of many around him that the probability of success was low, VJ knew that making a difference in the heart of Hewlett Packard was exactly the contribution that was needed. Between 2000 and 2008, he built the platform for growth by winning the low end, leveraging scalable printing technology and connecting printers directly to the Internet, which allowed the company to build subscription-based models. The fruits of his labor were stunning: he grew the Printing and Imaging group from $19 billion to $28 billion while improving operating profits from 10 percent to 16 percent. What initially was a disappointing setback became a valuable career lesson that helped VJ focus where it mattered most and paved the way to his CEO seat at 3D Systems.

As you build a bonfire, you have the best shot of being noticed when people can readily answer yes to the question: *Is this person known for something important for the business?* For example, getting involved in a major initiative to change the business, such as M&A, is an excellent opportunity to both hone your skills and raise your profile. This applies whether you happen to be on the side of the acquirer or the company being acquired. Acquired executives get exposure far above the level they would normally have in their own business. If you are on the side of the acquirer, leading merger integration is a crash course in understanding the entire business and puts you in regular dialogue with the most senior people in the business.

Visibility in the Right Way

1. Ask for what you want.

There's one thing that will help you be noticed for the right opportunities, and it's ridiculously simple. So simple that even some of the most competent senior executives we know fail to do it. *You have to ask.*

Few things are more important in accelerating your career than asking for what you want. Those on the path to CEO—or leadership roles of any kind—show confidence and conviction by doing exactly that. *Almost 60 percent of Sprinters we studied took the initiative and at*

some point in their career proactively asked for their next responsibility.[2]
Here are a few representative examples of asking we heard from those
who got to the top faster than might have been expected:

- "I was an unknown when I started. Six months later, I
  told my supervisor that I wanted more. We had to move
  an entire production line from one facility to another
  over the Thanksgiving holiday. I lobbied hard to get that
  project because I knew it was a big priority for the business."

- "My company knew I wanted to run a P&L and promised me the opportunity when one opened up. But after
  a few months of waiting, a bigger job opened up in the
  Quality function that would allow me a lot more exposure to the senior team. I asked for it. It meant a longer
  runway to get a P&L, but ultimately it led to a shorter
  runway to CEO."

One caveat to this—you have to have earned the right to ask by
delivering a strong performance. If you have not earned it, you will
be seen as an overly ambitious climber rather than someone with the
good of the company or organization at heart. As you read this, if you
find yourself worried whether you've earned the right to ask, you probably have. Not surprisingly, overly ambitious climbers rarely lose sleep
over being too ambitious.

What if you are unsure of what, exactly, you want? Yes, ask even
then. You don't need to be locked in on a specific long-term destination.
It's absolutely fine if you are considering different paths—most people
do. Flex your **Decisiveness** muscles to pick and commit to a next step,
and get others to help you. You can always change direction later.

How you ask for what you want is at least as important as whom
you ask. Your tone must be that of aspiration, not desperation. The

first common mistake is coming to sponsors with problems rather than requests. The management refrain "Don't bring me problems— bring me solutions" applies equally to enlisting sponsorship. If you want sympathy, go to a friend. If you are going to a sponsor, make requests, not complaints.

When making a request, your goal is to enlist support by exuding positive energy and alignment with the goals of your business and your sponsor. *Here's where I'm excited to go. Here's why it will be great for the enterprise and why I'm the right person to do it. I'd love your help if possible.*

2. Rock the boat.

You might assume that highly visible rising stars work hard to please people in power. In fact, the opposite is true. *We found a strong theme of creating productive conflict on the path toward results. Conflict, so often perceived as a negative, can, when done for the right reasons in the right way, strengthen relationships and create powerful reputational tailwinds that establish you as a leader with conviction and power.* What makes a conflict productive? When it's aimed at producing a result valuable for the business.

One of the CEO candidates, "Carly," owes her fast-rising career to her willingness to trample hierarchy and break rules when a problem needs fixing. Early in her career, Carly was working as an entry-level Web developer at a telecom company in Texas. She became increasingly concerned that her company's network infrastructure was leaving their data wide open to hackers. No one listened to her concerns, so she found a surefire way to get heard: She went rogue. She hacked into the poorly protected servers.

Company executives were infuriated and fired her immediately— only to backtrack almost as quickly. Not only was her subterfuge carried out in the company's interest, they came to realize, but its success had proven that Carly was uniquely qualified to build better defenses. She was invited back to head the security team, a major promotion that put her on the fast track to the C-suite positions she's held ever since.

Carly wasn't looking to create conflict. She was bold in her commitment to do what was right for the business, and it thrust her into the spotlight. Rocking the boat to get the organization to sunnier shores—i.e., pursuing conflict in the interest of getting something productive done—can help you get ahead. Rocking the boat to get a better seat for yourself—i.e., to feed your personal ambition—will sooner or later land you in the water gasping for breath. We've seen countless political maneuvers. The person perpetrating the maneuvering is often the only one who is oblivious to how blatantly obvious those maneuvers are.

We saw this recently with an ambitious CFO we'll call Jason. Jason had actively campaigned to succeed the CEO, befriending four board members and getting employees to write letters of support. He was bright, had strong commercial instincts, and was professionally poised. His ascent seemed all but assured. Then he went a step too far. Jason decided to seal the deal on his promotion by negotiating a major M&A transaction without informing the current CEO or the board. He argued that the company was moving too slowly to capture what he saw as a strategic opportunity. The board saw him as a loose cannon and fired him a week later.

"Wow! It's good thing we didn't make him CEO," a board member later told us. "He was totally focused on advancing his own personal agenda without regard for what's best for the business."

The question is: How do you manage yourself so that your actions are understood as brave contributions to the collective good, not inadvertently read as reckless self-promotion? We'll tackle that question in the next section. Just remember, if you're not comfortable rocking the boat, you're probably not on the road to becoming a CEO.

The Self-Interest Torpedo

Recently Kim worked with "Phil," an executive who was on his company's CEO successor list. At first glance, he looked like a perfect candidate. He hit or exceeded targets in every role. He had successfully led a complicated merger integration at this multibillion-dollar construction and infrastructure business. He was charismatic and could spin a compelling vision. On the surface, he looked like the kind of leader the company could be proud of. Unfortunately, people who worked with him closely saw a starkly different picture. Phil was single-mindedly focused on his own success above all else. Every one of his "successful" conquests had left broken and crippled bodies along the road. Phil was the model of collegiality when he needed someone's help to achieve his own objectives. But once he got what he wanted, he didn't even say hello when passing the person in the hallway. He never reciprocated or supported anyone else's initiatives. If it wasn't his agenda, he moved on. After a while, his self-interested behavior became widely known. He started to lose some of his key team members. When we were asked to evaluate several CEO candidates for this company, Phil received the lowest feedback ratings from the entire executive team. This caught the attention of the board. Phil was ultimately dropped from their list of CEO candidates.

Selfishness or blatant self-promotion can help one get ahead in the short term, but it often backfires in the long run. "Kissing up and kicking down" is not a long-term strategy. Boards look for CEOs who are ambitious on behalf of the company—not for their own personal advancement or ego.

3. Look and speak the part.

You're willing to be a renegade—but how do you get heard rather than cordoned off to the side and labeled a rogue or a nut? The first key is obvious: Your ideas need to generate the results you promise. That track record creates confidence. A track record takes time, though. The second key to instilling confidence in you and your ideas is to *look and speak the part.*

"Fred," an executive we recently assessed, had a history of creating conflict that looked at first glance like a surefire way to get fired. For example, while working in sales, he had fought his boss tooth and nail over personnel decisions and major operational changes that he thought were necessary to move the organization forward. Did he have the authority to do so? No. Did the boss listen? Yes.

Why? First, Fred's changes worked. Fred grew revenues by implementing his approach. But before Fred could prove that his way would be successful, he had to get his boss to agree to even give it a try. He constantly humbled himself to ask for advice and smoothed friction with agreeable compromise: "Let me try it my way for six months, and if I fail, we'll do it your way." He would get agreement to test his ideas in low-risk ways such as changing sales force incentives for one small sales team. When it was successful, he'd get a commitment to broaden the change to the sales team that sold the most profitable product. His most brash, aggressive actions were always justified by the value they created for the organization. He saw creating value and building an enduring organization as his best route to the top.

The way Fred carried himself and communicated engendered confidence. Fred is a master of what Lynda Spillane, a celebrated public speaking coach who works with CEOs, royalties, and top government leaders, calls "permanent public speaking mode." It is an almost guaranteed generator of executive presence. According to Lynda, executives are perceived as strong and capable when they:

- **Speak a little louder.** This immediately communicates authority, competence, and confidence—whether or not the individual has any of those.

- **Speak more slowly.** This is generous to their audience, as it allows the time for them to digest the message. It also shows that the speaker believes he or she is worthy of airtime, another sign of confidence.

- **Master the deliberate pause.** Those with executive presence use pauses sometimes for clarity, sometimes for dramatic effect.

- **Make every word count.** In America, we typically use three times as many words as needed to communicate a point. Fewer wasted words compel the audience to pay attention.

- **Know their opening and closing sentences before they enter a room.** They never stumble their way through greetings. They understand that "Good morning" and "Good afternoon" are what everyone else says and does. Strong CEOs make themselves and their points memorable.

- **Constantly scan for cues that their message is gaining traction.** This allows them to custom-tailor their approach to the room.

- **"Borrow from Frank Sinatra."** The strongest CEOs, as Lynda likes to say—"they do it their way. And their way is authentic to them."

We know from experience that executive presence can be developed with practice and conscientiousness. Often, it's a matter of self-awareness and building more effective habits.

. . .

Getting noticed by the right people in the right way can become yet another catapult to the top. As promised, we now return to Christopher. With Elena's advice, he reengineered the way he was spending his time. He joined an industry board to increase his visibility and exposure to people who could open doors to CEO opportunities. He created a "kitchen cabinet" of informal advisors dedicated to his CEO search. He proactively reached out to private equity firms active in the relevant industries. And most of all, he invested more time reaching out and discussing the types of opportunities he wanted. One day, after Christopher had been offered two other CEO opportunities that weren't quite right, a recruiter with whom he had built a relationship called him with the perfect opportunity. The last time Elena saw Christopher, he had just come from his first industry conference as a CEO. He told her, "All these guys I've always looked up to—now we're at the same table."

The Yelp Effect

In the days of Glassdoor, Twitter, and other fast-moving social media, reputations build quickly and can be hard to change. We've seen seemingly minor missteps torpedo careers. It's a lot easier to avoid these behaviors than to clean up your reputation after. Among the top missteps to avoid:

- Being rude to receptionists, administrative assistants, and other people of perceived lower status. They will go out of their way to tell all their friends that you're someone to avoid. Unfortunately, Travis Kalanick, CEO of Uber, learned this the hard way when a video surfaced showing him berate one of his own Uber drivers. This video brought to public attention a broader issue of a hostile work environment which precipitated his slide into resignation in 2017.[3]

- Acting like a sycophant toward those in power. Confident leaders treat a CEO and a janitor with equal respect and graciousness.

- Being disrespectful or annoying to others in small but habitual ways. One leader we worked with was notoriously late. Her executive team felt constantly disrespected, and their low degree of loyalty and morale reflected it.

- Blowing up or losing your temper in front of people— especially those who see you rarely. Virtual teams and long-distance relationships are tough; every interaction is interpreted in the most paranoid light. Fraught interactions linger.

- Ignoring or patronizing a colleague's spouse or children at an event.

- Poor judgment in social media. Assume that anything you ever e-mail, tweet, or put anywhere in social media will be seen by potential employers. Does your online footprint shows you as a CEO-ready leader?

KEY TAKEAWAYS

1. Career success = Get Results x Get Known. Work on both parts of this equation.
2. Invest in your relationship with your boss and her boss.
3. Actively build sponsorship.
4. Build critical mass of relationships with key people rather than spreading yourself too thin.
5. Ask for what you want.
6. Rock the boat—for the sake of business results.
7. Speak as if you belong at the executive table.

chapter 8

Close the Deal

Death will be a great relief. No more interviews.
—Katharine Hepburn

CONGRATULATIONS, YOU'VE MADE THE SHORT LIST OF CANDIDATES!
Now all you have to do is pass the final test: *How do I walk into the room and convince the decision makers that I'm their best choice, whether for a CEO or another role?*

This is the question on the mind of anyone, everywhere, who's ever competed for a job. But it's exactly the wrong question to ask if you want to raise your odds of success. If you're on the short list for a job, your accomplishments are likely already hire-worthy. So what else does it take to get to a yes?

In Chapter 3, we learned about the power of perspective getting. Now it's time to put that learning into practice. *To ace an interview, ask not what the interviewer can do for you but what you can do for the interviewer.* Nothing gives you a greater edge in getting hired than an intimate understanding of the mind of your interviewer. In the case of a typical board member in the midst of a CEO succession, it's something like this:

Oh, boy! This feels very risky and very uncomfortable! CEO successions don't happen so often. We're all hired to be expert advisors, and here's something most of us have done only once at best. This is my single most important responsibility as a board member. . . . We've talked about succession for years, but now it's decision time. Big decision time!

If I were unlucky and replacing a failed CEO, I'd be anxious about finding someone up to the task of fixing the mess. But instead I'm lucky. Our CEO has done a great job. On the other hand, if we pick the wrong person, it will be painfully obvious that we screwed up.

Board members better than I, more accomplished than I, at some of America's top companies, who supposedly had a great succession plan in place, still picked the wrong person 50 percent of the time. Hewlett Packard, Disney, P&G . . .

And the stakes! Make the wrong decision, and I've simultaneously put a bullet through the head of our company and my own reputation. It's Russian roulette.

That, future CEOs, is what you're up against. In fact, managers hiring for any position are typically facing some version of that anxiety: Time is short. No one seems like the perfect fit. Their expertise around making the right selection is limited. The chances for failure are uncomfortably high. The cost of a wrong decision is astronomical.

More than anything, hiring decision makers want to make a *safe* choice. Our point is this: Get out of your own head and your own anxieties over proving you are worthy of the role. *Safety*, and the means to bestow it on the decision makers, is your key to the kingdom.

This is not an easy notion to accept if you're an accomplished fast-track executive who has dedicated the last two sleep-deprived decades of your life to making the necessary sacrifices to vigilantly mold yourself into "the right stuff." There's only one statistically significant variable that both increases the chances you'll get hired *and* suggests you'll be successful as a CEO. It's **Reliability.** *No* other factors overlapped. None at all. Reliably delivering on expectations time after time gives decision makers a sense of safety that you will continue to deliver in the future. Feeling safe makes them more likely to bet on you.

Recently, we worked with a very successful investment firm that needed to replace the CEO for one of their largest acquisitions, a consumer services company that was losing market share to new competitors. The lead investor was a young, hypersuccessful overachiever. So far, everything he had touched had turned to gold, but his biggest-ever investment was on the rocks. For everyone involved, the financial and reputational stakes were huge. There was a lot of disagreement about what they needed, but the one thing everyone wanted? "A safe pair of hands." And to them, "safe" meant candidates who had big, impressive, household names of companies on their résumés. To investors it seemed obvious that someone who ran a $5 billion division could run an $800 million business.

As we saw it, a big company guy wasn't a safe choice at all. This was a middle-market business. We encouraged investors to consider several decisive, execution-oriented candidates who had done great things with companies of a similar size. Their "brand name" choice lacked several critical behaviors we knew he'd need to turn things around. But at the end of the day, our recommendation went out the window.

As one powerful board member and CEO recently told us in a moment of candor, "Let's face it, boards want to go with the safe choice. Not the one with the highest upside." Why? Because the highest upside often comes with high variability, and most boards don't want to bear that risk.

A year later, we got a call from the investors: "Elena, here's your 'I told you so' moment. The guy we hired is too slow for a small company bleeding cash. It's been a year, and he hasn't even upgraded the team or gone out to see customers. He is smart but is struggling making decisions without full information and absent the resources of a large business. We are back to the drawing board looking for a CEO."

The bottom line is this: *You get fired on results but hired on perception.* Whether you have the perfect pedigree or not, this chapter will set you up for success in getting picked for your dream job.

Become the Happy Warrior

Bill Fry has delivered many tens of millions of dollars of value to shareholders of companies he ran. He grew the vacuum company Oreck during an economic downturn—no easy feat. Before that, he led Bell Sports through a major acquisition and then a merger. Before starting his corporate career, he spent eight years in the Navy, after an ROTC scholarship took him to Ole Miss. Bill is competitive and as sharp as a tack. Sounds formidable, right? *He must be one intense guy!* Elena thought, prior to meeting him to assess him for the CEO role at Oreck.

It took one minute in his presence to prove that assumption wrong. Bill radiates an *I'm OK, you're OK* vibe that sets you immediately at ease. Eye contact, friendly questions, self-effacing humor, and calm but confident demeanor. Bill listens intently no matter who is in front of him—a CEO or a mailroom clerk—and makes you feel respected. Bill Fry gets results, without a doubt, but darned if he isn't the nicest guy you ever met.

Earlier we warned you of the pitfalls of aiming to be a nice CEO. Prioritizing how people feel over getting things done doesn't help you get results. It may even get you fired. Well, *surprise!* It does help you get hired! In the interview process, nice guys and gals finish first.

Boards, and interviewers in general, consistently overemphasize soft skills in their hiring decisions. Can it be that the same comportment that helps attract a date also gives you an edge in getting hired? Sophisticated as they are in tackling most business problems, when sizing up people, board members and business leaders often hire under the heavy influence of gut feel. And gut feel leads them to the more likeable candidates.

Among the 2,600 candidates analyzed by Kaplan and Sørensen, the more likeable leaders had higher odds of getting hired for *any* leadership position.[1] They weren't necessarily the best of the best, but they were the friendliest of the best. SAS analysts found that highly confident candidates were 2.5 times more likely to be hired.[2] *Likeability and confidence impart no advantage in performance, but they definitely help you land the job.*

Bill Fry exudes the likeability and confidence of a "Happy Warrior." The Happy Warrior confidently says, "I love to solve the problems you have. Been there, done that, and liked it. Eager to do it again for you!" As these leaders talk about their most difficult projects and tough decisions, they exude joy, passion, and energy. In other words, they simultaneously create both emotional and practical safety. You know you've met a happy warrior when he or she leaves the room and you can't wait to put her or him in the job.

The people who ultimately get picked are those who lead with fierce competence delivered with genuine warmth. Good interviewees take a read on the room the moment they walk in and mirror the energy level. They pay close attention to body language to see how their words are landing: Are people's eyes lighting up? Do they sound hesitant? Are they checking their watches? Your goal is to connect with your audience and make them feel safe.

You may not look anything like the interviewers who will decide whether you get the job. You may not have gone to the same schools or played the same sports. But if you can leave them feeling safer and more energized than you found them, you've got a great shot at getting the job.

Safety of Language

The board and other stakeholders will decide whether you're their next CEO over the course of a series of interviews. This is unfortunate, since interviews—contrived, time-bound conversations between mutually stressed-out individuals—offer perfect laboratory conditions for drawing out the most ridiculous sorts of bias. The more senior the hire, the greater the pressure and the worse the effect. Jim Kilts, former CEO of Gillette and Nabisco and a director on seventeen boards, summed it up well: *"You can't win a CEO job in a single meeting, but you can surely lose it."*

So, how do you avoid the land mines in the interview process? We ran 212 CEO interview transcripts through SAS's text-mining software, searching for linguistic patterns behind hire and no-hire decisions. We found some ugly *hidden handicaps:* superficial factors that have little or nothing to do with what it takes to perform as a CEO yet that trigger biases that affect your odds of being hired.[3]

- **Foreign accents:** CEO candidates for United States–based companies who had a significant accent were, twelve to one (!), *less likely* to be hired. Yes, in the twenty-first century, when billions are spent on diversity initiatives, in-group bias continues to play an outsize role. It's bad enough that the bias exists. What's worse is that nobody will tell you as you are coming up the ranks that you may be the smartest person in the world but that others' perception of your capabilities may suffer because of your accent. Saying so is not polite and can even be risky. As a senior executive, if you ever hear about the need to polish your "communications skills" or "executive presence," listen carefully. Those comments may well be a polite euphemism for a deeper concern. Often brushed off by the executive in question as "not a big deal," we've seen it become a career derailer.

If, as an immigrant, you are hoping to helm a company, and your nationality of origin is not already prevalent among the decision makers, work on sloughing away the rough edges of your accent as you rise through the ranks. According to Lynda Spillane, who has helped many senior executives turn their accent from a handicap into an asset, speaking English at home is the fastest path to accent reduction and native fluency.

- **Elevated or pretentious language or affectations:** While accents are a handicap, so is using overly sophisticated language. Throwing the dictionary at your interviewers will not get you the job. Candidates who used more esoteric, intellectual, or "ivory tower" vocabulary were, eight to one, *less likely* to be hired. Candidates who used more colloquial language (e.g., phrases such as "shooting from the hip") were, eight to one, *more likely* to be hired. In our experience, down-to-earth storytelling, drawing on memorable results, is vastly more powerful than a cerebral, academic style.

- **Management platitudes, acronyms, consulting-ese:** Relying on empty buzzwords can be an interview killer. Kim sat with one candidate who kept saying he was "all about amplitude" and that he "liked to elevate people." Trouble was, he seemed to think that repeating these phrases removed the need to offer specific, quantifiable examples. Using generic language can come across as lacking authenticity and can trigger the board's ambiguity bias—the tendency to avoid those who appear to be missing information. This leads to a lack of credibility. Instead, be precise in your use of language and examples.

- **"We" and "I"**: Leadership is a team sport. The goal is to balance the "I" with the "We." In our assessment interviews, all candidates use "I" when describing their accomplishments at a higher rate than "We." But the weakest candidates used "I" at twice the rate of the rest of the CEO candidates. The best candidates are clear about their individual contributions without overusing "I." Candidates who go on and on with their own accolades and accomplishments impress decision makers less than the ones who say, "My proudest achievement was the moment the team began to knock it out of the park"—and then clearly explain their role in the team's achievement.

  Interestingly, when researchers at NYU compared linguistic patterns of women and men in our data set, they found that women who were hired as CEOs used "I" slightly more than their male counterparts.[4] Women who make it to the CEO seat are comfortable sharing what makes them great—while still remaining well below the ratio of "I" to "We" that sets off alarm bells. These women seemed to have realized the need to counter boards and bosses who are all too ready to see them as star position players rather than quarterbacks.

  Whether you are male or female, share stories of others' successes that you helped to enable. Brag about your team, your mentors, and your boss, and the board will embrace mentions of your own contributions as statement of fact, not signs of ego. It shows authority and showcases humility. And to state the obvious, an interview is *not* the place to disparage your boss or colleagues. If those you are interviewing with see you do it here, they'll assume you do it elsewhere as well. You don't want to be seen as the kind of leader who externalizes blame instead of owning your mistakes and doing the hard work of finding solutions. Moreover, your future bosses will rightfully fear that you might someday throw *them* under the bus!

Memorable and Relevant

How do the best candidates make sure their message lands and leads to a job offer? Their stories and details are both relevant and memorable. "Relevant" provides the safety. I've done this before and done it well. You can expect good results too. "Memorable" keeps you at the top of the interviewer's mind.

If you want people to listen, you need to know what they are interested in hearing. Do your homework long before the interview. Research the *who* and the *what*: Whom are you meeting with, and what problems do they need you to solve?

We once were debriefed by a board member who was shaking his head after watching a candidate spend a good chunk of his interview time spouting off ideas about why the company should consider alternatives to a planned IPO. He had a lot of impressive things to say about the pros and cons of various capital structures. The trouble was, he was interviewing to become the head of human resources, not CEO of the company. He must have thought his sophisticated finance knowledge would set him apart from other candidates—which it did. He was remembered as the HR guy who had nothing to say about HR. The board decided he wasn't the right fit.

Once you have figured out what is relevant, how do you make that information memorable?

Here are a few approaches we've seen to be particularly effective:

- **Meaningful numbers.** Data without context is information without insight. You won't engage anyone by sounding like a walking, talking spreadsheet, no matter how great the numbers. When you quantify your achievements, make sure you interpret them: "Everywhere I've been, I've hit my targets—but in that role I exceeded them by 20 percent." Provide the comparables—how did you exceed versus the target, versus the prior year, versus your peers or your competition? "I kept the revenue flat and grew profits in 2008, when a third of our competitors went out of business." When it comes to quantifiable results, what's your strongest, most attention-grabbing headline?

- **Bona fides and vivid stories.** Having a stamp of approval from a titan in the industry is both "sticky"— i.e., memorable—and safe. This is a good substitute if you don't have brand names on your résumé. Years ago, Elena assessed a candidate and gave him a strong recommendation. She still remembers a story he told about how Sam Walton jumped into a plane to convince him in person not to leave the company. Did the story influence her recommendation? Well, it obviously stuck with her. An interviewer tends to remember a vivid, meaningful, and personal connection you have to a known winner. Have you received awards? Mention them!

- **Address your blowups productively.** Lead with your strengths—but don't be afraid to take on your blowups and mistakes in an interview. A well-told tale of redemption and learning can be incredibly powerful and positive, to boot. In our research, CEO candidates who react well to failure are statistically more likely to get a hire recommendation.[5] Just remember that the story can't end in a pile of rubble. You have to show what you have learned and how you have changed your approach from that point on. One of the most unforgettable stories we've heard in an interview—out of thousands of hours of interviews—was also one of the most unfortunate. A CEO candidate recounted in vivid detail how, when he was a pilot trainer for an airline, one of his trainees crashed a plane into a hangar. He was animated as he described the danger and the flames from the fuel. We waited for the lesson from his experience, but there wasn't one. Luckily in this case, only the business sustained injuries—to the tune of over a million dollars—but no one was hurt. Later on in the interview, he recounted his business mistakes with similar candor and flair. But once again, he failed to paint a clear picture of what he had learned from those mistakes to ensure they would not be repeated the next time out. After the interview, the plane crash was all anyone could talk about. Again, almost half of our CEO candidates had a major blowup or two over the course of their careers. And that didn't stop them from getting hired.[6] The difference is in how you own your role in that blowup and convey what you learned and your evolution as a leader since.

Here's another way to put an indelible stamp on your interview: *Overinvest in "bookends."* Practice your stories before the interview. Know the details you want to tell, especially the "bookends." The first and the final minutes of your interview—how you meet and how you part—are most likely to be remembered. Make them special. Your expression, your voice, your hand gestures all need to telegraph, "I'm right, I'm ready, I won't let you down!" You are a safe choice, in other words.

Set the Agenda

You've worked hard to get here. Don't leave your fate to your interviewer's style and competence. You need to shape the agenda yourself.

Consider how the CEO of one of the world's most treasured food brands, Juan, told us he got the job. The board had reserved an Italian restaurant—not a table but *the entire restaurant*. As he walked into the looming, empty room to the round table where everybody sat, he grew more intimidated with each step.

The board fired questions at him throughout the lunch, jumping haphazardly from topic to topic, each board member interjecting his pet concerns. Juan kept up. Though they seemed satisfied with his answers, he left the lunch with the strong feeling that his answers didn't add up to a comprehensive, compelling picture of why he should be the company's next CEO. A strange, woolly atmosphere pervaded the lunch, and the conversation never quite came to life; he was fairly sure he wouldn't be called back.

To his surprise, he was. This time, after debriefing with a few trusted advisors, he decided to take a different tack. Instead of expecting *them* to establish a cohesive agenda, he stepped in with his own. He laid out his position: *Here's who I am. Here are the opportunities for your company today. Here's what I'm going to do about it.* That day, they hired him on the spot.

A successful first interview lies somewhere in between those two extremes. It's a delicate balance of push and pull. Of course you can't take total control, because you'll deprive the board of their authority.

Yet you'll be much more successful if you can take charge and show them the way while still being sensitive to their concerns.

You have to enter the room knowing what you want them to take away from the conversation. What do you want them to know and remember about you? Simply answering their questions leaves too much to chance. Apply your **Engage for Impact** muscle and think through what you want them to think, feel, and do as a result of the interview. Then build a simple list of three talking points to achieve those goals, with vivid examples for each. If the conversation falters, nudge it in a direction that allows you to speak to one of your topics.

Inevitably, being crystal clear about what you'll bring to the role and how you will deliver results may result in some doors shutting behind you. You won't win every job. That's not failure; it's the proof that your approach is working. Those were likely not the right roles for you. Remember, the only thing worse than not getting the job is getting the wrong job.

Doug Shipman is the president and CEO of the third largest arts center in the United States, The Woodruff Arts Center. He grew up in rural Arkansas, he traveled the world with the Boston Consulting Group, a premier management consulting firm, and he led a global creative consultancy, BrightHouse, as CEO.

Shipman recognizes, more than most executives, that not every CEO role will be a good fit for his unique interests and experience. So in every formal CEO search he's been a part of, he made a conscious choice to set the agenda. Before each interview was concluded, he had let the board know in clear terms what he brought to the table. His goal was always to make sure there was no distance between their expectations and his plans. In one case he even wrote a ten-page memo describing with exacting precision how he'd move the organization forward.

In five CEO opportunities, he landed three jobs and lost two— and they were all the right outcomes. The bottom line, says Shipman, is this: *"You interview the way you lead. You have to set the expectations."*

Your CEO Interview Talking Points

If any of the items below apply to you, be sure to include them in your talking points. Boards want to see these attributes in CEO candidates.

- **Industry experience.** Nothing speaks "safety" to a board member more than an "I've been there, done that" candidate. Experience in the relevant industry increases your odds of getting picked. If you have even tangential experience in the industry, be sure to mention it.

- **Being a general—not a foot soldier.** Be sure to highlight experiences where you proactively initiated major changes and set goals and strategies for your business. The board wants to know that you can set direction for their business—not just execute someone else's mandate from the top.

- **Having an accurate business GPS.** In 2013, Elena was a director on the board of Western Dental—an affordable dental care provider serving thousands of patients in more than two hundred offices. Investors were eager to get a new CEO for the business. As we screened candidates, Tom Erickson—executive chair at the time—kept coming back to the same question: Does this candidate have a comprehensive view of the business? Can they set the direction using many diverse inputs? Tom was looking for a CEO who had a full view of the entire business and all factors impacting it. He was not looking for a supersize version of a regional manager.

The Four Archetypes: Are You a Match to the Role?

So, the thrilling moment occurs. You get the call for the job you wanted. The offer is on the table. Your adrenaline is naturally pumping. You might even do a happy dance in your office (don't worry, we are dancing with you!).

You now face the toughest decision of all: *The number one success factor for a new CEO or a leader at any level is simply picking the right opportunity.* In over two decades of advising executives on critical hiring decisions, we've seen three factors come into play: 1. Does the business, or the division, or the team, have a shot at success, with or without you? 2. Are your strengths a true match for their needs? And 3. Are your style and values a match to the context and culture?

Don't accept just any CEO role. Accept the right role for your skills, strengths, and values.

Don't take the job if . . .

- Your gut tells you no. If it weren't for the title of CEO, you couldn't see yourself in this role or in this company.

- You don't have credible validation that the business is sound or can be fixed.

- You don't have a clear sense of why your predecessor left or was let go.

- You don't have the decision right to hire and fire.

- You don't get along with an important board member or several key board members who are unlikely to be moved off the board.

- You don't have complete visibility into the financial picture—especially the cash position—of the company.

- You see yourself having to change significantly who you are to succeed.

Robert Hanson, the CEO of the jewelry company John Hardy whom we met earlier, was one of those who admitted to us that his first role as CEO was a bad fit—and he knew it before he even accepted the offer. At the time, Robert was the global brand president of Levi's, living in San Francisco. His suitor was American Eagle, looking for a CEO who could revitalize a flagging brand.

"I remember standing in a hotel room in Pittsburgh, staring across the river, talking to my husband, saying, 'It's not the right fit.'" His gut was telling him that the founder would resist the very changes Robert thought were needed. The ultimate urbanite, Robert loved the cosmopolitan life he had in San Francisco. Pittsburgh just wasn't his speed. But Robert felt ready and eager for a CEO job, and they don't come along every day. So he squelched his concerns and accepted the offer. Less than two years later, before his contract was up, conflicts arose regarding many of the concerns he had worried about before taking the job, ultimately resulting in his departure.

In our analysis of over seventy situations where a CEO got fired, close to 40 percent were driven by a poor fit to what the job needed.[7] Remember Michael Jordan attempting to play professional baseball? It wasn't pretty. You may be a world-class athlete, but if you want to perform at the top of your game, make sure you are signing up for the right sport. If the board wants a steady hand to stay the course, and you're revving up for a high-octane turnaround, you're in trouble. If you set your sights on growing the company to be a $1 billion industry leader over the next ten years, and the board wants you to get the business ready for sale in eighteen months, you're in trouble. Likewise, you might have become a star by saving a brand with a whip-smart marketing and sales strategy—but then crash and burn when you're brought in to lead a company that's an operational mess.

How do you know if you're a fit? After assessing and coaching hundreds of CEOs, we have uncovered four common CEO archetypes. Most leaders don't perfectly fit a single archetype, but most can usually identify themselves in one or two. Likewise, companies may need a blend of skills in a new CEO, especially over time, but the role is likely to lean toward one of these archetypes. A candidate might be CEO material for *some* company but nevertheless ill-equipped to lead a *particular* company.

Where do you fit in with regard to the archetypes below? Figuring that out may save you from saying yes to the wrong challenge.

1. **The Sky's the Limit:** This CEO is relentlessly creative and entrepreneurial in the aggressive pursuit of growth. She spikes on **Adapting** and **Decisiveness**, sometimes at the expense of **Reliability**. Her natural habitat is rapidly changing industries and small high-growth companies. She is typically stronger at initiating bold breakthrough opportunities than at scaling businesses in a measured, predictable fashion. Many founders and entrepreneurs fit this archetype. Elon Musk is an iconic "Sky's the Limit" CEO. His SpaceX venture aims to colonize Mars.

   Eva Moskowitz is another example. A force of nature, Eva started and grew Success Academy Charter Schools from a single school in Harlem into the largest charter school network in New York City, with 15,500 scholars attending 46 schools. Undeterred by fierce union opposition, battles with the city government, death threats, and countless other obstacles, and inspired by an ambitious vision, Eva has built a network of public schools, enrolling mostly low-income minority children through random lottery, that are among the highest performing schools in New York State.

2. **The Lean, Mean, Operational Machine:** This CEO is a paragon of efficiency. He will reengineer process to maximize value and cut costs. These skills are best put to use in companies where cost is a key source of competitive advantage.

   An under-the-radar "Lean, Mean, Operational Machine" CEO is Larry Culp of Danaher. He built Danaher into a well-oiled machine, embedding Danaher's business system into the company's new acquisitions consistently and rewarding his shareholders with a long-term track record of consistent success. Only a few companies have delivered more impressive long-run returns than Danaher. Larry grew the value of Danaher stock from under $10 per share when he became CEO in 2000 to nearly $80 when he left.[8]

3. **The ER Surgeon:** This is the quintessential turnaround CEO. Such leaders tend to be adrenaline junkies who thrive on the intensity of dire situations and don't hesitate making tough calls. They are often skilled negotiators. They frequently move from one troubled company to the next, relying on their towering **Decisiveness** skills and bias toward action to turn things around.

   You may not have heard of David Siegel, but you know the companies he has rescued: Continental Airlines, Frontier Airlines, US Airways, Avis Budget Group, to name a few. David gets called when the going gets tough. He deftly wields a scalpel and a hammer to slash costs ($2 billion in a year in one of his jobs!), reduce head count, renegotiate with suppliers, and do anything else necessary to turn a business around.[9] Once shock therapy is no longer needed, he moves on. His typical tenure in each CEO role is approximately three years.

4. **The Safe Pair of Hands:** This CEO spikes on **Reliability** and is often also strong in **Engaging for Impact**. She pursues change with a consistent drumbeat, building buy-in and listening to ideas. A "Safe Hands" CEO is deliberate and relies on both culture and process to protect valued institutions. This archetype is typically found in slow-growth industries and mission-driven institutions such as nonprofits. This archetype is less commonly found in rapidly changing industries or private equity.

When a CEO's skills are well matched to the job, he can achieve great results. When a company or division fails to hire the kind of leader it needs, outcomes often disappoint. To avoid finding yourself in such a position, take advantage of the narrow window of the interview process. This isn't just the time for the company to vet you but for you to vet the company. Context is everything: What is the context and environment in which you can perform at the top of your potential? This is a function of your business values, your leadership style, and your life priorities. The answer looks different for everyone.

After leaving American Eagle, Robert Hanson spent six months considering what kind of role he should seek, he told us, with the help of "eighty interesting conversations with wicked-smart people." By the way, you'll get a much clearer read on your strengths and leadership style if you step out of your own head and ask people you trust to weigh in about you.

Robert developed a written statement of what he was looking for: an authentic global brand with high growth potential, in a mission-driven, values-based, high performance and entrepreneurial culture. A place where he could lead with his strengths, alongside smart partners who shared his perspective on how to both lead and grow. Writing down what you want is key; it creates a stark reference amid the distractions of excitement and flattery that accompany a CEO or top leadership search. It gives you the discipline to ask the tough questions that reveal whether you're truly aligned in your aspirations for the business and your expectations for the role.

In 2014, Robert's disciplined search paid off. He became the CEO of the jewelry company John Hardy, a small, private equity–backed company that met all his criteria. While in the role, he has focused on enriching the brand story, elevating the product, marketing and distribution, opening boutiques, expanding e-commerce and international, and improving operations. He's well past the two-year hurdle as CEO and has led his team to grow revenue and market share in a tough retail climate while putting in place the strategic platform to accelerate the brand transformation. The best litmus test in this case of leadership in the right context is that the founders, John and Cynthia Hardy, usually quite tough to impress, have been exuberant in their praise of how the brand has modernized to compete in today's marketplace while remaining authentic to the brand they founded.

As a leader, you will find much that you can't control. The job you choose is one thing that you can *control entirely. The opportunity matters more than the title—so slow down and pick the right conditions for your success.*

KEY TAKEAWAYS

1. Understand what is on the minds of your interviewers. What does a "safe choice" look like to them?
2. Make it clear you are the safe choice.
   a. Exude confidence, competence, and comfortable positive energy.
   b. Share memorable and relevant stories.
   c. Set the agenda.
3. Most important: Make sure you are taking the right job!

GET RESULTS

NAVIGATE THE CHALLENGES OF THE ROLE

1
GET STRONG

2
GET TO THE TOP

3
GET RESULTS

THE FIVE HIDDEN HAZARDS AT THE TOP

NOT JUST ANY TEAM—YOUR TEAM

DANCING WITH THE TITANS—THE BOARD

chapter 9

The Five Hidden Hazards at the Top

"You're off to Great Places!
Today is your day!
Your mountain is waiting.
So . . . get on your way!"

—Dr. Seuss, *Oh, the Places You'll Go*

MADELINE BELL WAS SITTING IN HER OFFICE ON THE TWELFTH FLOOR
of the Children's Hospital of Philadelphia (CHOP) on a bright June
day in 2015 when she got the call: The position of CEO was hers.

Madeline was elated. Thirty-two years of devoted work had culminated in her being selected to lead one of the world's most renowned
pediatric hospitals, saving children's lives and shaping standards of pediatric care globally. She felt a rush of emotions probably akin to what
world-class athletes feel as they step onto the track at the Olympic
Games: "You've spent your whole life preparing for this. There's joy,
and fear, doubt, and hope, all wrapped together," she recalls. It would
be a breathtaking moment for anyone. For Madeline, the first female
and the first nurse to rise to the top of CHOP in its 160-year history,
it was a landmark achievement.

Six weeks later, Madeline stepped into the role—and like most
new CEOs, she instantly found herself at the epicenter of a torrent
of issues, urgent queries, and requests. Madeline's CFO and general
counsel quickly brought her up to speed on aspects of her job that were

completely off her radar. For example, she was now the hospital's representative as a major shareholder of Spark Therapeutics, a $2 billion-a-year gene-therapy company that had been spun off from CHOP. *Who knew?* Requests for her presence inside and outside of the organization were pouring in. After every appearance she made, a line of people formed to grab a few moments of her attention.

She quickly saw her role with new eyes: "Before, it was actually easy. I had one boss. I had thought CEOs don't have a boss. Now instead of one boss, I have thousands of bosses—all 14,000 employees, this whole community, the donors, the board members, everybody who cares about us. In my first year, I woke up in the middle of the night and felt literally a wave of anxiety wash over me. They're all depending on me to deliver. What if something big goes wrong?! I felt grave responsibility on my shoulders."

An MRI able to track the emotions of any new CEO's brain would reveal a pattern of thoughts and reactions similar to Madeline's. The initial elated *Wow, I did it! Could it really be me?* careens to the anxious *Oh, boy! What did I walk into?* and bottoms out with the grave *It's all on me now. Am I ready? What if I fail?*

Madeline spoke for many when she told us the CEO role was "so much weightier than I expected, in terms of eyes on you as the leader. There really are very few people who understand it. It's a lonely place."

Madeline had become a celebrity overnight. Wherever she went, she was now onstage. "Every meeting that I'm in, I'm under the microscope," she says. "They are thinking: *What's her reaction? What's her body language? What's she saying?* When I wake up in the morning, I look at my calendar: I'm going to the audit committee meeting of our board, where I have an important sticky topic; then I'm going to be running to kick off a big fund-raising event, and so on. It's just being on, on, on—and in every different place, how do I want to show up?"

In our experience, *a typical CEO takes roughly two years to feel comfortable in the role.* Guess how long it takes for a typical board to fire a CEO who has demonstrated fatal flaws? Roughly two years. There's not a lot of time to prove yourself. The big question on every new CEO's mind and on the minds of anyone in a new role: *What is it that I don't know that can kill me?*

To answer that question, we dove deep into seventy situations where CEOs were fired so we could understand the root causes. We also closely analyzed common patterns of mistakes made by first-time CEOs. We interviewed investors, board members, team members, and others to analyze the reasons, circumstances, and outcomes. The third section of this book is dedicated to helping leaders avoid the biggest mistakes first-time CEOs make. Many of these insights are applicable for anyone entering a new role.

Here's what many first-time CEOs understand only in the rear-view mirror: Their new role isn't just a more difficult, supersized version of leadership positions they've held in the past. It is a completely different job, requiring shifts in their habits, assumptions, attention, and time, new filters, new relationships, and more. When we analyzed patterns of mistakes among first-time CEOs, we found that over 40 percent of them struggled to adapt their leadership style to the unique contours of their new position quickly enough.[1]

If you have been with us for the last eight chapters of this book, you are already coming into the CEO role better prepared than most. This chapter is dedicated to uncovering and arming you to navigate the five most common hazards that first-time CEOs—and, in many cases, any senior leader—must navigate in order to adapt to the needs of the new role. The next chapter then dives into the single most common mistake of new CEOs: failure to quickly get your team in place. And Chapter 11 closes out this section by parting the veil on the number one concern for most new CEOs: navigating the new world of the board of directors. Applying the lessons in this section can help prevent avoidable "should've known" mistakes, leaving more of your energy to leading the company to success and to handling the inevitable surprises that come your way. Even more important, knowing what you should and should not worry about can free your mind to play to win.

To paraphrase Groucho Marx: Learn from the mistakes of others, or you may not be in the job long enough to make them all yourself.

Hazard #1: The Ghouls in the Supply Closet

You've taken the helm. More than anything, you want to prove yourself worthy of the job. You've heard about "the vision thing" and can't wait to wow the board and the team with your inspiring vision for the future. Or maybe you pride yourself on getting things done and are raring to show how quickly you can knock off items on the endless list of priorities. Whatever your style, you are hungry to start strong out of the gate. Therefore, our first piece of advice may be the hardest to heed. . . .

Stop.

Pause.

Before you paint a picture of the bright future, and even before you go knocking off the tempting "low-hanging fruit," take a very close look at what you have walked into. Whether you've been promoted into the role or brought in from the outside, you are moving into a new, unfamiliar house, and before you start your renovation projects, you would do well to acquaint yourself with what you have inherited to begin with. Your first task: to reenact that harrowing scene you find in every horror film. The one where the movie's hero walks through the house, opening doors and pulling back curtains, trying to find and contain the ghoul before the ghoul stabs her in the back.

No matter how well you've been briefed by the board, they probably failed to tell you about the serial killer in the shower. Chances are that they have no idea he's there. The first order of business is to search every dark corner, decide what's a genuine threat versus just a creepy but harmless shadow, and then decide how to best deal with it.

Take "Paul," who stepped in to run our client's recycling company. He had been told the company had a groundbreaking new technology for turning dirty plastic into clean, reusable plastic. It sounded great—until Paul showed up for duty and discovered his first ghoul: The product was not performing in the field as well as it was supposed to. As a result, the sales cycles lagged, and they ran out of cash. Paul didn't get fired, but he had to leave the company, because they could no longer afford to pay him. Not every ghoul is survivable. But the earlier you find them, the better your chances of survival are.

What kinds of threats might you find? Here are some common examples:

- A critical gap between the board's expectations and the reality inside the business

- A hidden financial or operational bomb that's now in your lap; e.g., loss of a major customer, cost overruns on a large project, IT implementation problems

- A sacred cow or cultural blind spot that has the potential to stymie exactly the changes needed to grow the business

- Signs coming from a level or two down that one of your critical people isn't up to his or her job or is on the way out

The best way to conquer the ghouls? Let the light in. Lay out the ghouls and goblins in front of your board, team, and others, to show: "This is where we are. This is what we're up against. Here's how we're going to fix it." The clock is ticking: *Anything you bring to light in the first six months in the role will be viewed as part of what you walked into, setting the baseline. After that, it's your problem.* If you fail to parade the ghouls early, you'll own them forever. Use what you have learned to set realistic expectations and develop well-informed plans for delivering on those expectations. As hard as it is to start your brand-new CEO role with a bit of sobering news, it beats failing on expectations that were never realistic in the first place.

When Scott Clawson arrived to take the helm at Culligan, a water treatment company that had been purchased by a private equity firm, he pulled up the financial floorboards and found that the business was behind plan. "When prior management sold the company to investors, they predicted that the company would produce $60 million EBITDA. As I dug into the details, the number was much closer to $45 million. I flew to New York for a few very tough conversations with my board. Ultimately, they supported me."

Scott was fortunate that this was his second CEO position with these investors. He had just delivered nearly fourfold returns on another company he had run for the same private equity firm. So even when there was no growth the first year, his board stood by him: "We get it, we trust you, let's go." Over the next three years, Scott grew EBITDA by about $10 million a year, culminating in a successful sale and a remarkable turnaround of a brand that was once a household name.

Your first step as you pause in the new job: Hear your major stakeholders out. This is true whether you are the CEO, a middle manager, or an individual contributor. We'll talk in detail in Chapter 11 about how to build an effective partnership with the board, to develop a clear picture of how they view your business now, their needs, and their expectations for the future. Once you understand where they sit, you've got the much harder job of gathering the data to develop your own point of view. It's time for your listening tour. Neil Fiske, CEO of Billabong whom you first met in Chapter 3, kicked off the early weeks of his CEO tenure by spending an hour daily interviewing his senior team and the managers at least two levels down. The feedback from these conversations produced, in his words, "a rich road map of issues that need to be addressed and questions to be confronted."

Go even farther: Walk the floors. Visit the field offices. Ask people what they think is working and what isn't. And go outside the organization to get a broader perspective on your industry. Interview outsiders and the most important experts of all: the customers.

"You would not believe the stuff I heard," Mary Berner, the CEO of Cumulus Media, told us of the listening tours she conducted as the CEO of *Reader's Digest* between 2007 and 2011. Mary regularly visited the company's many field offices, scattered across fifty countries, and randomly sat down with groups of ten employees, from the mailroom on up, for off-the-record conversations. She asked them what they would do in her shoes. She asked for their thoughts on what would help the company get even better. She took notes. In this way, she heard about problems ranging from the absurd ("There was a serious goose-poop issue on our main campus's lawn") to the serious ("We found a case of expense fraud").

Even if you're lucky enough to inherit a basically stable business—PG-level thrills, not an R-rated slasher—you will often hear conflicting views from the board, corporate staff, line employees, and customers. All of that helps you build a realistic baseline on the business, set goals grounded in reality, and identify risks you have to attend to.

You may not be able to banish every ghoul. But understanding even the intractable issues protects you from surprises, giving you space to develop work-arounds while you still have the luxury of a clean slate. Get skeletons out of the closet and into the light so that you can start the process of getting everyone excited about the inspirational new script: yours.

Your Year One Checklist:

- Assess the shape of the business and get skeletons out of the closet

- Set vision and strategy

- Set the baseline and new expectations for plans, budgets, and projections with your board (and the market if applicable)

- Score a couple of early wins

- Assess and upgrade the team (as required)

Hazard #2: Entering Warp Speed

E-mails, keynote opportunities, media requests, meetings, fund-raisers, galas, small decisions, big decisions, new information, responsibilities—oh, my! A simple walk to the bathroom is now an impromptu meet-and-greet (and a major commitment of time). Kevin Cox, the CHRO of American Express, who sits on several boards and is often sought after for leadership advice, likens the first CEO role to being a new quarterback: "The game looks awfully fast to a rookie quarterback! Good coaches attempt to simplify the game to slow it down. Just the same, the game looks fast to a new CEO. They are instantly inundated. They just need to slow the game down enough to play it well. This is very important. You only get so many chances and then you get benched."

While this time crunch is especially acute for CEOs, *any* leader who makes the transition to leading a larger organization will experience some degree of it.

We asked CEOs how their focus shifted when they reached the top. For non-CEO executives outside of sales, an average of 80 percent of their time was focused internally. For CEOs, that dropped to 55 percent.[2] The time they spent externally more than doubled from 20 to 45 percent. A vast multitude of new stakeholders requires CEO attention: on the board, with shareholders, regulators, government, customers, partners, reaching out to the industry, the media, and the broader world. In other words, *you're going to have to take on the most challenging job of your life—running an enterprise—in significantly less time than you devoted to running the business in previous positions.* Can you imagine doing your current job in only two thirds of the time? How do you make that seemingly impossible math work? How do you stretch time?

The first step isn't to change *what* you focus your attention on, but *when*. Time is moving faster, so look forward. Set coordinates in the future so that warp drive will take you to your desired destination. CEOs who shift their time horizon farther out are more successful at adapting their organizations to change. *While non-CEO executives typically spend almost 80 percent of their time focused on issues affecting the next twelve months, CEOs spend over 40 percent of their attention focused more than a year into the future.*[3] This practice instantly creates a filter for all those incoming demands on their time: *One or two years from now, is this going to matter?* Such filters are key to managing the crushing cognitive load of this new role.

The second important filter is your administrative assistant. A CEO produces results by deploying people, time, and capital. Your assistant steers a key lever—your time. When Madeline Bell became CEO, she brought her assistant with her. The assistant had competently supported Madeline while she was the COO. Madeline welcomed this small but important island of stability amidst all the turmoil of a new role. Unfortunately, as Madeline's role and priorities shifted dramatically, her assistant kept managing her calendar in the same way she had for years: prioritizing calendar time for one-on-ones with internal people. She treated requests from the board and other external constituents as a distraction. Madeline sat her down to tell her, "As a CEO, I need to spend time differently than I have previously. The board and external constituents are now my priority. And many of the people who used to get a lot of access now need to go to my COO instead."

Flexing a strong **Reliability** muscle, Madeline coached her assistant to train *everyone else* how to interact with her. As COO, she had had time, for example, to read an entire merger agreement and offer her thoughts to the general counsel. Now she needed bullet points. "I've had to create a system of people who are filtering and packaging for me in a way that I never had before," she says. When something comes in that's not ready, her assistant punts it back. Everything needs to come in summarized.

For you to step up to the new responsibilities of a more senior role, *you often need to train others around you how to work with you.* One of the CEOs had his assistant send out a structured format for his one-on-one meetings with direct reports. Their agenda can cover any or all of six prescribed priority areas, including progress on key initiatives, issues of material consequence, and professional satisfaction. Two business days before meetings, his directs are required to submit a bulleted outline of their agenda.

Does this level of structure feel overly exacting and pedantic? A few may chafe at the new rules, but many will appreciate clarity about how to work with you effectively. Even if you are at the helm of a $20 million company, and two days' advance preparation seems like a ridiculous dream, ask yourself what steps you can be taking to allocate most of your time and attention to the top priorities. Something as simple as delegating control of your calendar to an assistant can free up a lot of time and energy but could also be hard to do, especially for an entrepreneur. Rob Wenger, CEO of a quickly growing small software company told us, "Empowering an assistant can be hard when you've been used to doing everything yourself, but life-changing. Having support has changed my life; my days are efficient, and my time is spent linked to my goals instead of reacting to what comes at me."

After coaching and interviewing dozens of CEOs on surviving business at the speed of sound, we've distilled a few more tactics for mastering warp speed:

Fit to Size: Whether your default time window for a meeting is fifteen minutes or thirty, actively manage your calendar to ensure that you allocate appropriate time and attention depending on the level of priority and complexity of an issue. Make a disciplined habit of getting in, getting to the point, and getting out of meetings and conversations. Kim worked with a CEO who never spent more than fifteen minutes on a phone call with her—unless an important issue came up that was too complex and consequential to handle in fifteen minutes. Then he called her at 6:00 A.M. from California for a thorough, unhurried conversation. Six in the morning, it turned out, was when he took his dog on her daily walk. It was the time he preserved for decisions and conversations that required more space and consideration.

The Calendar Reality Check: We've shocked many CEOs by leading them and their assistants through calendar reviews. These are leaders who know their priorities. They believe they're aggressively focused on their priorities, and they are confident that they know where they spend their time. Their calendars often tell a very different story. We analyze every appointment and map exactly which stakeholders and what priorities are getting the most and least time and attention.

The results of these reviews are always eye-opening. We recently had one CEO, for example, tell us her first priority that year had been to expand into China. That "top priority" turned out to be receiving 3 percent of her time. So it wasn't surprising that the company was still (literally) thousands of miles from its goal. Calendar reviews are a revealing exercise, helpful at any stage, to make sure that your time, attention, and actions are aligned with your stated priorities. First, ask yourself, if anything were possible, how would you allocate your time in line with your priorities? Then ask your assistant to compare your goals to how you actually spend your time. We recommend you conduct this exercise twice in your first year and annually thereafter, with four questions in mind:

1) How well does your time allocation represent your business and life priorities?

2) How well does your time allocation represent your relationship priorities?

3) How much time are you spending on short- versus long-term issues?

4) How much time are you spending internally versus externally?

The Polite No: When Andy Silvernail became the CEO of IDEX Corporation, a wise mentor in his seventies took him to a congratulatory lunch. "I've seen this movie a few times before, so here's my advice, take it or leave it," he told Andy. "The CEO role is a different beast. It is demanding, and it is seductive. There's just two things you need to understand to make it work. Number one, nothing's more important than your team. But, number two, you need to know when you need to appear and when you don't," he said.

Once you get appointed CEO, your popularity index soars in an instant. You have new access to elite corners of business and society. You get gilded invitations to enticing events. Invitations to sit on a variety of boards. Requests to speak at conferences. Just yesterday you were in the back row taking notes as other industry CEOs shared their wisdom. So when you are invited to be one of them, it is easy to be seduced. Thanks to his mentor, Andy learned quicker than most to relentlessly filter these requests with the choosy eye of a veteran rather than the hungry enthusiasm of a rookie. What seemed tantalizingly out of reach just yesterday might well be a distraction you can no longer afford. Too many new CEOs, faced with their newfound popularity, set their bar for "yes" far too low. *We often coach first-time CEOs to shift perspectives from "new kid on the block" to imagine they already are a leading CEO in the industry before deciding what they say yes or no to.* This enables them to redirect precious time and energy from subpar engagements to delivering results that would indeed make them into a leading CEO.

Before you get flooded and seduced, be clear about your goals. What do you really want? To advance your business? To learn from the best? To elevate your status? One new CEO was recently reprimanded by his board for jumping into the company jet to visit the White House in his first months on the job. The company was bleeding cash in the midst of a tough turnaround, and the CEO was seen as advancing his own agenda rather than helping the business by accepting the high-profile invitation. Everyone's situation and filter will be slightly different, but in the first year, you're in safe territory if you only accept invitations that move specific goals forward or make you a better CEO. Andy Silvernail uses those criteria but with an additional personal filter: He chooses the opportunities that interfere the least with his family time.

Hazard #3: Amplification
and the Permanent Spotlight

"As CEO, everything you do is amplified. Every pat on the back. Every e-mail. Every compliment. You don't just casually stop by somebody's desk anymore. They think it is a signal of how they're doing, when, in fact, you had to go to the bathroom. Your kid's sick, and you didn't go to their meeting, and they think that that means that you hate their idea. Everything is viewed through the role of you as CEO."

That reflection is from Doug Shipman, president and CEO of The Woodruff Arts Center. When you ask anyone about the most surprising shocks of becoming a boss, you'll inevitably hear some version of it.

We call this phenomenon "amplification." *You are now the face of your company, the bellwether of its future, the embodiment of its values. Your smallest motion ripples across the organization.* You are constantly under a spotlight as people scrutinize every twitch of your eyebrow, the words you choose, the way you spend your time. They're not just curious, they're on the hunt for clues to direct their own behavior. The bottom line is, the way people relate to you as the boss—even people who were just yesterday your peers—is completely and utterly different. Understand this, adapt your leadership style accordingly, and amplification stops being a hazard. In fact, it becomes one of the most potent tools in your new kit.

At the most basic level, fine-tune your body language. If the entire organization is cueing off your mood, you need to radiate positivity or at least have a good poker face. Jim Harrison, the CEO of Party City, has embraced what he calls the "Smile Rule" for twenty-five years: "As a leadership team, we can argue, debate, whatever. . . . But when we leave here, we all smile," he says. He's been smiling ever since an employee told him that his default expression, a scowl, was terrifying every employee he crossed paths with. And so he shifted to a smile. "When I'm at a facility, I walk around, say hello, ask how they're doing—so they know I'm not a bad guy and things are going well," he says. While the "Smile Rule" may not work in all cultures and contexts, employ the body language that conveys confidence and a positive outlook to your organization.

The days are over when you can lose your temper and unconsciously wear your emotions on your sleeve. As a CEO, transmit negative emotions with care and precision to achieve a desired outcome—not because you are at the mercy of your emotions. Know your triggers, and work to manage them. As Larry Prior, CEO of technology services company CSRA, likes to say: *"As a CEO, you are too senior to lose your temper not on purpose."* One executive we've been advising puts his hand in his pocket during difficult conversations so that he can pinch himself, "a sharp, physical reminder to stay calm when I'm seeing something coming that I know will upset me."

CEO amplification runs deeper than mood swings: People seize upon everything you say and do as a potential call to action. When Tom Monahan, the first non-founder CEO of business information company CEB, spent a day in the company's Boston offices, he shared a nostalgic moment with one of his team members. "I told him that I grew up in Boston, and I could see my whole life from this office window," he told us. "My high school, the train I took to school, my dad's office . . . I could see it all from this vantage point." Years later CEB was consolidating its office footprint. Tom was surprised that Boston was nowhere on the list of potential closures. He learned that everyone had assumed the current location of the Boston office was untouchable because "it had a special place in Tom's heart."

Tom's brief moment of nostalgia, shared years earlier, now echoed back to him as a rationale for a costly decision that was not his intention. "How many other things are out there like this?" he wondered.

Once you recognize the incredible power of amplification, look for opportunities to use it to its greatest positive effect. Thomson Reuters CEO Jim Smith, for example, told us about a conference call he had the day after Brexit, the United Kingdom's vote to withdraw from the European Union. Harvard economist and former Treasury Secretary

Larry Summers had called it the single worst thing to happen to Europe since World War II.[4] Jim asked the folks from his London office, "How's it feeling there today?" Their response: "Like ground zero." It was a casual conversation before the real business of the meeting, but a thought flashed through Jim's mind: "It's my job to lead us through this." Instead of echoing their low spirits, he took a positive tone. "Let's remember, folks, in any disruption, there's always opportunity." He talked about the company's responsibility to help customers find those opportunities. "We stay focused on the customers. Let's stay focused on what we can control and do our best at that," he said. With a few simple lines, he gave his employees the comforting knowledge that despite upheaval, their power was real and important—reassurance that would impact their behavior in the hours, days, and weeks that followed.

Your new reality is this: Every move matters. Every gesture is profound. Your words are no longer musings, banter, input, or casual thoughts. They are declarations with the power to shape the future. Use them to create the future you want for your business.

Hazard #4: It's a Smartphone, Not a Calculator

Maybe you've seen that old Seinfeld episode where Jerry loses his head because his father will only use his new Wizard organizer as a tip calculator. (Jerry: "It does other things!") That phenomenon is not so different when an executive moves into the CEO role—but it's far more costly. In our review of seventy CEO firings, *a fifth of the CEOs were fired because they didn't use the full set of business levers available to them—the CEO-specific means of influencing outcomes.*[5] Many first-time CEOs come up via a specific professional track, like finance or marketing. Suddenly, these new CEOs are responsible for the full enterprise, including the functions they have never run. CEOs have at their disposal levers of value creation that are unique and often unfamiliar. First and foremost, the CEO's role is setting the strategy and vision for the enterprise. Prior to being CEO, the focus was likely on executing a strategy in a single function or business segment. Now as CEO, job number one is to set a strategic direction for the company grounded in understanding of internal and external conditions and a full view of the entire business.

An investment firm recently engaged us to help them understand why a CEO of one of their retail businesses was severely underperforming and what to do about it. "Sandy" had been a fantastic general manager, squeezing impressive growth out of her handful of locations. Her wheelhouse was the in-store experience: fine-tuning product and merchandising, promotions, and staffing to get customers to buy. When she became CEO, her focus never shifted from inside the stores. Meanwhile, the real threats were outside. A tightening credit market made it harder for the company to get required financing. Several downward industry trends created "perfect storm" conditions leading to slower growth. She was struggling because she led exclusively through the filter of her prior expertise. She never stepped back to set the course for the business. The company needed a strong CEO, not a great general manager.

We see some CEOs stumble because they fall back on their historical strengths: the former CFO who over-indexes on cost reduction in a business that desperately needs to grow; the operational whiz who makes incremental productivity gains only to lose hundreds of millions on foreign exchange rates; the sales leader who expands the customer base but not the production capacity and quickly hits a wall. Beware of a hammer perpetually seeing nails.

As a CEO now, you need to work from the satellite view to rise above individual functions to see the full enterprise, spotting chokepoints and directing resources to where they can have the most impact.

So what, exactly, are the new levers available to a CEO? Here are three that new CEOs often don't sufficiently attend to.

Lever 1: Culture Shaping

In our advisory work, we are often struck by the contrast between first-time CEOs and the CEOs who are ready to pass the baton after a successful tenure. Many of the retiring CEOs reflect in hindsight that cultural change was by far the hardest and yet the most impactful change they had instilled in the business. They frequently wish they had placed more attention on culture earlier. Even as they prepare to pass the reins, many of them are eager to reinforce the culture and values that they hope will transcend their tenure in the business.

Ironically, when we advise recently appointed CEOs, culture is often something they readily agree is important but often don't act on early enough because there are more pressing, "harder" business priorities at hand. Neglecting the company culture is akin to training for a marathon in a city with dangerously elevated air pollution and ignoring the warnings because you've got to keep up with your training regimen. You may train yourself into your grave. On the other hand, CEOs who make culture a priority early often see exponential returns on their efforts.

Ian Read was appointed CEO of Pfizer in 2010 when the company was in dire straits. He inherited a corrosive political culture devoid of trust and innovation, a cliff of expiring patents on the most profitable medicines, and a stock trading around $15 per share (down from $24 in 2006). A lot of hard business issues needed attention. Ian's first order of business? In his very first days as the CEO, Ian put forward cultural imperatives that he believed were foundational to turning around performance. Ian and his CHRO, Chuck Hill, spared no effort to improve the culture and to back it up with action. Today, terms like "Straight Talk" and "Dare to Try" are increasingly the way of life at Pfizer.

Ian and Chuck viewed every interaction and major decision as an opportunity to reinforce the desired culture. In 2014, Pfizer sought to buy AstraZeneca for $118 billion—a very high-profile deal. When

AstraZeneca's board demanded a 10 percent higher price for the company, Ian decided to walk away. Ian held a global, company-wide town hall the next morning. He candidly acknowledged his disappointment that the deal didn't happen and seized the opportunity to reinforce the cultural message: "To be a leading pharmaceutical company, we have to 'Dare to Try.' We have to take risks. This deal was my 'Dare to Try' move. It didn't work out, but it was the right deal to pursue initially and the right deal to walk away from when the price got too high. You've seen me try and fail and live to fight another day. I encourage you each to take risks for the sake of making us better. Dare to Try!" Ian's clarity of message and his role modeling have paid off. The company is much healthier today than it was seven years ago when Ian took the helm. The stock price has more than doubled and company culture has turned from a source of consternation into a source of pride.

Tomes have been written about corporate culture, and we won't repeat them here. Just remember: *Whether you intend to focus on your company culture or not, much like air, it will have an ever-present impact on your results. You'll want to be intentional about it.* For a busy and maybe even slightly overwhelmed leader new to a role, we offer three ways to shape the cultural imprint you leave on the organization.

1. How consistently you articulate and model the behaviors you seek

2. Where you put your time and attention

3. Whom you hire, fire, and promote

If you do nothing else, ask yourself once a year what your aspirational intent as CEO is and how well you translate this intent into the three sets of actions above.

Lever 2: Financial Strategy

By the time you become CEO, chances are that you're an expert at operating a business. As a division president or general manager, you have been laser focused on driving the bottom line. As CEO, you've got to use both the balance sheet and the P&L to create shareholder value. How are you making capital allocation decisions? How are you managing cash flow? Optimizing taxes? Investing capital? Scouting potential acquisitions?

Five years ago, Elena introduced Seth Segel to the board of the company that hired him for his first CEO job—Woodbury Products. Near the top of his list of a new CEO's most important to-dos is this: Carve out dedicated time with the CFO so that he or she can walk you through the P&L, balance sheet, and cash flow. Get answers to questions such as, "How much control exists over the largest expense line items? What is the cash conversion cycle and the projected CapEx? What are the policies on such key items as revenue recognition and depreciation? What are our terms with key lenders?"

If finance isn't your strength, you've got to find someone who can help you learn. When Steve Kaufman was promoted from a division president to CEO of Arrow Electronics, he was "totally unprepared for the Wall Street part of it." A typical operator, he knew the P&L statement well. "But I didn't really understand the financial engineering of the balance sheet or how to deal with analysts and investors."

Steve partnered with the chairman at the time to get a crash course on financial engineering and investor relations.

Lever 3: Corporate Diplomacy

A CEO's satellite view naturally extends your area of influence beyond the walls of your company. Your company success is impacted by the ecosystem you inhabit and your role in this ecosystem. No matter whether you are a flagship global company shaping the industry, a disruptive new entrant, or a small local player looking to fly under the radar, ignore at your peril the industry and broader geopolitical, regulatory, and macroeconomic dynamics. To set the right course and steer the business, a CEO must understand (and often attempt to influence) the terrain and context the company operates in. Building alliances, shaping PR, and interfacing with government at the local, industry, country, and at times even the global level—these are all tools for amassing the influence required to fully set the agenda as CEO.

On September 15, 2001, Leo Mullin, the CEO of Delta Air Lines, was watching from his office window as Delta's first plane took off following the terrorist attacks of September 11. But even as the plane rose safely into the air, Leo knew that his company—and the whole industry—was in deep trouble. In the aftermath of the horrifying events, people were simply not flying. Ticket sales, and therefore revenue, dried up.

In an industry with enormous fixed costs, this amounted to a rapid downward spiral. Delta, even with the strongest balance sheet in the industry, had but a few short months' worth of cash to cover its huge impending operating losses.

Leo recalls waking at 5:00 A.M. the next morning, looking in the mirror, and saying to himself, "I've got to handle this. It's on me." He realized Delta could not do this alone, given the magnitude of the problem. All the other major carriers were in the same or worse positions. In the urgency of the moment, it was never more apparent that the responsibility of CEOs goes beyond the walls of the company or personal interests. By 10:00 A.M., Leo was on the phone with CEOs of other airlines. Within a week, he was testifying on behalf of the airline industry in the packed Senate and House chambers, steering key players in the industry and government toward a painful but necessary solution. This fast action led to the approval of a $15 billion governmental support package that saved the industry.

These were extraordinary measures in extraordinary times. Whether confronting a national crisis at the helm of a Fortune 500 company or negotiating with local authorities over medical reimbursement or real estate permits, a CEO must be ready to fulfill the role of the company's chief ambassador to the outside world.

Recalibrate Your Power

The CEO role is new and different from anything you've done before, and your historical sources of power aren't necessarily going to apply. What got you here? Knowing the business closely? Being the smartest one in the room? Owning key customer relationships? Being loved by the CEO? Every CEO needs to candidly assess her capabilities and sources of power that have helped her to date, then deliberately recalibrate her tools (time, attention, and team) to ensure the appropriate focus in her new role as CEO. Every company is different, every CEO position is different, but some common patterns apply.

- *Knowledge and insight.* The knowledge that gives a CEO power is a broad understanding of the business, not specialized knowledge of a function or business segment.

- *Access to information.* The information that gives a CEO power is predominately interpreting big picture patterns from outside the company and their implications on the business, rather than detailed information from inside the business.

- *Formal and informal network.* CEOs focus on building networks outside the company and recalibrate their views on their preexisting internal network.

- *Loyalty.* Followership and loyalty of your team are now much more important than the loyalty of your boss.

- *Positional authority.* The best CEOs use positional authority sparingly.

Hazard #5: The C-Suite Is a Psychological Thunder Dome

The ghouls. The time warp. The spotlight. The explosive pressure. We've covered some intense territory so far, and it all comes together to create the perfect conditions for Hazard #5: Every day as a CEO can be a psychological maelstrom. Every day you are tested. Stakes are high. Fates and fortunes of hundreds or thousands of employees and customers are affected by your daily decisions. You often feel you are walking on a knife's edge between success and failure. In this role of seemingly ultimate authority and power, a lot is still outside of your control.

The one thing utterly within your control is showing up to this high-stakes obstacle course in your absolute best condition to perform and win.

In some CEOs, we've seen the heady mix of power and celebrity lead to an inflated ego and entitled behavior. Caught up in the pressure and responsibility of the role, they risk losing sight of civility and even ethics. We were recently coaching a leader who was at the top of his company's short list of CEO candidates but feeling hesitant about stepping up because he had seen close-up how power can corrupt. "I have seen so much crazy," he told us. "I don't want to get drunk and throw a chair through a plate glass mirror or sleep with my assistant like my last CEO, and I definitely don't want to go to jail like the guy three CEOs ago." Another CEO told us that he was divorced because he'd neglected his marriage—not so much because he was buried in the business but because he was jumping into the company jet to be at every high-cachet event, no matter how many time zones it removed him from his wife.

And finally, the most persistent and pervasive psychological challenge of all: loneliness. Wary of the stereotypical "lonely at the top" notion when we interviewed CEOs for the book, we never asked them if they were lonely. And yet time and again, they brought it up unprompted, eager to help prepare others for the weighty isolation of the role. Within the walls of the company, you are a cohort of one. People who were your peers just yesterday are now treating you with deference or, worse, are distant and aloof because you got the job they wanted. You've got a lot of people depending on you and nobody with whom you can be completely candid and unfiltered. As Jim Smith of Thomson Reuters put it, "At times it can feel like everybody's working you for something. They may be positioning for more investment in their business unit. They may be trying to manage down my expectations. Whatever it is, once you are a CEO, nothing is 'just a conversation.'"

You *can* thrive, even in this pressure cooker, but self-regulation has never been as important or as hard to maintain. Here are some proven approaches from successful CEOs.

1. Create winning routines.

Major League Baseball players are famous for their elaborate superstitions: Turk Wendell famously pitched without socks and while chewing black licorice, brushing his teeth every inning without fail. Braves player Elliot Johnson chews grape gum for defense and watermelon for hitting. Olympic swimmer Michael Phelps has a routine circumscribing every move he makes in the two hours before any major event. More than superstitions, these are rituals that world-class athletes use to get their mind ready for peak performance, to silence all the noise and distraction of an arena and their life beyond it and focus on the demands of their sport.

CEOs are no different. They need disciplined rituals and routines that keep them consistent and grounded and that simplify life. Such tools enable them to hit a mental "reset" button after a bad customer meeting and walk into a board meeting a minute later fresh and ready to engage. They also serve as grounding to stave off daily anxiety and get a good night's sleep. Just like athletes, a CEO benefits from consistent routines that reliably put her in peak condition.

Krista Endsley, former CEO of Abila software company, likes self-talk, constantly reminding herself: "I don't have a liver in my office in a cooler. This isn't life and death here." Wendy Kopp, the founder of Teach For America, goes running every single morning. As Matt Kramer, her successor as CEO there, told us, "No matter how tired she is, no matter the time, she gets up. If it has to be four in the morning, then it's four in the morning. That is her time for setting things aside and thinking about the world." One CEO we work with knew there was one place he could go if he needed some quiet time, uninterrupted by people constantly asking him questions: the dentist!

Whatever winning routines work best for you, build them now. Turn them into daily habits so that when you need them most, they are there to serve you.

2. Protect against "identity theft."

Thanks to twenty minutes in a Singaporean cab with legendary McKinsey alum Ted Hall, Dom Barton, the managing partner (i.e., CEO) of McKinsey, learned he had been the victim of "identity theft." It was 7:30 A.M., and the two men were to connect in the hotel lobby to head to an 8:00 A.M. meeting with the finance minister of Singapore. When Ted showed up, Dom's jaw dropped.

"Ted Hall is a big, intense guy," he recalls. "And he's wearing this big red Hawaiian shirt." Dom immediately pleaded with him to go change. "You can't wear that to a meeting with the finance minister!"

Ted was completely unmoved. Dom had a choice: this shirt or no shirt at all. Finally, they got into the cab, and Dom wanted to prep. He asked Ted for the document he was supposed to bring. Ted shrugged: *What document?* Dom started to lay into him, but Ted cut him off. "Dom, if I had a document, I'd rip it up and throw it out the door," he said. Shocked, Dom muttered, "Maybe we should cancel this meeting, you're tired. I think you have jet lag. . . ."

Ted cut him off: "Let me ask you a rhetorical question: Are you an interesting person? The answer is: no, you're not. In fact, I think you are the most boring person I have ever met. I know you had hobbies when you joined the firm, but we've sucked it all out of you. That's a problem. I'm a musician. I play the French horn. I founded a jazz record label. I've sailed a sailboat across the Pacific. What have *you* done that isn't work related? Why should people want to be around you?"

They were harsh words, tough love from a man Dom revered. The truth set in: Like so many present and future CEOs, he had succumbed to "identity theft." His corporate identity, his hyperfocus on the work, had subsumed his humanity. It happens all too easily and leads to problems that get magnified the further you climb. If you become a hollow husk of a human, you burn out fast—but that's not the worst of it. You can't lead effectively if people don't see signs there's a person behind the title.

Protect your identity from theft. Invest time in nurturing aspects of yourself that are unrelated to your CEO job or status. Today Dom dedicates time to the activities he loves—to running marathons, to spending time with friends and loved ones, and to reading books for both pleasure and perspective on the world outside of immediate business concerns. As a top leader, he's formalized his efforts to stay well-rounded. Dom has developed a dashboard of sixteen metrics that he tracks, including several well-being indicators to make sure that he doesn't neglect his personal life. He may never pick up the French horn or win an award for his Napa Valley–grown Rutherford grapes (one of Ted Hall's more recent adventures), but he doesn't need to. The point is, Dom Barton devotes time and attention to being Dom Barton. He's also made a point of making growth and learning part of his public persona. The mantle of CEO isn't so heavy if you can admit to yourself and others that you are not an all-powerful superhuman: You, too, have weaknesses and make mistakes.

In the cab that day, Ted Hall offered Dom this leadership truth: "There are three stages to a leader's career. First, you're known for what you can do. Second, you're known for what you know. Third, people want to follow you because of who you are." This is true of all leaders and especially CEOs.

We've seen many leaders, as they get within reach of the CEO role, grapple with what such a role means to their identity, working hard to reconcile the needs of the role with who they are as a person. Craig Barnes, president of Princeton Theological Seminary, for example, told us that as he initially wrestled with whether to take the role, he was concerned that to run an organization of such renown spoke of pride and hubris antithetical to him as a Christian. Another leader, known for her irreverent humor and spontaneity, was worried that she had to put on an unnaturally stiff mask in the CEO role. Ultimately, leaders who find their own CEO voice authentic to them fare better than those who wear a mask.

3. Find confidants and consiglieri.

It's never too early to build a network of advisors outside of your business. These are people who understand what it feels like to wake up in the middle of the night thinking about the hundreds or thousands of employees and their families you're responsible for. They're also people who can offer business advice that's untainted by the authority of your title or their own agenda. Once you become CEO, myriad helpers will flock to you with advice: consultants, bankers, lawyers, coaches, and business acquaintances you haven't heard from in years. Overnight you become a magnet for a crowd of well-wishers eager to help you. You are looking for a small trusted circle, not an army. The following filters could help you:

- **Agenda:** Are your potential helpers free of self-interest when it comes to the advice you seek? If not, are they at least transparent with you and with themselves about their agenda? Where does their agenda conflict or align with yours? Are your bankers or attorneys, for example, telling you to pursue a much larger acquisition because it will quickly make you a market share leader—or because it will bring them larger deal fees? Unless you can have a candid conversation and they are willing to be transparent about their agenda, move on.

- **Chemistry:** It's hard to trust someone you don't like, particularly when you are looking for support that's as much emotional as practical. A CEO once told us that she would pick a coach only when she found someone she "couldn't wait to spend more time with." Whatever your bar for chemistry is, make sure you feel it with the advisors you select.

- **Competence:** Do these individuals know what "great" looks like? Can they challenge and offer new or broader perspective? Are they among the best at what they do? Chances are, by the time you get to the CEO role, you already have trusted advisors. Now is the time to think carefully about whether they are strong enough to take you forward.

. . .

This has been a "fly in the ointment" chapter by necessity. Sections I and II of *The CEO Next Door* focused on helping you land your dream job. In Section III of the book we try to protect you from the common stumbles and explosive land mines you can encounter when you step into the CEO role. We have deliberately focused on what is most likely to go wrong and how to prevent it. With so much to manage, you might wonder if CEOs actually like their work. The answer we heard hundreds of times: *Yes. Yes. Yes.* Take Madeline Bell. Where she is today looks a lot different from where she was in her first year as a CEO. These days her life is full of "pinch me" moments—for example, a recent public showcase of the hospital's genetic scientists, one superstar after another. "In these moments, and I definitely have quite a few of them, I feel very proud and very excited," she says. "I finally have that feeling that our board chair talked to me about eighteen months ago, excited and really happy to be at the pinnacle of my career."

When we asked CEOs about their "pinch me" moments in the role, we expected to hear about meetings at the White House, invitation-only gatherings at the World Economic Forum, or flights to private islands on the corporate jet. CEOs thoroughly enjoy the perks and privileges of the role. Yet when asked about their best moments, we heard a similar story from most of them, whether it was a $50 million firm or the Fortune 500. Their greatest moments come when they see their team revel in a victory, and they know that they, as the leader, helped make the team's pride possible. Which leads us to the next chapter—and the most commonly mentioned pitfall of first-time CEOs: choosing the right team.

KEY TAKEAWAYS

1. Congratulations! You've made it! No matter how excited or stressed you feel right now, it's normal. It takes about two years to get comfortable in the CEO role.

2. Overinvest in figuring out what you walked into. What you don't know *will* hurt you.

3. Own your calendar and the incoming requests for your time—don't let them own you.

4. Get used to life in the permanent spotlight. Smile! It's good business.

5. Use all the levers of the CEO role. If you are seeing the world through your old lens, you are not doing your job.

6. Breathe. And get support to help you navigate the trials and tribulations in the CEO seat.

chapter 10

Not Just Any Team—Your Team

It ain't what you don't know that gets you into trouble.
It's what you know for sure that just ain't so.

—Mark Twain

YOU PROBABLY GOT WHERE YOU ARE TODAY AT LEAST IN PART BECAUSE you've earned a reputation for building world-class teams. In fact the leaders you've hired and mentored may be a great source of pride for you. You've got committed, talented people who followed you from job to job. You know how painful it is to fire someone but also that waiting to remove an underperformer serves no one.

That's why almost every CEO we meet comes into the role feeling fairly confident about building his team. "I've got this," they say. Here's the reality: *Challenges building the team are the single most common setback for new CEOs. Seventy-five percent of CEOs we interviewed made painful mistakes in building their team, despite coming into the role with a lot of management experience.*[1]

How is it possible that most executives spend their careers thinking they're great on talent, only to pay the price when they become CEO? At this level, the cost of a bad hire is more severe and more public than ever before. Under the spotlight of the CEO position and the unrelenting pressure of running the company, the problem becomes magnified.

Take the situation Raj Gupta stepped into in 1999 when he became CEO of the specialty chemical company Rohm and Haas, now part of Dow Chemical. Raj came to the United States from India in his early twenties with eight dollars in his pocket and no inkling that he might someday have a shot at becoming a CEO. As a mechanical engineer building a career amid a company of chemists, he knew how critical a strong team was. Promoted to CEO from within the company, he knew all the players and had strong instincts about who should stay and who should go.

Then those instincts collided with reality. Raj inherited a seemingly intractable problem: what to do about the runner-up to the CEO position. "Arthur" had been with the company for a long time and was respected for his experience and credentials by the board and employees alike. Raj had grown up in a culture in which firing a guy like Arthur "wasn't the kind of thing that one did, especially since the board made it clear they wanted to keep him," Raj recalls. Arthur was untouchable. Visibly disappointed about not getting the CEO role, Arthur became a drag on morale and eventually on performance. Raj resigned himself to live with the problem, finding Band-Aids and work-arounds. Meanwhile, the business was on a wild ride in the early years of his tenure. The financial crisis of 2001 hit Rohm and Haas hard—the stock price plunged, the company had to take a major write-off, customers were reducing their spending with the company. A challenging start for any new CEO. To Raj, it felt like professional life or death. Raj discovered, as so many do, that it's easy enough to say "you need to get the right team in place fast" but very, very difficult to do in practice. Under tremendous pressure to prove himself, Raj simply didn't feel he had the freedom to move on Arthur. He kept the underperforming executive on the team until the moment that the board called *him* and said, "Raj, are you going to fire this guy, or should we?"

Raj not only survived but went on to lead the company successfully for nine years. In July 2008, he capped off his CEO run by selling the company to Dow Chemical for $18 billion in the midst of the financial crisis. But looking back on those early talent problems, Raj is clear-eyed. "Did we lose momentum? Did we lose some traction?" he says. "Yes, we did. If I were to do it all over again, I would do it differently." Raj knew the right answer but felt his hands were tied. It was only obvious in hindsight that he could have and needed to move faster.

We see different versions of this movie play out time and again. The specific reasons may be different, but the result is the same: "I know it's the right thing to do, but I just can't afford to do it right now." The risk of taking difficult action to make personnel changes feels overwhelmingly real and tangible, while the upside to getting the right person on board can feel ephemeral and uncertain.

Team problems cause CEOs more difficulty than board relations— or than any of the five hidden hazards we've already discussed. And if you are reading this chapter earlier in your career, imagine how much career acceleration you could enjoy by getting ahead of this, by becoming adept at building winning teams early on.

Approaches we share in this chapter are designed for real-world conditions. While designing that perfect, handpicked, all-star team the moment you ascend to the CEO role may be a fantasy, you must make necessary talent changes quickly. Successful CEOs we inter-viewed proactively upgraded up their teams, changing 40 to 60 percent of direct reports they inherited within the first eighteen to twenty-four months.[2]

The first question every new leader should ask when it comes to talent is this: "How can I move this from being the team to being my team as quickly as possible?"

The Inaugural Address

You've heard Jim Collins's enduring dictum: *First who, then what.*[3] His emphasis on talent is correct, but when we advise new CEOs, we actually flip Collins's advice on its head. It turns out that the best way to figure out *who* is to start by telling your team *what*. What do you stand for as a leader, and what does your arrival mean for the organization and for each person in it?

Everyone knows a new leader will put her imprint on the organization. A new leader's arrival often brings new energy and builds momentum for positive change. It also causes much anxiety among the troops. As a new leader, you might have barely found the route from your office to the bathroom, but your employees have already spent a lot of time googling, speculating and making assumptions about who you are, how you will lead, and what that means to them. Your arrival signals uncertainty and potential threat, which can quickly turn into disengagement and even the risk of losing your best employees. You never get a second chance to make a first impression, and you can bet that the team is watching and interpreting every word you say, every move you make. Under uncertainty, most people assume the worst, shifting their attention from productive pursuits to disaster planning. *How you enter the CEO role has enormous power to set the right momentum and tone for your tenure.* The best CEOs seize this opportunity to shape the story of their leadership from the first moment with what we call the *inaugural address.*

In 2006, when the legendary Silicon Valley investor Maynard Webb became the CEO of the call center provider LiveOps, his reputation as a demanding leader preceded him. In his prior role as COO of eBay, he was a critical player in growing the company of 250 employees and $140 million in revenue to an over $4.5 billion tech behemoth with 12,000 people. His accomplishments were well known in the tight-knit technology community—as was his hard-charging style. At the time Maynard walked into LiveOps, the company had a young, dynamic team that prized a culture of fun.

As Maynard got up to the podium for his first CEO town hall, he was eager to share his vision for the company and his excitement for its future. When he opened the floor for questions, the team had other concerns on their mind. "I heard you worked people hard at eBay," said one of the senior engineers, speaking for many. "How is that going to impact us?" For some members of the team, fear that they would not be able to balance the demands of the job with the rest of their life was eclipsing the opportunity in front of them.

While the question surprised him, he didn't back away from the chance to set the tone. "I know you at LiveOps have high aspirations. eBay was a hugely successful public company. We are not there yet. So, yes, we're going to have to work hard," he told the crowd. "In fact, we're going to have to work even harder than we had to at eBay. If you don't want that, you shouldn't be at a startup."

Courageously, he used the opportunity to announce what he stood for: high aspirations, high standards, and frank realism about the challenges before them. And then he gave them the big finish: "Because we worked so hard at eBay, a lot of people don't have to work at all now, and I hope we can do that for many here." His point was clear: *Working hard can get us all somewhere pretty amazing collectively and individually.*

In this short speech, Maynard had delivered a much-abbreviated version of a great inaugural. It is far more than a pep talk. It's a concrete, unvarnished statement of who you are, where you are going, and what it will require to get there. It is too important to leave anyone guessing. Among the key points to consider as you prepare your inaugural address:

- **Your assessment of today**: What is your take on the current health of the organization? As you reflect on what you have learned about the business, it is critical to show genuine respect for the accomplishments and wins that came before you. It is also important to frame gaps and opportunities. Vivid personal details and examples will demonstrate your connection to the people and the business.

- **Your vision for tomorrow:** Average CEOs have a task list. Great ones paint a picture of a point of arrival. JFK's daring challenge to *put the man on the moon and bring him back down to earth safely before this decade is out* is aspirational and concrete at the same time.[4] They make the destination crystal clear, specific, and compelling. That's the level you're shooting for when it comes to conveying your vision: a tantalizing glimpse at a future that is both aspirational and supremely concrete.

- **Your values for the organization:** What values do you see as essential to achieving that vision? Mary Berner, while at *Reader's Digest*, for example, committed herself (and the organization) to six principles, with operational efficiency at the top of the list.

- **Your broader view:** What do you see happening in the world that will affect the industry, the company, and your own decision making?

- **Your call to action:** Remember Bill Amelio, who was charged with turning around the turbulent helicopter company? He credits an early call-to-action speech to his senior team with creating the needed momentum. After laying out the severity of the company's financial situation, he said, "We are getting killed—in the market, by creditors, and by the board. We are in a battle together. I need everyone's best ideas and nobody shooting each other in the ass. We're gonna go get this done. You're either in or you're out. Put your hands on the table. If you don't want to be in, tell me, and you'll be out tomorrow. Now let's come up with the best ideas we can."

- **Your leadership style:** Your people are preoccupied with figuring out how to work with you. Getting ahead of this is actually simple: Tell them. How do you plan to involve yourself in the organization? How will you spend your time? How do you like to be communicated with?

    We recently worked with a CEO who had a background in sales. When he took the helm of a tech company, the other senior executives assumed he'd be so sales-driven that he'd ignore technical and product constraints and sell things that weren't deliverable. In an early meeting, he reset their expectations: "You probably think all I care about is the new deal pipeline. It's not. I'll be spending time with the product team and with customers in my first year to make sure I understand how our product works, what we can deliver, and what we can't. I expect you to hold me accountable to that."

During your first three to six months, you'll be delivering versions of your inaugural address many times, in many mediums, to many audiences. Every week, Maynard Webb sent a weekly update to the entire company to share the issues he had at the top of his mind, along with positive employee interactions from the week past. He sent out his objectives, and every quarter he had his own performance graded by the board—the results of which he then sent to every employee.

The goal of all this communication was to "set the tone that I was very approachable and would share everything I could with them." It also made clear to employees that, as hard-driving as he might be, he held himself to the same standards as everyone else.

Your inaugural address prepares the organization for what's coming, but your daily actions must constantly reinforce the message.

The Six "Safe" People Bets That Put You in Peril

You've laid the groundwork throughout the organization for who you are as a leader and what you expect. You know you need to—and you want to—upgrade the team. Yet even the most decisive CEOs often get stuck in the dangerous stalemate of: "Yes, he's got to go . . . *just not now.*" Certainly, as we saw in Raj's experience at Rohm and Haas, it is never easy to fire people. Organizational politics can create friction and noise. So does pressure. So does the innate humanity of these leaders: The challenges of moving fast on people are real and understandable.

But of all these brakes on forward momentum, the sharpest and the most common is fear. *New leaders feel vulnerable. And that vulnerability can lead to inertia and poor judgment at the very moment when bold, decisive moves are critical.* The problem we've found that is at the core of most CEO's people mistakes is this: Your human bias for safety is once again leading you astray. The status quo inherently feels safer to us. But this attitude is nothing short of reckless conservatism. Suddenly, instead of taking swift action, you second-guess yourself or cling to your security blanket.

People issues are like fish rather than fine wines: The problems you see on your team now are not going to improve with age. If you tolerate underperformance on your senior team, you put your company, your job, and possibly the jobs of thousands of other talented, hardworking folks in jeopardy. And you won't be doing the failing individual any favors either.

What follows are the top six miscalculated "safe" people bets we see leaders fall prey to again and again.

1. **Maintain the status quo.** Leaders stick with the incumbent team or pull up their trusted lieutenants, clinging to their security blanket without evaluating these loyal soldiers anew for the role. They choose the "devils they know."

2. **Favor pedigree over relevant track record.** Instead of judiciously matching candidates' previous results to future needs, leaders pick the candidate with the most impressive credentials.

3. **Acquiesce to the board.** Board members or even a former CEO often have recommendations on talent. Leaders assume they're "stuck" with these options and fail to insist on a fully objective approach.

4. **Over-rely on people who helped them land the top job.** A leader ascending to any coveted position often feels grateful to those who helped him win the role. Gratitude and loyalty are essential building blocks for lasting personal relationships. Unfortunately, they can also dangerously cloud hiring decisions. We have seen leaders brought to the point of failure by hiring and keeping people out of loyalty rather than with a dispassionate view focused on capabilities.

5. **Hire people who are clones of themselves.** People who look like them and have similar backgrounds feel safe to new leaders. So instead of finding people who add diversity and complementary skills to their talent

portfolio—so critical to the success of a team—they hire people who are carbon copies of their skill set and experience.

6. **Avoid talent that could become "competition."** Being a leader is hard enough without an ambitious go-getter breathing down one's neck. So new leaders might settle for "good enough," because the person is nonthreatening.

This last "safe" bet may be the worst of all. We recently worked with a first-time CEO who set the gold standard for avoiding the "competition" trap. Before he assumed the top position, one of his biggest advocates was the head of HR. Everyone, including the board, considered the HR leader untouchable. Nonetheless, he was the first senior executive the new CEO let go, when the HR executive rejected an extremely qualified candidate by saying, "You don't want to hire this guy—he's so good, he'll be your rival." At that moment, the CEO realized his HR leader's thinking was incompatible with his vision and values. "I didn't want just one leader who was that good; I wanted to hire fifty people that good," he said.

Draft the Right Team Quickly

What follows are four fail-safe principles we've gleaned from the CEOs who have avoided the six "safe" people bets and quickly and successfully rebuilt their teams. These are applicable at any stage of one's career.

1. Develop your people plan. In writing.

If you are planning an investment in technology, opening a new location, downsizing your manufacturing footprint, or implementing any other significant business initiative, you likely have many pages documenting the business case, success metrics, and implementation plans. When was the last time you applied equal rigor to developing and documenting a robust, "no excuses" people plan for the long, medium, and short term?

Figuring out who belongs on the team isn't just about assessing raw capability. Building a strong team requires considering three factors:

- **Vision:** Does this individual have the specific skills to advance your vision and strategy as well as the track record to prove it?

- **Alignment:** Is she aligned with your values and the direction you are setting for the business? Strong voices and diverse views are essential on any team, but someone who is misaligned on values or doesn't buy into your leadership won't help you take the business forward.

- **Portfolio:** How well does this individual complement your own and other team members' capabilities and personal styles?

Assess your team looking forward through the windshield, not backward through the rearview mirror: How well suited are each person's capabilities and experiences to what you'll need over the next one to two years? Over five years? As a team, do you have the capabilities to take the business into the future?

Once you're clear, put a people plan in writing that includes specific milestones and timing—the only way to keep yourself honest and on track. For any team members you are not sure about, write down specific metrics and upcoming milestones that you'll use to make the decision on whether they should stay or go and how to best support them.

2. Starring roles require stars.

Tom Monahan is the cerebral former CEO of CEB, a business information services company where hard analytics reign supreme. So, frankly, it surprised us when he told us that he learned one of his most important lessons about talent on a beach boardwalk in Salisbury, Massachusetts, where his family owned a carnival business. There were two types of attractions on the boardwalk, rides and games. When it came to rides, the quality of the machine itself drew the crowd, and the team needed to focus on safety and efficiency. Games were another story. Talented carnival callers made all the difference between a hot attraction pulling in long lines of visitors and a forgotten kiosk losing money. Beloved characters—Larry the Gypsy! General Store Jake!— were their own attraction. Without top "talent" in those roles, the carnival couldn't survive.

In your business, you need to know where you need a Larry the Gypsy—a top-tier, A-player talent—and where just turning on the machine at 11:00 A.M. sharp every summer morning is good enough. As you consider each position, ask yourself, "How important is this role to the delivery of my vision and objectives? Do we need this person to be a source of competitive advantage for our team or mainly to make the trains run on time?"

3. People projects are costly.

In the past, as you moved up through the ranks, you could prop up underperformers on your team and still get your job done. Do that as CEO, and you put your company on the line. *Every minute you spend putting Band-Aids on someone else's subpar performance, you are not doing the one job you were hired to do—be a CEO.* You no longer have the time (and often not the experience) to dive into the weeds and do others' jobs for them. As CEO, you have significantly less time to run the business as you did in your prior positions. Say you have two personnel "projects"—underproducing staff members—on your team. If two of your five P&L presidents or general managers each deliver only 80 percent, you're already way off target for the quarter.

We recently saw a CEO lose his job because he kept a weak chief technology officer in a company whose business model lived and died on the quality and development speed of its technology. The business required an extremely talented CTO. The CEO had strong technical chops himself and thought he'd compensate for the CTO's weakness. He was wrong. Key projects fell behind schedule, costs started to balloon, and he was spending less time with customers at the time when his touch was needed the most. Business suffered. The CEO lost credibility with his board, and in nineteen months he was out.

The fact that you don't have time for "projects" doesn't mean you can't have key players who still have room to grow. You want leaders with upside potential. But having too many people projects will weigh you down. People in the most critical roles need to be ready to deliver in the role today, and you don't want to be the only development support they have. Top leaders evaluate the broader executive team portfolio and ask: Across the team, do we cover all the critical skills and experience we require? What is the full set of internal and external development support we can engage to perform to full potential?

4. Set a higher bar for what "great" looks like in each role.

You may not always be the best judge of who's a budding superstar and who is a personnel project, especially in areas outside your expertise. A new CEO with a reputation for being smart on talent (Frank) recently ran down his early assessment of his team with Elena. When he got to general counsel, he shrugged: "Eh, not the worst I've ever seen. He stays." The general counsel was a five out of ten at best. Frank expected to grow the business aggressively through acquisitions and long-term customer contracts—both of which required a strong legal function. This business needed a ten, yet Frank grossly underestimated the importance of the role. Seven months later, a board member pulled him aside to share his grave concerns about the weak legal team, skyrocketing legal costs, and slow contract execution. Frank, in hindsight, saw these setbacks as costly and unnecessary self-inflicted wounds. He didn't realize how a strong general counsel needs to support the business.

Similarly, CEOs (and especially founders) of high-growth businesses often struggle setting their sights high enough for talent needed to take the company into the future—not simply deliver at current scale. McKinney, Texas–based SRS Distribution is among the most successful and fastest growing roofing products distributors in the nation. Headed by industry veterans Ron Ross and Dan Tinker, SRS delivered a whopping 7.6 times return to investors between 2008 and 2013. Far from resting on their laurels, Ron and Dan asked us in 2014 what it would take from the leadership perspective to triple the business over five years and win the talent war. The management team rated themselves as a 6.5 out of 10 in terms of readiness to scale the business. They have been wildly successful to date, but they recognized a new set of capabilities was required going forward. Through a series of interviews and analyses of the entire team, SRS built a talent plan for the future organization that they strived to become. Among other recommendations, this work led Ron and Dan to rethink what they needed from the entire leadership team. SRS continues to thrive, and Ron and Dan credit the lessons in this chapter for giving them a winning talent playbook.

So how do the best leaders protect themselves from the six "safe" people bets? They start talent discussions from a **zero base.** *Rather than assuming that you have to live with what you have, imagine you had to redraft your entire team for the sole purpose of winning against company vision and goals.* Strip away all the perceived constraints, and take a hard look at the future needs of the organization. Reset your lens in terms of the capabilities, skills, and experience you need to deliver the future direction of the business. Only then do you turn to assessing the team to understand fit or gaps. This should become a ritual not just at the start of your tenure, but every single year.

Successful CEOs also don't do it alone. They know when to bring in an outside perspective to push their thinking forward. Asking someone to explicitly play watchdog, testing your assumptions against the facts, can help. If there's an area of the business where you don't have a depth of experience, consider bringing in someone who can guide you—as did the CEO with a sales background who, when he took the helm of a tech firm, brought in a trusted CTO from a prior business as a consultant to assess the capabilities of his product team. Finally, you might also benefit from the advice of someone who has solved similar business challenges as a CEO. For example, if you're running a $500 million firm, consult on talent with a CEO who grew a business from $200 million to $2 billion.

Build Your New Language

Another challenge of your powerful new platform is how to stay connected at the right level to your team and to the business. How do you drive the business yet step back enough to get all those people you so carefully selected to do their very best?

In the past, you likely added value by being the one with the knowledge and insight to make the big decisions. But the higher you go, the less your value proceeds directly from your insight, information, or experience. We like the way Tom Erickson, who has been a CEO and chairman of several companies, put it: "Ninety percent of CEO leadership is behavior modification." Behavior modification is all about getting scores of people acting in an aligned fashion to achieve the goals of the organization. Trust people enough to step back and let them do their job, but also find opportunities to use your presence to keep people honest and on point and to keep them moving. Choose where you get involved based on what signals need to be sent to an employee, to your team, or to the broader organization.

The most important decision you'll make is when to be a cheerleader, inspiring and engaging others, and when to wield the hammer of accountability. Each has its time and purpose, and the best CEOs make the choice thoughtfully and strategically, not reactively. Thanks to "amplification"—the outsize effect the power of the CEO role has on those around you—any suggestion, no matter how gently you deliver it, feels like a pronouncement. The best CEOs deliberately develop their own idiosyncratic repertoire of small gestures that send big signals. Here are a few examples of the symbolic language of CEOs we've noticed:

- **CEO for *"This* matters"**: When Tom Monahan was CEO at CEB, he read every benchmarking report the company produced. Every so often he'd follow up to offer a specific point of view on something he'd read. The point he was making wasn't as important as his sending a powerful message that product quality and customer experience were top priorities for the CEO.

- **CEO for "I'm paying attention"**: When a CEO drops in for a surprise plant visit or walks the halls to smile and shake hands, he or she does so in part to remind people that every single day they have an opportunity to excel or to slip up—and, yes, their efforts count.

- **CEO for "I know you've got this"**: You go to the meeting—just to listen. John Zillmer, the highly successful CEO of Allied Waste, completely turned that company around. Yet, if you attended one of his management meetings, you'd be shocked to see that he often barely said a word. He was present where it mattered, and his silence said, "I've got the right people at the table doing the right thing."

- **CEO for "We're discussing, not deciding"**: When former CEO of Arrow Electronics Steve Kaufman wants to remind his staff that his participation in discussion and debate is meant to explore—not direct—he literally takes off his CEO hat (it's a baseball cap) and puts on a second hat that says TEAMMATE. "Otherwise, when I ask questions, people think I'm giving answers they have to run with," he says.

- **CEO for "I want the truth"**: Steve Kaufman doesn't just explicitly ask direct reports to tell him the unvarnished truth, he ensures that bad news travels up to him fast by thanking the bearer and reacting calmly and graciously every single time he's given information, even when the responses aren't what he wanted to hear.

- **CEO for "I'm never too busy for *you*"**: Marc Tessier-Lavigne, president of Stanford University, a school with more than 16,000 students, has office hours for students. Through an online signup sheet, anyone enrolled can get ten minutes with the president, with priority given to first-time visitors.[5]

- **CEO for "I'm human"**: Whether you wear a Hawaiian shirt à la Ted Hall or find other ways to bring your personality to work, people want to follow full human beings, not walking suits. For some CEOs, self-effacing humor goes a long way. After replacing half her team at *Reader's Digest*, Mary Berner passed out Halloween costumes at a leadership off-site. Her costume? The Wicked Witch of the West.

The language of leadership has to do with actions, not words; signals, not demands. Success is no longer your success. It's your team's.

KEY TAKEAWAYS

1. You probably think you've got it all figured out with your team. There is a one-out-of-four chance that you are right. *Seventy-five percent of first-time CEO mistakes are about not moving quickly enough to build the right team.*

2. There is never a second chance to make the first impression. Seize the moment with a powerful inaugural address.

3. Develop your people plan—in writing. Use at least as much objectivity and analytical rigor in your people assessment as you use for other business decisions.

4. Know where stars are needed.

5. Minimize personnel "projects."

6. Use small gestures to connect with your team.

7. For additional help on building your team take a look at *Who: The A Method for Hiring* and *Power Score: Your Formula for Leadership Success,* both written by Geoff Smart and Randy Street. Alan Foster is a co-author.[6]

chapter 11

Dancing with the Titans—The Board

He is pulling the load of an ox and walking on eggshells.
—Stieg Larsson, *The Girl with the Dragon Tattoo*

"JOE" ATTENDED A RESPECTABLE UNIVERSITY, THEN FLEW UP THE management chain of two world-class corporations known for two things: operational excellence and producing future CEOs. As VP and eventually president, he built a reputation as a "lean, mean, operational machine" who could rebuild an organization from the ground up.

At last, twenty-two years into his career, his well-deserved shot arrived. When the private equity firm called to offer him the helm of a mid-cap farming equipment company in the Midwest, after hanging up, Joe let out a victory cry in his hotel room. His moment had come!

He rolled into town with his trademark energetic intensity, ready to tackle tough changes. The PE firm was confident they had hired exactly the right guy, even though he didn't have a background in farming. To make sure he had the domain expertise he needed, they loaded the board with industry-savvy advisors who could fill any gap.

Conditions seemed perfect for a quick win. Instead, Joe discovered exactly what many CEOs find out when they earn that first coveted

CEO job: that just running the business is only part of the work. How well you work with your board of directors can make all the difference between success and failure. Six months in, Joe's board was about to fire him.

A typical first-time CEO feels incredible pressure. The group of people whose job it is to hear your challenges and offer wise, dispassionate counsel is the *very same group* judging your performance. Every challenge you bring them, you rightly fear, is weighted with a question: *Has this guy screwed up and outstayed his welcome?* Boards have the ultimate power and responsibility to give you the CEO job—and to usher you out. No wonder working with the board may feel like handling an interpersonal powder keg.

Boards are intended to represent shareholders' interests by holding a CEO accountable and supporting her with savvy counsel. They can bring wisdom, experience, and a fresh point of view to push a CEO's thinking and provide a valuable sounding board. A strong board can serve as a periscope to help a CEO rise above the business, above his individual experience, to spot and prevent problems before he rounds a corner. Unfortunately, not every CEO walks into a ready-made, highly functioning board. In fact, only 57 percent of CEOs we interviewed rated their boards above a 3 out of 5 on adding value to the business.[1]

Whether facing a strong or a struggling board, working with the board is the number one concern of incoming first-time CEOs. And for good reason: *Failure to manage the board is among the top three most commonly cited mistakes made by new CEOs.* In our review of over seventy CEO firings, broken board relationships caused a quarter of the dismissals. What starts as a love affair can end as a painful breakup. *Once a board gets concerned about a CEO, if that concern is not resolved, on average it takes boards just under two years to move out a CEO.*[2]

This was almost the case for Joe, our Midwest farming CEO. While he was busy putting his initiatives into motion, the chairman of his board, "Keith," was eyeing every move with skepticism. Keith was the former CEO of the company, which he had grown successfully until it changed ownership. The new investor wanted the value of his expertise, but Keith had trouble handing off authority. And so when Joe's sweeping changes ruffled feathers with the old guard, Keith was all too happy to hear them out and conclude that his successor was screwing things up. He began to actively campaign against Joe, providing a sympathetic ear to employees resistant to change and agitating the board to change the CEO.

A tireless operator, Joe was consumed by the task of restructuring the company for aggressive growth. He was missing a crucial part of a CEO's job: building an effective partnership with the board. He fell into a trap common for first-time CEOs in which they assume that as long as they report out strong results, the board will be happy. When we see a CEO struggling with a board, the first question we ask the CEO is how much time and attention she is devoting to building a strong partnership with the board. For many relentless operators, building board relationships is seen as a necessary evil. They are concerned about being in good stead with the board but don't necessarily invest the time or take the steps required to build a strong relationship. *On average, successful CEOs we've interviewed spent between 10 and 20 percent of their time working with the board.*[3] That percentage can go over 30 percent at key inflection points, such as stepping into a new CEO job, taking the company public, a major M&A transaction, or selling the business. Much like with any other aspect of a CEO's job, allocating time and attention in line with key priorities pays dividends.

Joe was the rare CEO who got a second chance. When his board chair aired his concerns to the investors, they asked us to help them understand what was really going on. After detailed interviews with everyone involved, our conclusion was that Joe was the right leader for the business, but had underinvested in his relationship with the board and that Keith, the former CEO, was a big problem. The investors were the power center of this board. Joe had assumed that as long as he delivered results, they would be in his corner. The problem was that it takes time to deliver results. Joe diligently reported on the project plans and milestones, but he hadn't invested enough or in the right way to build deeper trust to turn the investors from watchdogs into allies. He also didn't share strongly enough with them how Keith's meddling was setting the business back and creating morale issues on the team. Absent this deeper relationship building, in the eyes of the investors, Joe was merely a CEO on training wheels, and Keith was the accomplished CEO who had just delivered home-run results for the previous owners of the company. It's easy to see that Joe was in a precarious position. We coached the investors and Joe to help them build a deeper relationship. Some of Joe's initiatives were starting to bear fruit, giving investors greater confidence that they'd picked the right guy to run the company.

As Joe got stronger, Keith got weaker—and he, not Joe, soon got moved out of the business. Three years later, Joe had grown the company 50 percent and doubled earnings, then sold the company in a successful deal. Joe is well into another CEO role now and has been proactively building alignment and trust with the board from day one.

Managing the board can feel like a daunting and at times even frustrating task to most new CEOs. The board is an important asset to a new CEO, but it may not be functioning as well as it could. With the advice in this chapter, you will walk into the CEO role better equipped to create the best-case scenario: an active partnership with a group of thoughtful, experienced individuals who can push your thinking to help the business and you perform at full potential.

How Not to Do It

CEOs who fail to partner with the board tend to fit one of the following four personas.

SUPER OPERATOR: "MY JOB IS TO RUN THE BUSINESS. AS LONG AS RESULTS ARE GOOD, THE BOARD WILL TAKE CARE OF ITSELF."

To the "Super Operator," board management is "noise" and annoying bureaucracy, serviced with the bare-minimum interaction. Eager to move forward quickly and efficiently, a Super Operator soon learns the dire cost of not bringing the board along. Seemingly simple decisions devolve into long, tedious discussions, ultimately blocking progress.

THE HEISMAN: "I'VE GOT THIS."

"Heismans" have a strong need for both being and looking in charge. They keep the board at arm's length, especially when things aren't going well.

As one of the board chairs reflected on a CEO who had recently been fired: "He treated the board like mushrooms. Kept us in the dark and fed us crap. That simply couldn't continue." Boards quickly lose trust and tolerate the Heisman CEO only as long as he or she delivers outstanding results. The smallest fumble quickly escalates to an early departure.

THE POLLYANNA: "GREAT, GREAT, GREAT, NO PROBLEM!"

Eager to score a perfect grade, a "Pollyanna" avoids the tough, awkward, uncomfortable discussions. Board members are initially happy: It's all good news. But when the cracks show up, and Pollyanna glosses over them, the board grows increasingly impatient and distrustful. Pollyannas also tend to overpromise and underdeliver. Their optimism and desire to prove themselves often lead to unrealistic expectations, setting up their team and them for failure.

THE OVERSHARER: "BY THE WAY . . ."

Overly needy for board approval, an "Oversharer" runs to the board with every mundane issue, pulling them so far into the trees that they can't see the forest. Board members can and should help a CEO with perspective, but when lines between governance and management get blurred, chaos ensues. Teams chafe under CEOs who can't work with the board in a way that keeps board members focused on governance and out of daily operations.

Who Is Really in Charge?

Your first puzzle to solve: What are the power dynamics on this board? Who are the strongest influencers on the board, and how do they wield power? On paper, this is straightforward. The board chair (or lead director) is often (but not always) the most influential member, followed by committee heads, with governance and compensation typically being the two most powerful committees. And if your company is owned by investors, deal partners generally outrank operators. These rules of thumb are a helpful start, but in practice the rules of power can be idiosyncratic and unwritten.

New CEOs often feel they need to prove themselves before they earn their seat at the board table. They are often reluctant to establish their leadership role with the board early enough. Here's the paradox: The more power you claim (within reason and in the right way), the more power you will earn. Board members are first to point out that a CEO who is looking for the board to set direction is not fully doing the job he's been hired for.

Take the experience of one first-time CEO we coached, "Mark." Mark was the head of a midsize consumer products business. Mark didn't inherit a functioning board as much as a firing squad of seventeen with no commander. The prior CEO had been fired, and only a slim majority of board members had backed Mark's promotion to CEO. The board chairman supported Mark but was on his way out, and his political capital had been depleted. Three board members were actively lobbying for the chairman role. One of them, "Oliver," was a meddling micromanager determined to undermine Mark. Several capable board members were disengaged, and some were looking to resign, unable to contribute amid so much dysfunction.

More than anything, Mark wanted to focus on the business. He needed board support for a major acquisition and had a complex IT decision to consider. With the board in disarray, decisions weren't moving forward. He anxiously lamented the hand he was dealt but knew he couldn't ignore it. If Oliver won the chairman title, Mark was prepared to quit. Mark turned to us in angst and exasperation. He initially thought that as a newly appointed CEO, his role was to patiently let the board sort itself out. Mark loathed to be seen as overreaching, but he was emphatic that the company needed a well-functioning board to succeed. After we carefully analyzed the situation, it was increasingly clear that the board wouldn't get there on their own. We helped Mark understand the power dynamics on the board, find his voice, and gradually guide the board to a successful outcome for the business.

Getting the right chairperson in place and neutralizing Oliver was Mark's first concern. We examined the sources of Oliver's power on the board. First, Oliver had what you might call "bullhorn power." Without a strong chairman or lead director, a mediocre board member can capture undue influence by forcefully asserting himself in meetings. Share of voice often translates into real power and influence.

Second, Oliver had "busybody power." He inserted himself in

managing key initiatives, convening meetings, and minding the administrative details. He was at the center of every conversation, giving him ample opportunity to build relationships and lobby behind the scenes.

Oliver had a lot of informal power and was on a mission to become the chairman. Mark was up against a big challenge. Fortunately, Mark was one of the most gifted CEOs we've met when it comes to **Engaging for Impact**. Rather than confront Oliver directly, we advised Mark to focus his energies on building relationships with capable board members who'd been previously disengaged. Mark enlisted each of them in a business initiative that fit their skills and interests. He made their roles clear and visibly appreciated their contributions. The mood on the board started to shift. With board agenda refocused from squabbling to business priorities, Oliver's voice was muted by the more capable contributors empowered by Mark. Not one to give up, the less relevance Oliver had in business conversations, the more vehemently he politicked behind the scenes. When the time came to select the new chair, Mark worked hand-in-hand with the outgoing chairman and head of the governance committee to put in place an objective and transparent process with clear selection criteria. Oliver didn't even make the list of finalists. His ego-driven gamesmanship was so extreme, other board members reached their own conclusions. He had self-destructed. As we wrote this chapter, Oliver was retiring from the board.

Mark never imagined that his first task as a CEO would be to help restructure the board. Had the situation not been so dire and so risky for the company, he might have shied away from asserting that much leadership with the board in his first year. He learned a valuable lesson. *The CEO may not have the formal authority to lead the board, but he has the responsibility to put the company on a path to success, even if that means taking risks with the board.*

No matter whether your board functions as a well-oiled machine or suffers from a *Game of Thrones* level of intrigue, your job is to understand what you walked into and how to engage with the board to make the business successful.

The board dynamic is far more complex than that of a simple collection of individuals, and it needs to be understood. To start with, find out how the board has functioned in the past: How often did they meet; how often did they interface with the previous CEO and other management team members; what level of detail did they involve themselves in; were there other means by which information flowed outside of formal meetings; how were decisions made; how did the board tackle the last crisis?

As you become acquainted with your board, be on the lookout for these common archetypes among board members:

- **The Engaged Partner:** This is the board member you want. The CEOs we interviewed told us that 63 percent of their board members are engaged partners.[4] This board member has good judgment, invests the time to understand your business, and provides candid, thoughtful perspectives and pushback that help you and the business succeed. He understands that his role is to provide advice and accountability, not to manage the business. Proactively look to develop and add engaged partners so that they comprise at least three-quarters of your board. Lean on them to help push your thinking and help you be the best CEO you can be.

- **The Quiet Expert:** This board member has good ideas and relevant experience but won't weigh in on board debates unless you specifically ask her to. She's unlikely to take risks or stick her neck out to support you. Typically, the quiet expert has more competence than influence. Create structured opportunities for the quiet expert to add value. For example, if she is an M&A expert, and you are looking to raise your game in M&A, ask her to meet with your team to share best practices and to help you get an independent point of view on your team and approach in this area. Proactively ask for her perspective in board discussions within her area of expertise.

- **The Rubber Stamper:** This is a board member who follows the lead of the CEO and the most powerful board members. His primary goal is to establish an agreeable reputation that gets him hired to other boards. When conflicts and challenges arise, seemingly innocuous rubber stampers can become liabilities, because their primary instinct is self-protection; they are, therefore, not reliable allies. Ignore a rubber stamper at your peril. From early on, understand whom they hold in high regard. As big decisions come up, rubber stampers will be looking for indications of where you and other influential board members are leaning.

- **The Micromanager:** This board member is eager to prove his value and, at times, superiority. His actions can undermine the CEO and be disruptive to board dynamics. If a micromanager is well intentioned and competent but misguided about his role, actively enlist him in activities that are helpful to the company and to you. Set clear parameters, and give him candid feedback on what is and isn't helpful to you and the company. If he is disruptive, engage your chairperson or lead director to help coach him. If all else fails, work with the governance committee to remove him from the board.

- **The CEO-in-waiting:** This is the person who wants your job. You'll often find one or even more board members who would like to run the company. Sometimes that person is actually brought on board as a contingency plan. Other times she has "unfinished business" in her own career and is eager to prove she could do the job better, whether or not she'll ever get a shot. When you are offered a CEO job, ask who else wanted the job and how prepared is the chair/lead director to address any issues should that board member be disruptive. As hard as it is, approach those board members initially with an open mind. Understand their contribution, power on the board, and motivations. If they bring value, find a way to work with them. If they are disruptive and seek to undermine you, work with the chair/lead director to move them out when possible.

- **The Activist:** This is someone who is put on the board by a hedge fund or private equity firm to drive a specific agenda or is an activist investor himself. Don't try to win over activists with your relationship skills. Their primary allegiance is to the hedge fund, not you. Instead, understand the agenda they represent and look for common ground.

Now, with the scan of surroundings completed, you are ready to move from learning what you have walked into to building an effective partnership with the board.

The Best Questions No One Asks
Their Board Members

CEOs in their first two years feel especially vulnerable and eager to prove themselves. As a result, they often take a "report out" posture with the board: dutifully reporting results, summarizing actions completed and milestones met, and pedantically following up on board members' suggestions. The very same CEOs who can effortlessly charm a customer and have built enviable relationships with their previous bosses seem to lose their mojo when dealing with the all-powerful board. Recall the lessons from Chapter 3, "Engage for Impact," and Chapter 8, "Close the Deal." They can be simply summarized as: "If you want to win people over, first understand who they are and what they care about." Sounds simple enough? Yet it is too often forgotten in the anxiety-ridden first two years at the top.

Kim was recently called to Chicago to coach a CEO of a $75 million private equity–backed retailer whose lead director's frustration was moving toward detonation. When she arrived, the CEO's attitude was combative. As he saw it, he was hamstrung by a board of finance types who had no respect for the level of experimentation needed to achieve the desired growth. Kim listened to him for an hour while asking some basic questions about his plans for the business, his expectations for organic growth, and the like. He finished with an exasperated request: "Just tell me what to do to get this board off my back!"

So Kim asked a new question: "Have you ever tried to put yourself in the lead director's head? Do you know how his broader portfolio is doing and how this business fits in?"

No, he admitted.

"Then let me tell you about your lead director. He's young, just like you. This is one of his very first big investments. He's proving himself, just like you. He has to work hard to get his investors to trust him with their capital. That's how he invests in companies like yours. His partners want to see him driving this company and you to results. They want to know you're not making haphazard bets. Numbers are his one and only opportunity to show that. Meanwhile, in an hour of talking about the business with me, you haven't used a single number. You want him to be comfortable with risky moves? Then talk to him in a way that shows you appreciate where he's coming from. You've got to speak spreadsheet to him, or you're never going to earn the trust you need to be bold."

Succeeding with your board (or with anyone else, for that matter) starts with understanding how *their* performance is measured and motivated. With that grounding, you also need to go beyond the numbers. Get to know your board members one-on-one and understand their context and their pressures, dreams, and fears. So often in problematic CEO-board relationships, the fundamental problem is a lack of shared context. Here you are, playing the highest-stakes game of your career, with a roomful of people you barely know. They feel the exact same way about you. You need them to trust you. Trust is built on alignment of interest, credibility, and familiarity. Underinvest in any of these three ingredients and the breaches in the relationship are sure to show up at a time when you need board support the most.

Susan Cameron, the former CEO and current board chair of Reynolds American Inc. (RAI), led the tobacco giant with a board of accomplished leaders—former House Speaker John Boehner, former Univar CEO John Zillmer, and Jerome Abelman, the general counsel for British American Tobacco, which during Susan's tenure owned 42 percent of RAI, to name a few heavyweights. Susan describes having had supportive, productive relationships with them all, but not by accident: She invested in a one-on-one relationship with each member. Aside from regular conversations, she visited each of them in person every other year.

"I made an explicit gesture to go to them," she says. "Doing it on their turf, they're more comfortable," she says. "It shows you value them." From Susan's point of view, every new CEO needs to set aside time to communicate directly with her board members as individuals, "so they get to know you and they understand your priorities and character. If nothing else, reaching out and discussing things with them will give them a level of comfort, and they will support you." In other words, adding familiarity to the relationship can cement support, which could be the difference between whether they back or balk at your next strategic initiative.

Think of these meetings as your chance, at last, to interview *them*, albeit in a comfortable context that demonstrates respect. Your goal is to build a relationship and to establish the foundation for alignment and trust with the board. Here are some of the questions to ask your board members one-on-one within six months of your hiring:

- **What excites you the most about being on this board?** With these questions, you're looking for clues to their primary motivations: *Relevance? Status? Stimulation? Compensation?* Most board members genuinely want to add value, but understanding *why* can help you engage them more deeply.

- **How did you get connected with this board?** The answer may lend insight about whether they're likely to have an independent point of view or be beholden to a founder or investor.

- **Whom on the board do you talk with most often?** This seemingly innocent question is a giant tell, often answering a key question: *Who's influencing whom?* This question will help you understand the behind-the-scenes coalitions so that you can manage them and bring back-channel conversations into the light.

- **Where have you focused your time and efforts in the past?** This question will help you understand the person's competencies and also shed light on how (and how well) the board has functioned prior to your arrival.

- **Where and how would you like to engage in the future?** This is an opportunity to proactively engage board members on issues where they feel they can add value. It will ease their doubts about how to participate and be useful and also give you a clearer picture of how much of their time and attention you're likely to get.

- **What does success look like, for the company and for me as CEO, in one year? In three years?** This is the start of many conversations you'll have around expectations and strategy.

Invest in these relationships appropriately, and you should never have an iota of doubt about where you stand with your board. Regular one-on-ones are your chance to "connect the dots," as Susan Cameron puts it, and make sure everyone's belted in and along for the ride.

From Lunch Function to Functional

As you have seen above, the initial investment into understanding board members plants very important seeds for a strong partnership. To bear fruits, these seeds must be continually watered and fertilized through deliberate ongoing engagement and communication.

Kevin Cox of American Express likes to show CEOs the chart we've reproduced for you on the next page. The first CEO he showed it to immediately balked: "The board shouldn't be at the center; that's giving it too much prominence." But that's exactly where it belongs, Cox told him. "If I were to animate this, you would draw lines going

THE CEO ECOSYSTEM

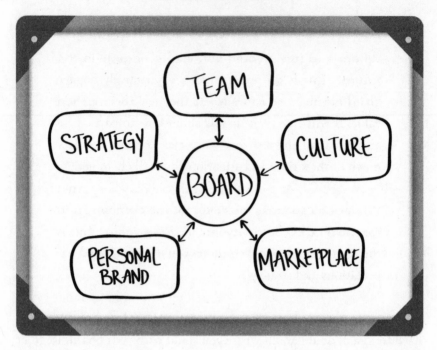

back and forth. You are constantly pinging the board, for example on strategy. Develop the strategy, go back and triangulate it with the board. Take their feedback. Adapt it."

Reade Fahs, the CEO of National Vision, serves on nine boards. Reade believes it is the CEO's job to ensure that his board sleeps better at night. As tight as you may be with your board, as earnest as you are about the spirit of partnership, there is still a need for influence and persuasion. There should be a robust flow of information to ensure there are no surprises in board meetings. Each director should have a preview and a chance to voice concerns, giving you time to prepare your thoughts and anticipate questions and debate. A lack of information creates a vacuum that board members will fill, says Reade. In silence, people will assume the worst. Then, when problems arise, the board rushes in to manage things without giving you time to solve them.

You have to remember that you are living and breathing the business. Any given decision you make is the result of hundreds of data points that all add up to what, in that context, seems obvious to you. In contrast, your board member who is not as deeply involved in the business sees a blank space between the problem and your proposed solution. It's on you to communicate with enough frequency and depth to fill that space. Here is a short list of practices that have helped CEOs build effective partnerships with boards:

Align on what success looks like. It sounds obvious, but often we see CEOs trip up over this because they avoid the tough conversations that emerge once you dig into details. Failure could be fatal: One study of 246 board members found that alignment of the board and CEO on strategy and goals was the most important determinant of success or failure of the CEO.[5]

Jason Blessing, the CEO of Plex Systems, told us about his challenges with board members and financial sponsors over how to measure performance early on. The cure, he's found, is to be as specific as possible as soon as possible. He learned this the hard way as the CEO of a growing SaaS business. Everyone agreed that customer retention was an incredibly important metric. But over the course of several board meetings, it became clear that the way he and the board were measuring and interpreting the results of their retention metric were quite different, causing unnecessary friction. To move forward, Blessing met one-on-one with each board member and the CFO, getting everyone on the same page about how they'd measure retention going forward and what was the range of acceptable outcomes. Looking back, Blessing only wished he had pushed the issue much sooner, at the very first moment he saw that there might be a discrepancy in thinking.

Align on the rules of engagement early. Be up front and explicit in creating clarity around roles: yours and theirs. Reade

Fahs shared his list of the six responsibilities of a good board. They are to:

1) Hire and fire the CEO and hold her accountable.

2) Agree on strategic vision and plans.

3) Agree to an annual budget.

4) Advise on any substantive risks.

5) Approve the annual audit.

6) Don't get in the way.

That's it—everything else is at the discretion of the CEO to involve the board. But it's up to you to make that clear, particularly if you're dealing with an inexperienced board. Find out up front if they have special concerns: What *can't* the board be surprised by? What decisions, at what level, would they prefer to be involved in?

Assign homework. The best way to productively engage directors and bring the best of their expertise to the business is by setting clear and real priorities for each board member. You already have committee charters, but does each of your board members know what, specifically, you are counting on her or him for?

Elena once counseled a CEO who had a potentially valuable board member who was ready to resign. "Give him something meaningful to do!" she told her client. "Something he'll enjoy and that will add real value." The CEO thought Elena was way off base, because this board member's stated reason for leaving was not having the time to contribute. But the CEO agreed to try it, asking him to lead a board task force on a major acquisition, his area of expertise. Sure enough, the board member walked out of the room reenergized and excited to contribute. "He told me he'd never been more excited about this board!" the CEO said.

Partner with your chairperson or lead director. Some CEOs make the mistake of thinking that a weak board chair or lead director will give them more power, but the opposite is true: It takes a strong, credible leader with time and discipline to corral a group of peers, all of whom should be coming to the table with distinct points of view. If you align with your chairperson, she'll be your best partner for harnessing different viewpoints to push the business forward, not disintegrate into unproductive conflict.

Bring in fresh talent. The board that hired you may or may not be the right board to support you as CEO. Whether the business has scaled from $35 million to $500 million or whether your agenda is a significantly different one from that of the previous regime, the board is unlikely to be the same one you will need going forward. Board development is a very delicate dance and can backfire easily if not well handled. Ideally, company bylaws and power dynamics on the board allow you to bring on board a couple of trusted and competent people in the first couple of years.

When Vicki Escarra was the CEO of Feeding America, she proactively rebuilt her board. She started the conversations with her chair, David Taylor, the current CEO of P&G, about the composition of the board during her very first week.

Call out unproductive behavior. Jack Krol, the former chairman and CEO of DuPont, told us that he found that board meetings tended to be dominated by two or three voices. The other members were silent, because they were either not paying attention or unsure of what they had to contribute. Jack adopted the practice of calling on each member individually. That kept everyone thinking actively. By doing this, he found out that the silent folks were often the source of great ideas.

Take a shareholder's perspective. An investor recently shared that the company had fired a CEO because he was acting like an advocate for employees instead of a shareholder for the business. Ultimately, a CEO's job is to create value for shareholders. A CEO is uniquely at the "pinch point" among many constituencies with often divergent interests. You may need to talk the board down from unrealistic expectations while pushing the team up to reach higher levels of performance. To deliver, a CEO must think and act like an owner.

How to Deliver Bad News

Even the highest-achieving CEOs can stumble at the moment when they're most vulnerable: when they need to deliver bad news. Faced with a painful setback, they suddenly resemble John Wayne, seized by the impulse to ride solo until he can fix what's broken. Or they may genuinely think they have the issue under control. Solve the problem first, they think, *then* report to the board. Delivering bad news is never easy. In the earlier chapters, we shared that mistakes and even major blowups are common.

"Communicate early and communicate often," says Krista Endsley, recounting the hardest, most stressful time in her entire career. It was September of her first year as CEO of the nonprofit financial management software firm Abila. She'd sat down to review her third-quarter P&L statement, and she nearly had a heart attack: They were going to miss their bottom line at the end of the year by $800,000. She was blindsided by what was a "dramatic failure."

In hindsight, the problem was obvious: She didn't have the right support around her. She had never hired a CFO. Her VP of finance was inexperienced and, like Krista, had never worked with a board before. "Having a new relationship with the board, I didn't know how or when to communicate things," she says. She was also investing energy explaining in gory, 150-slide detail the operations and activities of the business. Meanwhile, the financial investors who comprised the full board just wanted to understand what was driving value and by how much. "It was a miserable time," she recalls. "They honestly had every right to get rid of me."

She walked into the next board meeting in Austin, Texas, unsure whether she'd have a job by the time it was over. She shared the P&L, and, though she was frustrated, she owned the results. But then she asked the board to look forward with her. The shortfall had not shaken her conviction that their strategy was strong. "I assured them. I showed them plans," she said. "I knew that we were doing the right thing for the future growth of the business." And deep down, she believed she had the experience needed to run the business.

In that meeting, Krista did everything right. She didn't show up and lay an open-ended problem at the board's feet. Instead, she accepted fault, transparently laid out the facts, and offered a clear, confident plan to go forward, including strengthening the team around her. The only thing she could have done better was to see trouble early enough to be able to say, "Hey, this is coming," and ask for help. Trouble was, she didn't have the experience to know what help to ask for.

The board decided to stand behind her. As the months went on, in addition to hiring the support she needed, she added an external board member, a fellow CEO who had a strong sales background but who also understood operations and could mediate between the two perspectives. The conversation at board meetings went from detailed reporting with a retrospective view to a forward-looking perspective of leading indicators (such as customer churn or potential deals in the pipeline) and how they would drive value.

By the time she stepped down as Abila's CEO in 2017, she had added two product lines, fully integrated three acquisitions, and more than tripled the size of the business. She exited 2016 with double-digit growth for the year. "With the right team, the right bets, and me being a better CEO, we've turned the entire business," she says with humility. "It's got to be how people climb big mountains. You do it one step at a time, and you look back from the top, and you're, like, 'Wow, when did that happen?'" At the time, bad news seemed like an unsurmountable obstacle, but, taking the long view, it was actually a stepping stone paving the path to Krista's success. Mostly because she quickly learned from those early experiences to get ahead of bad news.

Successful CEOs stand out not for lack of setbacks but for how they deal with them. Here are the key lessons from the CEOs we have advised and interviewed:

- Communicate early and often to ensure no surprises.

- Own the issues, and aim for a tone that is balanced and focused on course-correcting the business; don't be overly apologetic or defensive.

- Don't be defensive. Clear and succinct root cause analysis shows you own the issue. Excessive explanations that sound like excuses and deflect responsibility will only put you deeper in the hole and erode trust and credibility.

- Apologize if an apology is warranted and then move on. Don't let your energy wane or your tone become obsequious.

- Discuss forward-looking early-warning operating metrics, not just the rear-view prior-month revenue and profits. By the time you miss P&L targets, it is too late to adjust course.

- Come with a plan that identifies what is happening, the ultimate impact to the business, the root cause, and the roadmap to address it. If the plan is not yet clear, discuss what you need to know or what help you require to get there.

- An occasional "I don't know. We'll look into it and get back to you" builds a lot more trust and credibility than trying to wing it.

Make It Count

Even the best CEOs at times lament the time and energy it takes to build an effective partnership with the board. How you work with your board will to a large degree determine whether they are the strong arms that support you—or the ones that push you out. When done well, the payoff for the business and for you as the CEO is well worth the investment.

We asked Art Collins to name a CEO who stands out for building a productive partnership with a board. Art has worked with over a dozen boards and numerous CEOs during a career that included the chairman and CEO roles at Medtronic and director positions at a wide range of nonprofit and for-profit boards such as Boeing, U.S. Bancorp, Alcoa, and Cargill. He instantly named Richard Davis, former chairman and CEO of Minneapolis-based U.S. Bancorp, as a gold standard.

Richard grew up as a latchkey kid in Los Angeles and rose from a bank teller to CEO. He transformed U.S. Bancorp from a patchwork of regional banks into the fifth-largest commercial bank in the United States. During his more than twenty years on the U.S. Bancorp board, Art worked closely with Richard, serving as chair of the governance, finance, and compensation committees and as lead director at different points during Richard's CEO tenure. Among the world-class CEOs Art has observed, Richard stands out as a phenomenal communicator who engaged deeply with the board to gain alignment on priorities, shared his views and concerns, and continually sought candid board feedback, which he then put into action. Once he became CEO, Richard immediately reached out to each board member to obtain views on what was going well and what needed to change. Art reflects: "Richard's communication was always transparent, proactive, timely, and complete. He candidly shared unvarnished facts as best he knew them. If he had a recommendation on an issue, we heard it early. If he wasn't yet clear on the course of action, he always laid out his plan to figure out the solution and then told us when we should expect to hear back from him. Very importantly, we never felt that Richard was trying to sell us a bill of goods or spinning facts to support his point of view. As a result, the board trusted Richard."

This trust and alignment with the board made all the difference during the financial crisis of 2008. Richard was barely into his second year as CEO when the country spiraled into the Great Recession, with banks being hit especially hard. While many corporate boards were playing defense, focused on risk mitigation, Richard advocated that U.S. Bancorp continue to invest in infrastructure and customer support in order to position the company for growth. Art recalls that trying time for the bank: "The global financial system was in peril. Most of our competitors were retrenching. While we were in much better shape than others in the industry, we still were under tremendous pressure to cut costs. However, Richard saw opportunity and wanted to invest to better serve customers and capture share from competitors. We debated Richard's proposal at the board, recognizing that if the increased expense profile didn't sufficiently result in revenue growth, our profits and stock price would suffer. It was an especially big bet at the time because we didn't know how long it would take before the economy would begin to recover. Richard was completely candid with the board about opportunities and risks during this time of unbelievable pressure. The board ultimately supported his investment program in large part because he was honest and we trusted his judgment."

The growth strategy implemented during the financial crisis was a turning point for U.S. Bancorp, setting the corporation on a path to grow into one of the largest and most profitable banks in the country, with 58,000 employees and $21 billion in revenue.[6] The financial company the Motley Fool reported recently: "As hundreds of banks failed during and after the crisis, and many more were forced to sell out at a discount or to egregiously dilute shareholders by issuing capital at the nadir of the crisis, U.S. Bancorp never once recorded a quarterly net loss."[7]

Having successfully passed the CEO baton to Andy Cecere, Richard is now contemplating the next chapter in his professional life. He reflected on how the U.S. Bancorp board helped him to mature and succeed as a CEO. "Having accomplished leaders like Art and others provide an outside perspective, constructively challenge me, and push my thinking has definitely made me a more effective leader and a better CEO. When I stepped into the CEO position, Art told me that I should always view the board as a valuable resource rather than a threat. Well, I took his advice to heart, and there's no doubt in my mind that the board's collective knowledge and counsel allowed me to make better decisions that in turn benefited our employees, customers, and shareholders."

Armed with the insights in this chapter, you have greater odds than most first-time CEOs of turning your relationship with the board from a source of anxiety to a competitive edge for your business and a source of growth and support for you.

KEY TAKEAWAYS

1. Take an active role in building a highly effective board, starting early in your CEO tenure.

2. Get "up close and personal" with each board member. Understand individual needs, agendas, and interests. Gauge group interactions and power dynamics on the board.

3. Engage board members actively to support the business and align with them on clear roles and rules of engagement.

4. Avoid surprises!

From Ordinary to Extraordinary

There is no passion to be found playing small.
—Nelson Mandela

WE ARE OFTEN ASKED TO NAME THE "PERFECT" CEO. HAVING PER-
sonally advised or assessed over 300, we've learned that the only perfect CEOs we know are the ones we don't know well. Successful CEOs
come from all backgrounds. Many of the CEOs regarded as extraordinary today had very ordinary beginnings. Every single one of them
lived through messy struggles and devastating defeats—much like
those you may have already experienced in your own career.

In this book we have introduced you to many CEOs to illustrate
and enhance the insights from ten years of research based on the track
records of over 17,000 leaders. We hope that you see what we see,
amid the drama of their stories, victories, and stumbles: The lessons
of CEOs serve everyone. Whether you aspire to lead an organization
or simply to advance in your career and contribute, this book is your
opportunity to learn directly from the wisdom and experience of the
most successful people in business.

As we complete this journey together, we find ourselves coming back to this question of the "perfect" CEO. While a perfect CEO doesn't exist, there is a particular type of leader that earns our highest regard.

These are what we call "high-purpose, high-performance" leaders. In addition to mastering the four CEO Genome behaviors, these leaders create extraordinary *value* for shareholders as an outcome of two distinguishing actions. They lead with clarity of purpose, and they create a culture grounded in strong *values*.

We've been fortunate to encounter several high-purpose, high-performance leaders. Raj Gupta (whom you met in Chapter 10) is one of them. Raj was raised in India as one of six children of a civil engineer father and a homemaker mother.[1] Who could know that he would one day helm a Fortune 500 company, much less that he would lead Rohm and Haas to become the second-best-performing Fortune 500 stock during his decade-long tenure, a mark of **Reliable Delivery** that most could only dream of. Raj transformed Rohm and Haas from a midsized specialty chemical company into an industry leader. At the very outset, he acted **Decisively**, completing three acquisitions in a single quarter. The Dow Jones Industrial average lost 27 percent of its value between 1999 and 2009. Over that same period under Raj's leadership, Rohm and Haas's stock shot up 117 percent.[2] Raj produced these victories while facing many of the exact same hazards that have torpedoed many CEOs. Since successfully selling Rohm and Haas to Dow, Raj has dedicated himself to service. In addition to his charitable activities, he has supported twenty-four CEOs as an advisor and has served as a director on fifteen boards, including Vanguard, HP, Delphi Automotive, and others.

When asked to reflect on his proudest achievements, Raj happily agreed to get on a Skype call with us at 7:00 A.M. "I still wake up at 4:00 A.M. every day," he says. "Back at Rohm and Haas, mornings were my most productive time. Old habits die hard."

When we spoke, the question of legacy was fresh on Raj's mind. He had just helped his younger daughter, Vanita Gupta, CEO of the

Leadership Conference on Civil and Human Rights, host a charity event. Many of Raj's former colleagues flew to Philadelphia from all over the country to support him, his daughter, and a mission they all believed in. "I firmly believe that this country stands on two fundamental principles: rule of law and equal opportunity for all," says Raj. "As an immigrant, I have been a direct beneficiary of those principles. It's my duty and the duty of every leader to ensure those values remain strong. These are the same values that enabled me to rise to the top. The same values I embedded into the Rohm and Haas culture as CEO."

You can immediately see those values reflected in the team Raj built, with women, Latinos, African Americans, Asians, and Europeans all strongly represented. It was one of the most diverse leadership teams among Fortune 500 companies at the time. In years since, thirteen of Raj's direct reports have become CEOs of companies all over the world, a powerful legacy itself.

"It didn't matter where you came from," says Raj. "As long as you delivered, there were no limitations to how far you could go at Rohm and Haas. That's how we exceeded all expectations as a business. That's why we've become known as a 'CEO factory.' Long-term shareholder returns are the ultimate metric for a CEO. But returns are an output, not an input. We focused on building a great team and on doing the right thing for our customers and for our 23,000 employees worldwide, whose families counted on Rohm and Haas for their livelihood."

For Raj, this mission was and is personal. We all know the CEO role brings power, perks, rewards, and accolades. And yet, Raj says the only thing he misses about the job is the people. Raj knew close to one thousand employees around the world by their first names. "My favorite part of being a CEO was making a difference in the life of individuals, encouraging them, helping them realize their potential beyond what they thought was possible. That's what I've done post-retirement with my board work, my book, and advising, teaching, and mentoring," he says.

Raj's story is extraordinary but not exceptional. *High-purpose, high-performance leaders get up in the morning to achieve better outcomes for others.* CEOs and other leaders can have a powerful impact on hundreds, thousands, and sometimes millions of lives.

In closing, we hope that you help us achieve our purpose in writing this book. Each of us is a mother of two young children. Like any parent anywhere in the world, our biggest hope is that our children grow up in a safe, fair, and prosperous world where they can realize their own potential. Leaders have a disproportionate power to shape this world. Leaders helped put a man on the moon. Leaders helped bring down the Berlin Wall. Leaders unlocked the secrets of strep bacteria to create possible cures for genetic disorders. But leaders can also build walls, stymie progress, and marginalize people.

We want to help the good leaders win. With this book, we are eager to encourage and help you achieve your full potential, no matter your starting point or the ultimate destination, so that you can be the leader who makes the world a better place.

Stare down your doubts and flaws, and use the lessons in this book to overcome them. We want you to see what we, at the close of this adventure together with you, believe is a demonstrable fact:

You, too, are a CEO. At least, you could be.

And remember to pass on to others the advice and support that helped you succeed.

acknowledgments

To our ghSMART clients who allow us the privilege to serve as their leadership advisors.

To the fearless leaders of our firm, Geoff Smart and Randy Street, without whom this would not be possible.

To the leaders who shared their perspective and stories with us, including: Bill Amelio, Andrew Appel, Claire (Yum) Arnold, Shanti Atkins, Craig Barnes, Dom Barton, Tom Bell, Madeline Bell, Mary Berner, Jason Blessing, Jerry Bowe, Susan Cameron, Karen Cariss, Bob Carr, Simon Castellanos, Stephen Cerrone, Zia Chishti, Amy Churgin, Scott Clawson, David Coleman, Art Collins, Scott Cook, Kevin Cox, Richard Davis, Will Dean, Jim Donald, Ann Drake, Krista Endsley, Tom Erickson, Vicki Escarra, Reade Fahs, Mike Feiner, Neil Fiske, Richard Foster, Bill Fry, Atul Gawande, Ben Geyerhahn, Shikhar Ghosh, Matthew Goldstein, Lisa Gordon, Steve Gorman, Patrick Gross, Raj Gupta, Ted Hall, Robert Hanson, Jim Harrison, Fred Hassan, Frank Hermance, Chuck Hill, Jean Hoffman, Ali Jameel, Vyomesh (VJ) Joshi, Steve Kaufman, Robert Keane, Jim Kilts, Nataly Kogan, Wendy Kopp, Matt Kramer, John (Jack) Krol, Cidalia Luis-Akbar, Damien McDonald, Tom Monahan, Eva Moskowitz, Leo Mullin, Woodrow Myers, Elizabeth Nabel, Christian Nahas, Lara O'Connor Hodgson, Susan Packard, Doug Peterson, Mary Petrovich, Nancy Phillips, Will Powell, Larry Prior, Ian Read, Ron Ross, Seth

Segel, Glen Senk, Doug Shipman, Andy Silvernail, Matthew Simoncini, Don Slager, Brad Smith, Jim Smith, Robert Spano, Lynda Spillane, Kurt Strovink, Sally Susman, Ashu Suyash, Dan Tinker, Bhairav Trivedi, Elisa Villanueva Beard, Gene Wade, Maynard Webb, Christophe Weber, Rob Wenger, Ashley Wheater, Anne Williams-Isom, David Works, Dawn Zier, John Zillmer.

To our research teams, including Steve Kaplan, Morten Sørensen, Arthur Spirling, Andrew Peterson, Leslie Rith-Najarian, Kimie Ono, and Lisa Hecht, and to Fiona McNeill, Beverly Brown, and the rest of the team at SAS.

To Lorin Rees, our literary agent.

To Roger Scholl, our editor, and the team at Currency.

To Mark Fortier, our publicist, and his team.

To Amy Bernstein, Susan Donovan, Sara Green Carmichael, and Amy Poftak for your laser-sharp insights and relentless standards of excellence in challenging us to hone our ideas.

To Sara Grace and Tahl Raz, without whom this book would still be a glimmer in our eyes and who have made *The CEO Next Door* so much better than we originally imagined.

To insightful thought partners who reviewed manuscript drafts and helped us in other insightful ways, including George Anders, Karen Dillon, Mary Anne Nahas, Howard Means, Nathan Means, Stephanie Pitts, Paige Ross, Mukul Pandya, Glenn Rosenkoetter, Jackie Reses, and Andrew Feiler, each of whom generously offered their time and care to give us exceedingly helpful feedback.

To Jeanette Messina and Beth Olenski, without whom we would have lost our way.

To our colleagues, many of whom read early versions of the chapters and who are helping in various ways to amplify the positive impact leaders have on this world and to bring *The CEO Next Door* to life. We are particularly thankful for the hundreds of hours that Nicole Wong, Steve Kincaid, Vamsi Tetali, Jason Fiftal, Claudio Waller, Sanja Kos, and Kim Lemmonds Henry freely gave to the effort.

chapter 1
Unlocking the Secrets of the CEO Genome

1. "Highest-rated CEOs 2017: Employees Choice," Glassdoor, 2017, https://www.glassdoor.com/Award/Highest-Rated-CEOs-LST_KQ0,18.htm.

2. Geoff Smart, Randy Street, and Alan Foster. *Power Score: Your Formula for Leadership Success* (New York: Ballantine Books, 2015), 56.

3. "2014 Study of CEOs, Governance, and Success," Strategy&, 2014, https://www.strategyand.pwc.com/media/file/2014-Study-of-CEOs-Governance-and-Success.pdf.

4. Nelson D. Schwartz, "The Decline of the Baronial C.E.O.," *New York Times*, June 17, 2017.

5. "Statistics of U.S. Businesses: 2008," U.S. Census Bureau, 2008, https://www.census.gov/epcd/susb/latest/us/US--.HTM.

6. Katheryn Kobe, "Small Business GDP: Update 2002–2010," Small Business Administration, January 2012, https://www.sba.gov/content/small-business-gdp-update-2002-2010.

7. "Statistics of U.S. Businesses: 2008," U.S. Census Bureau, 2008.

8. George Anders, "Tough CEOs Often Most Successful, A Study Finds," *Wall Street Journal*, November 19, 2007.

9. Steven N. Kaplan and Morten Sørensen, "Are CEOs Different? Characteristics of Top Managers," Columbia Business School Research Paper Series, presented at Paris Finance Meeting, December 2016, https://ssrn.com/abstract=2747691.

10. Brett Collins, "Projections of Federal Tax Return Filings: Calendar Years

2011–2018," Internal Revenue Service, 2012, https://www.irs.gov/pub/irs-soi/12rswinbulreturnfilings.pdf.

11. "CEO Genome Project," ghSMART, 1995–2017, http://ceogenome.com/about/.

12. Kaplan and Sørensen, "Are CEOs Different? Characteristics of Top Managers," Columbia Business School Research Paper Series, presented at the Paris Finance Meeting, December 2016, http://ssrn.com/abstract =2747691.

13. "Women CEOs of the S&P 500," Catalyst, August 4, 2017, http://www.catalyst.org/knowledge/women-ceos-sp-500.

14. F. L. Schmidt and J. E. Hunter, "The Validity and Utility of Selection Methods in Personnel Psychology: Practical and Theoretical Implications of 85 Years of Research Findings," *Psychological Bulletin*, 124 (1998): 262–74.

15. "CEO Genome Project," ghSMART, SAS, 1995–2017, http://ceogenome.com/about/.

16. "2014 Study of CEOs, Governance, and Success," Strategy&, 2014.

17. "CEO Genome Project," ghSMART, SAS, 1995–2017.

18. Richard Boyatzis, *Competent Manager: A Model for Effective Performance* (Hoboken, NJ: John Wiley & Sons, 1982), 4.

19. Benedetto De Martino, Dharshan Kumaran, Ben Seymour, and Raymond J. Dolan, "Frames, Biases, and Rational Decision-Making in the Human Brain," *Science* 313.57 (2009): 684–87.

20. Geoff Smart and Randy Street, *Who: The A Method for Hiring* (New York: Ballantine Books, 2008).

chapter 2

Decide: Speed Over Precision

1. "CEO Genome Project," ghSMART, SAS, 1995–2017, http://ceogenome.com/about/.

2. John Antonakis, Robert J. House, and Dean Keith Simonton, "Can Super Smart Leaders Suffer from Too Much of a Good Thing? The Curvilinear Effect of Intelligence on Perceived Leadership Behavior," *Journal of Applied Psychology* 102.7 (2017): 1003–21.

3. "CEO Genome Project," ghSMART, 1995–2017, http://ceogenome.com/about/.

4. Noel Tichy and Ram Charan, "Speed, Simplicity, Self-Confidence: An Interview with Jack Welch," *Harvard Business Review*, September/October 1989.

5.   Bob Evans, "How Google and Amazon Are Torpedoing the Retail Industry with Data, AI, and Advertising," Forbes.com, June 20, 2017.

6.   Purva Mathur, "Hand Hygiene: Back to the Basics of Infection Control," *Indian Journal of Medical Research* 134.5 (2011): 611–20.

7.   Brad Smith, "Three Things I Wish I'd Known Before Becoming a CEO," LinkedIn, 2016, https://www.linkedin.com/pulse/three-things-i-wish-id-known-before-becoming-ceo-brad-smith?trk=v-feed.

8.   Ben Casnocha, "Reid Hoffman's Two Rules for Strategy Decisions," *Harvard Business Review,* March 2015.

9.   "CEO Genome Project," ghSMART, SAS, 1995–2017.

10. Daniel Kahneman, *Thinking, Fast and Slow* (New York: Farrar, Straus and Giroux, 2011), 13.

11. George S. Patton, Paul D. Harkins, and Beatrice Banning Ayer Patton, *War as I Knew It* (Boston: Houghton Mifflin Co., 1947), 402.

12. Chip Heath and Dan Heath, *Decisive: How to Make Better Choices in Life and Work* (New York: Crown Business, 2013).

13. Michael Norton, Daniel Mochon, and Dan Ariely, "The IKEA Effect: When Labor Leads to Love." *Journal of Consumer Psychology* 22.3 (2012): 453–60.

14. Ben Horowitz, *The Hard Thing About Hard Things: Building a Business When There Are No Easy Answers* (New York: HarperBusiness, 2014), 183.

chapter 3

Engage for Impact: Orchestrate Stakeholders to Drive Results

1.   "CEO Genome Project," ghSMART, SAS, 1995–2017, http://ceogenome.com/about/.

2.   Steven Kaplan, Mark Klebanov, and Morten Sørensen, "Which CEO Characteristics and Abilities Matter?" Working paper, University of Chicago, 2007.

3.   Sucheta Nadkarni and Pol Herrmann, "CEO Personality, Strategic Flexibility, and Firm Performance: The Case of the Indian Business Process Outsourcing Industry," *Academy of Management Journal* 53.5 (2010): 1050–73.

4.   Matthew J. Belvedere, "Warren Buffett Wants to End Wall Street's Broken Earnings Game." CNBC.com, August 15, 2016.

5.   "Orchestra," Wikipedia, https://en.wikipedia.org/wiki/Orchestra.

6. Lucinda Shen, "United Airlines Stock Drops $1.4 Billion After Passenger-Removal Controversy," Fortune.com, April 11, 2017.

7. Jon Ostrower, "The 10 Things United Is Doing to Avoid Another Dust-up, Drag-out Passenger Fiasco," Money.CNN.com, April 27, 2017.

8. "CEO Genome Project," ghSMART, 1995–2017, http://ceogenome.com/about/.

9. Nicholas Epley, *Mindwise: How We Understand What Others Think, Believe, Feel, and Want* (New York: Alfred A. Knopf, 2014).

10. Susan Cain, *Quiet: The Power of Introverts in a World that Can't Stop Talking* (New York: Crown Publishing, 2012), 11, 264.

11. "CEO Genome Project," ghSMART, SAS, 1995–2017.

12. Ibid.

chapter 4

Relentless Reliability: Deliver Consistently

1. "CEO Genome Project," ghSMART, SAS, 1995–2017, http://ceogenome.com/about/.

2. Ibid.

3. "CEO Genome Project," ghSMART, 1995–2017, http://ceogenome.com/about/.

4. Thomas W. H. Ng and Lillian Eby, "Predictors of Objective and Subjective Career Success: A Meta-Analysis," *Personnel Psychology* 58 (2005): 367–408.

5. Teresa Amabile and Steven Kramer, *The Progress Principle: Using Small Wins to Ignite Joy, Engagement, and Creativity at Work* (Boston: Harvard Business Press, 2011), 3.

6. Adam Bryant and Jeffrey Swartz, "What Makes You Roar? He Wants to Know," *New York Times*, December 19, 2009.

7. Warren Bennis, *On Becoming a Leader* (New York: Basic Books, 2009), 152.

8. Karl E. Weick and Kathleen M. Sutcliffe, *Managing the Unexpected: Resilient Performance in an Age of Uncertainty* (Hoboken, NJ: Jossey-Bass, 2007).

9. John T. James, "A New, Evidence-Based Estimate of Patient Harms Associated with Hospital Care," *Journal of Patient Safety* 9.3 (2013): 122–28.

10. Edgar H. Schein, "On Dialogue, Culture, and Organizational Learning,"

Reflections: The Society of Organizational Learning Journal 4.4 (2003): 27–38.

11. "CEO Genome Project," ghSMART, 1995–2017.

12. Ibid.

13. Atul Gawande, *The Checklist Manifesto: How to Get Things Right* (New York: Metropolitan Books, 2010), 177 (emphasis added).

chapter 5

Adapt Boldly: Ride the Discomfort of the Unknown

1. Richard Foster, e-mail message to authors, July 23, 2017.

2. "CEO Genome Project," ghSMART, 1995–2017, http://ceogenome.com/about/.

3. "CEO Genome Project," ghSMART, SAS, 1995–2017, http://ceogenome.com/about/.

4. Richard S. Tedlow, "Fortune Classic: The Education of Andy Grove," Fortune.com, March 21, 2016.

5. Andrew S. Grove, *Only the Paranoid Survive: How to Exploit the Crisis Points That Challenge Every Company and Career* (New York: Currency Doubleday, 1996), 89.

6. "CEO Genome Project," ghSMART, 1995–2017.

7. Jianhong Chen and Sucheta Nadkarni, "It's About Time! CEOs' Temporal Dispositions, Temporal Leadership, and Corporate Entrepreneurship," *Administrative Science Quarterly* 62.1 (2017): 31–66.

8. Brad Smith, "Three Things I Wish I'd Known Before Becoming a CEO," LinkedIn, 2016, https://www.linkedin.com/pulse/three-things-i-wish -id-known-before-becoming-ceo-brad-smith?trk=v-feed.

9. "CEO Genome Project," ghSMART, 1995–2017.

10. Hal Gregersen, "Bursting the CEO Bubble," *Harvard Business Review*, March/April 2017.

11. Herbert A. Simon, "Designing Organizations for an Information-Rich World," chapter published in *Computers, Communication, and the Public Interest* (Baltimore: The Johns Hopkins Press, 1971), 40–41.

12. "CEO Genome Project," ghSMART, 1995–2017.

Adding It All Up

1. Jeff Bezos, "2016 Letter to Shareholders," Amazon, April 12, 2017, https://www.amazon.com/p/feature/z6o9g6sysxur57t.

2. "CEO Genome Project," ghSMART, 1995–2017, http://ceogenome.com/about/.

chapter 6
Career Catapults: Fast-Track Your Future

1. "CEO Genome Project," ghSMART, 1995–2017, http://ceogenome.com/about/.

2. "Korn Ferry Survey: 87 Percent of Executives Want to Be CEO, Yet, Only 15 Percent of Execs Are 'Learning Agile,' a Key to Effective Leadership," Korn Ferry, October 2, 2014, https://www.kornferry.com/press/korn-ferry-survey-87-percent-of-executives-want-to-be-ceo-yet-only-15-percent-of-execs-are-learning-agile-a-key-to-effective-leadership/.

3. Christian Stadler, "How to Become a CEO: These Are the Steps You Should Take," Forbes.com, March 12, 2015.

4. "CEO Genome Project," ghSMART, 1995–2017.

5. "Best Business Schools," *U.S. News & World Report*, https://www.usnews.com/best-graduate-schools/top-business-schools/mba-rankings?int=9dc208

6. "CEO Genome Project," ghSMART, 1995–2017.

7. Ibid.

8. Ibid.

9. Justin Fox, "What Makes Danaher Corp. Such a Star?" Bloomberg.com, May 19, 2015.

10. "CEO Genome Project," ghSMART, 1995–2017.

11. "CEO Genome Project," ghSMART, SAS, 1995–2017, http://ceogenome.com/about/.

12. "CEO Genome Project," ghSMART, 1995-2017.

chapter 7
Stand Out: How to Become Known

1. "CEO Genome Project," ghSMART, 1995–2017, http://ceogenome.com/about/.

2. Ibid.

3. Polina Marinova, "Read Benchmark's Letter to Uber Employees Explaining Why It's Suing Former CEO Travis Kalanick," Fortune.com, August 14, 2017.

chapter 8
Close the Deal

1. Steven N. Kaplan and Morten Sørensen. "Are CEOs Different? Characteristics of Top Managers," Columbia Business School Research Paper Series, presented at the Paris Finance Meeting, December 2016, https://ssrn.com/abstract=2747691.

2. "CEO Genome Project," ghSMART, SAS, 1995–2017, http://ceogenome.com/about/.

3. Ibid.

4. "CEO Genome Project," ghSMART, Arthur Spirling, 1995–2017, http://ceogenome.com/about/.

5. "CEO Genome Project," ghSMART, SAS, 1995–2017.

6. "CEO Genome Project," ghSMART, 1995–2017, http://ceogenome.com/about/.

7. Ibid.

8. Justin Fox, "What Makes Danaher Corp. Such a Star?" Bloomberg.com, May 19, 2015.

9. Keith L. Alex, "Chief Executive of US Airways Resigns," *Washington Post*, April 20, 2004.

chapter 9
The Five Hidden Hazards at the Top

1. "CEO Genome Project," ghSMART, 1995–2017, http://ceogenome.com/about/.

2. Ibid.

3. Ibid.

4. Matthew J. Belvedere, "Larry Summers: Brexit Worst Shock Since WWII and Central Banks Are Out of Ammo." CNBC.com, June 28, 2016.

5. "CEO Genome Project," ghSMART, 1995–2017.

chapter 10
Not Just Any Team—Your Team

1. "CEO Genome Project," ghSMART, 1995–2017, http://ceogenome.com/about/.

2. Ibid.

3. James C. Collins, *Good to Great: Why Some Companies Make the Leap . . . and Others Don't* (New York: HarperBusiness, 2001), 13.

4. President John F. Kennedy, delivered in person before a joint session of Congress, May 25, 1961.

5. "Office Hours with the President," https://president.stanford.edu/office-hours/.

6. Geoff Smart, Randy Street, and Alan Foster, *Power Score: Your Formula for Leadership Success* (New York: Ballantine Books, 2015); Geoff Smart and Randy Street, *Who: The A Method for Hiring.* (New York: Ballantine Books, 2008).

chapter 11
Dancing with the Titans—The Board

1. "CEO Genome Project," ghSMART, 1995–2017, http://ceogenome.com/about/.

2. Ibid.

3. Ibid.

4. Ibid.

5. "Transitions in Leadership: A 2011 Corporate Board Member/RHR International Study on Managing Successful CEO Transitions," RHR International, 2011, http://www.rhrinternational.com/sites/default/files/pdf_files/Transitions%20in%20Leadership%20A%202011%20Corporate%20Board%20Member%20RHR%20International%20Study.pdf.

6. "U.S. Bancorp," Wikipedia, https://en.wikipedia.org/wiki/U.S._Bancorp.

7. John Maxfield, "Is U.S. Bancorp Stock Safe?," fool.com, July 8, 2017.

epilogue
From Ordinary to Extraordinary

1. Raj Gupta, *Eight Dollars and a Dream: My American Journey* (Lulu Publishing Services, 2016).

2. Bloomberg database, accessed August 16, 2017.

Elena Lytkina Botelho: I am an unlikely success story, or so people tell me. I was born in Russia at a time when private enterprise would land you in prison, not on a *Forbes* list. I grew up in a family of mathematicians, where money was as scarce as ideas were abundant. I made my way to the United States just as the Berlin Wall fell but with the Soviet Union still intact (not for long). My family's parting words rang in my ears: "Are you sure you can learn English?" I graduated from SUNY Binghamton and eventually joined the Corporate Finance group at Arthur Andersen as the only non–Ivy League graduate, the only foreigner, and the only transfer from the far-less-prestigious audit division. I was greeted with a skeptical: "Are you sure you can model?" (Meaning, create financial models in Excel. I think. At the time, my English wasn't good enough for me to be sure.) Later, when I was an MBA student at the Wharton School of the University of Pennsylvania, the first recruiter I encountered inquired, "How'd *you* get to Wharton? You must be really lucky." From there my unlikely trajectory continued to five years as a strategy consultant at McKinsey & Company and then on to ghSMART, advising leading CEOs and boards. With this book, I aim to bring unlikely possibilities within reach for many "lucky" others.

Kim Rosenkoetter Powell: My path followed a few unpredicted twists and turns. I finished college as a history major who'd never touched an Excel spreadsheet. I had a plan in hand to save the world by volunteering for a year after graduation. Due to serendipitous events, I found myself with offers from several global management consulting firms. When I ultimately decided to join the Boston Consulting Group, I was told they "took a flier" on hiring me, given that I had no business experience, no internships, and no relevant degree. Lucky for me, that opportunity expanded my horizons and led to an MBA at Northwestern's Kellogg School of Management. While I never intended to write a book, when I joined ghSMART and realized the gold mine of data we had at our fingertips, I couldn't resist diving in to understand and then share what differentiates successful leaders. I'm driven to bring a quantitative backbone to executive coaching. I apply my passion to ignite amazing leaders to aim high—and, in doing so, to positively impact the world, one employee, one company at a time.